FORTUNE
—— FAVORS ——
BOLDNESS

THE STORY OF NAVAL VALOR DURING
OPERATION IRAQI FREEDOM

BARRY M. COSTELLO
VICE ADMIRAL, USN (RETIRED)

F⊕RTIS

AN ADDUCENT NONFICTION IMPRINT

TITLES DISTRIBUTED IN
NORTH AMERICA
UNITED KINGDOM
WESTERN EUROPE
SOUTH AMERICA
AUSTRALIA
CHINA
INDIA

FORTUNE

—— FAVORS ——

BOLDNESS

BARRY M. COSTELLO
VICE ADMIRAL, USN (RETIRED)

FORTIS

FORTUNE FAVORS BOLDNESS

THE STORY OF NAVAL VALOR DURING OPERATION IRAQI FREEDOM

BARRY M. COSTELLO, VICE ADMIRAL, USN (RETIRED)

HARDBACK ISBN: 9781937592851
PAPERBACK ISBN: 9781937592868
PUBLISHED BY FORTIS (AN ADDUCENT NONFICTION IMPRINT)
WWW.ADDUCENTCREATIVE.COM

TABLE OF CONTENTS

Introduction i
Foreword ii
Reflections of a Blackshoe Sailor iv
Prologue 1
   Tradition 1
   9/11/2001 2
   Axis of Evil 4
   Genesis of Fortune Favors Boldness............................6
CHAPTER 1 | Cruiser-Destroyer Group 1 .... **14**
   Constellation Strike Group......................................15
   Strike Group Leadership..20
CHAPTER 2 | Pre-Deployment Training **24**
   Priorities 24
   Preparing for Battle 26
   Training Ashore 28
   9/11/2001 Anniversary 32
   Training at Sea...34
   Responsibility for Weapons Launch............................37
   "Man Overboard—This is Not a Drill"........................40
CHAPTER 3 | Deployment to the Arabian Gulf.......... **46**
   People 46
   Battle Rhythm 49
   Constellation Fire...52
   Train as We Would Fight..58
   Helicopter Deck Landing Qualifications......................60
   Veterans Day 61
   Blue Water Flight Operations.....................................63
   Communicating Intent 65
   Sailors as Ambassadors...66
   Transit to 5th Fleet (Arabian Gulf) 70
   Indian Navy Interaction and Strait of Hormuz Transit 71
CHAPTER 4 | On Station—Ready for Tasking.............. **74**
   Commander Task Force 50 74
   Medical Issues and Readiness 78
   Senior Leader Visits...80
CHAPTER 5 | Planning Across the Theater **89**
   Combatant Commands..89

General Franks and Component Commanders...........................90
Recrafting Strike Groups to Meet Warfighting Demands 91
Secretary of State Colin Powell 95
Secretary of Defense Rumsfeld and General Franks 97
Vice Admiral Keating and the 5th Fleet Team 98
CTF 50 and CTF 55 Coordination 99
CTF 55 Mission 104
Planning Considerations 105
CTF 55 Organization 106
CHAPTER 6 | Relationships Between Commanders...........108
Coalition Leadership...108
Order of Battle..123
CHAPTER 7 | Operations Part I: Setting the Force 127
Rotating the Clock for 24-Hour Air Coverage 127
Firepower Shift from the Mediterranean to the Red Sea 128
Commander's Guidance...131
Fog of War 136
Information Warfare 138
Media Embarkation 141
Mine Storage Areas and Rules of Engagement.......................153
Mine Clearance Operations 155
View from the Deck of USS *Raven* 162
Escort Operations 164
Maritime Interception Operations and Flushing the KAA 166
CHAPTER 8 | Operations Part II: Opening Strikes............177
War is Imminent..177
MABOT and KAAOT Oil Terminals Takedown 185
Tomahawk Strikes 192
Combined Air Operations Center..................................196
Flight Operations: *Air Wing of Destiny*...........................200
Decapitation Strike Support 201
In Harm's Way...203
Aviation Leadership Personal Perspectives 206
Quick Reaction Strike in Support of U.S. Marine Corps............223
Interviewing Returning Air Crews..................................225
Iranian Air Intrusion...226
Helicopter Operations..227
Saddam's Yacht—*al Mansur*......................................228
Carrier Night Operations...232
Submarine Operations..236
Naval Gunfire Support Operations (Al Faw Peninsula).............238

Joint Venture (HSV-X1)–The Mothership 242
Missile Defense Support to U.S. Army 245
CHAPTER 9 | Operations Part III: Clearing a Path for Relief Supplies **248**
Clearing the KAA 248
Naval Special Clearance Team 1 251
Securing Umm Qasr.. 255
PHOTO SECTION.. **263**
CHAPTER 10 | Wind Down of Navy Engagement................ **278**
Release of Carriers 278
Homeward Bound.. 284
Pacific Command Debrief 286
Return to San Diego 288
Post-Deployment Brief to Chief of Naval Operations................ 291
Lessons Identified 294
Recognizing a Job Well Done 298
British Empire Recognition 300
CHAPTER 11 | The Way Forward **302**
Leadership Assignments after Operation Iraqi Freedom 302
3rd Fleet Initiatives... 305
U.S. Navy and U.S. Marine Corps Relationships 309
Fleet Headquarters as Maritime Operations Centers............... 313
Combined Force Maritime Component Commander Course...... 314
Epilogue... **317**
Appendix A | Blessed **318**
Appendix B | Mentors and Early Leadership Lessons **321**
Appendix C | Letters **333**
Appendix D | Daily Press Briefings **337**
Acknowledgments **344**
Glossary **345**
Bibliography **353**

NOTES:

1. I refer to the waters between Saudi Arabia and Iran as the "*Arabian Gulf*." This body of water is also called the "*Persian Gulf*." There is a history to each of these names.

2. I refer to the groups of U.S. Navy ships as *strike groups*. These groups were formerly called *battle groups*, and the name change occurred during the period covered by this book, emphasizing

the focus on having an impact ashore in support of the ground force. I chose to use strike group throughout for consistency.

3. PUBLISHER'S NOTE: Making certain images—scanned letters, communication and correspondence—graphics or maps as large as possible for readability and collocating them in context has resulted in a few unavoidable gaps between blocks of text. There are not many.

Dedication

To the men and women of the *Constellation* Strike Group and all the Sailors, Marines, Coastguardsmen, Airmen, and Soldiers they represent, who deploy for extended periods of time away from their families on behalf of their country. They are motivated by patriotism and love of freedom, appreciating that freedom is not free. Their dedication inspired me every day and night during combat operations and continues to make me proud to have worn the cloth of our nation with them.

Introduction

Fortune Favors Boldness is the motto of the U.S. Navy's Cruiser-Destroyer Group 1 (CCDG–1). That team led the *Constellation* Strike Group throughout 2002–2003. This is when *"America's Flagship,"* USS *Constellation* (CV 64), made its historic last deployment to the Arabian Gulf in support of Operation Iraqi Freedom.

This story of epic events and bravery of Sailors and Marines in harm's way is told from the perspective of retired Vice Admiral Barry Costello who was the commander of this force. It reflects his view on the planning, preparation, and execution of operations in wartime. Leadership lessons are provided throughout this story.

FOREWORD

The seeds of *Fortune Favors Boldness* were planted by the September 11, 2001 attacks on the United States. Citizens awoke the next day to a new world reality, that fortress America was no longer impervious to the terrorism that was plaguing countries around the world.

Citizens came together and volunteers from all walks of life flooded military recruiting stations with a sense of duty to protect our foundation of freedom. Many volunteers became part of the *Constellation* Strike Group. They came from all parts of the country, and from all ethnic and cultural backgrounds. This team of 7,500 men and women became the heart and soul of the ships that constituted the strike group fighting force.

This group would begin training in June 2002 and would emerge five months later as a seasoned team focused on the details of warfighting. The hard-fought lessons learned off the waters of San Diego would prove to be critical. The subsequent transit west across the Pacific and Indian oceans provided additional opportunities to sharpen the sword. By December 2002, as the strike group transited the Strait of Hormuz into the Arabian Gulf, they were ready to take command of Task Force 50–directing coalition naval operations at sea in the Naval Forces Central Command/United States 5th Fleet area of operations, headquartered in Bahrain.

The *Constellation* Strike Group leadership team had experienced many deployments to the Arabian Gulf. As commander of 5th Fleet, I folded this talented group into my team as we prepared for a military response in Iraq against terrorism. Months of coordination at all levels by the U.S. military and coalition partners were required to groom war plan 1003V–named Operation Iraqi Freedom. Wartime operations would be dangerous. There was much to take into consideration to fight against a dug in adversary who could be expected to fight with chemical and mine warfare. We had the solemn responsibility of ensuring mission success while minimizing loss of life of our servicemen and the Iraqi people.

The opening days of Operation Iraqi Freedom were dynamic as we executed a complex war plan that involved thousands of moving parts at sea, in the air, and on the ground. The pace of success of the initial military operations against Saddam Hussein's forces exceeded all expectations.

Fortune Favors Boldness tells this story from Vice Admiral Costello's perspective at sea on *Constellation*. He provides insights into the thinking at all levels, from President Bush to the Sailors who plied the waters and dominated the airspace of the Northern Arabian Gulf and Southern Iraq. Like Admiral Costello, I feel fortunate to have had the opportunity to serve during this critical time in our nation's history and to have had the honor to lead. My note to the Sailors and Marines of 5th Fleet on 18 March 2003 set the tone for all that was to follow:

"... You will be called upon for sacrifice, for strenuous labor, for gut-wrenching, split-second decisions. You will make the right call; you will find a reservoir of strength and wisdom. I know you will because you have been schooled in the traditions of our glorious service, our United States Navy.

Now it is time for us to go to work. Do so aggressively, intelligently, with audacity and courage. Go fully confident that you have earned the support of your countrymen and of millions of freedom-loving people around the world.

May God continue to bless you and your families, and may He hold each of you in the palm of His hand now and always."

I hope you enjoy reading this story that captures the heroic combat action of the Navy/Marine/Coast Guard/Coalition team at sea as they supported the ground advance to Baghdad in 2003. Today's Navy continues to benefit from Operation Iraqi Freedom lessons learned as it prepares for potential future conflict in an increasingly dangerous world marked by great power competition.

–Timothy J. Keating, Admiral, USN (Retired)
July 6, 2018

REFLECTIONS OF A BLACKSHOE SAILOR

There is a long tradition associated with the color of shoe worn by naval officers. Surface and submarine officers wear black, while aviators wear brown (originally approved in 1913)—the distinction noted by each community with pride.

This poem, "Reflections of a Blackshoe Sailor," captures my love of the adventure of the sea. It was sent to me by retired Operations Specialist Senior Chief Ed Loudenslarger, a seasoned leader who fully appreciated his responsibility to train junior officers. He was wonderfully patient with Ensign Costello (gunnery liaison officer) on my first ship, the mighty USS *Brownson* (DD 868) in 1974. We were shooting for the Naval Gunfire Support (NGFS) qualification and succeeded because of his steady hand on the oar during the effort. Now it was 2002, and I was in command of the *Constellation* Strike Group. He thought it appropriate to remind me of my roots. This poem summarizes the experience of going to sea and encompasses my frame of reference for FORTUNE FAVORS BOLDNESS.

> I liked standing on the bridge wing at sunrise with salt spray in my face and clean ocean winds whipping in from the four quarters of the globe—the ship beneath me feeling like a living thing as her engines drove her swiftly through the sea.
>
> I liked the sounds of the Navy—the piercing trill of the boatswain's pipe, the syncopated clangor of the ship's bell on the quarterdeck, the harsh squawk of the 1MC (microphone), and the strong language and laughter of Sailors at work.
>
> I liked Navy vessels—darting destroyers, fleet auxiliaries and amphibious ships, sleek submarines and steady, solid aircraft carriers.

I liked the proud names of Navy ships: *Midway, Lexington, Saratoga, Coral Sea, Antietam, Valley Forge, Bunker Hill*—memorials of great battles won and tribulations overcome.

I liked the names of Navy "tin-cans"—*Milius, Higgins, Thach, Elliot*—mementos to heroes who went before us.

I liked the tempo of a Navy band blaring through the topside speakers as we pulled away from the oiler after refueling at sea.

I liked liberty call and the spicy scent of a foreign port.

I even liked the never-ending paperwork and the all-hands working parties as my ship filled herself with the multitude of supplies, both mundane and exotic, which she needed to cut ties to the land and carry out her mission anywhere on the globe where there was water to float her.

I liked Sailors, officers and enlisted from all parts of the land, farms of the Midwest, small towns from New England, from the cities, from the mountains and the prairies, from all walks of life. I trusted and depended on them as they trusted and depended on me, for professional competence, for comradeship, for strength and courage. In a word, they were "shipmates" then and forever.

I liked the surge of adventure in my heart when the word was passed: "Now set the sea and anchor detail—all hands to quarters for leaving port," and I liked the infectious thrill of sighting home again, with the waving hands of welcome from family and friends waiting pier side.

I liked the serenity of the sea after a day of hard ship's work, as flying fish flitted across the wave tops and sunset gave way to night.

I liked the feel of the Navy in darkness—the masthead and range lights, the red and green navigation lights and the stern light, the pulsating phosphorescence of radar repeaters—they cut through the dusk and joined with the mirror of stars overhead. And I liked drifting off to sleep lulled by the myriad noises large and small that told me that my ship was alive and well and that my shipmates on watch would keep me safe.

I liked quiet midwatches with the aroma of strong coffee—the lifeblood of the Navy—permeating everywhere.

I liked hectic watches when the exacting minuet of haze-gray shapes racing at flank speed kept all hands on a razor edge of alertness.

I liked the sudden electricity of "General Quarters, General Quarters, all hands man your battle stations," followed by the hurried clamor of running feet on ladders and the resounding thump of watertight doors as the ship transforms herself in a few brief seconds from a peaceful workplace into a weapon of war—ready for anything.

I liked the sight of space-age equipment manned by youngsters clad in dungarees and sound-powered phones that their grandfathers would still recognize.

I liked the traditions of the Navy and the men and women who made them. I liked the proud names of Navy heroes: Halsey, Nimitz, Perry, Farragut, John Paul Jones, and Burke. A Sailor could find much in the Navy: comrades in arms, pride in self and country, and mastery of the seaman's trade. An adolescent could find adulthood.

In years to come, when Sailors are home from the sea, they will still remember with fondness and respect, the ocean in all its moods—the impossible shimmering mirror calm and the storm-tossed green water surging over the bow. And then there will come again a faint whiff of stack gas, a faint echo of engine and rudder orders, a vision of the bright bunting of signal flags snapping at the yardarm, a refrain of hearty laughter in the wardroom and chief's quarters and the mess decks.

Gone ashore for good they will grow wistful about their Navy days when the seas belonged to them, and a new port of call was ever over the horizon.

Remembering this, they will stand taller and say, "I was a Sailor once. I was a part of the greatest Navy the world has ever seen, and the Navy will always be a part of me!"

> *–Vice Admiral Harold Koenig, USN (Retired)*
> [with slight modifications]

PROLOGUE

TRADITION

I often say that I am the luckiest guy on the planet. This is true for many reasons. In the context of this book, it is because the Navy leadership allowed me the privilege to command three units with sacred history. These were units led by heroes Elliot, Burke, and Halsey.

> **USS *Elliot*** (DD 967) (I served as the captain in 1992). This Spruance class destroyer was named after Lieutenant Commander Arthur J. Elliot II, commanding officer of Patrol Boat River Squadron 57, killed in action in Vietnam in 1968. Elliot was a native of Maine, the oldest of three brothers. They all served in Vietnam. He was awarded the Bronze Star for "heroic achievement and professional skill and courage," and the Purple Heart for his actions. His commander in Vietnam, former Chief of Naval Operations Admiral Elmo Zumwalt Jr., attended the ship's commissioning ceremony.

> **Destroyer Squadron 23, the "Little Beavers"** (I served as the commodore in 1996). This squadron received its nickname from Commodore Arleigh Burke during South Pacific operations in the early days of World War II. Burke led this squadron of destroyers to victory against the Japanese surface force, turning the tide of the fight for control of the waters in the Coral Sea northeast of Australia. He developed warfighting techniques that resulted in success for the remainder of the campaign. This tactical acumen and dynamic leadership in combat foreshadowed his later success as chief of naval operations.

1

3rd Fleet (I served as commander in 2005). This fleet was made famous because of its exploits in World War II. "Hit hard, hit fast, hit often," was Fleet Admiral "Bull" Halsey's guidance to the force as they took the fight to the Japanese in the Pacific. He was the driving force at sea, and his persistence led to the capitulation of the Japanese navy.

Tradition runs deep in our United States Navy. I am truly honored and humbled to follow in the footsteps of these three American Navy heroes. This story and lessons from my command of Cruiser-Destroyer Group 1, the *Constellation* Strike Group, and Task Force 55 follow the long tradition of learning from our predecessors.

9/11/2001

I was a rear admiral serving in the Pentagon on September 11, 2001. My assignment on the Joint Staff was deputy director for strategy and policy in the Strategic Plans and Policy Directorate (J5). The day was sunny and clear. As we began the business of the day, the TV pictures of a plane crashing into the World Trade Center flashed on the screen. The gravity of this was not lost on any of us. We watched in horror as the second tower was attacked, and a new reality set in.

My mind instantly went to my son Aidan, who was in New York City attending the School of Visual Arts on the lower east side, a few blocks from the tragedy. He would later tell of the flood of dust that poured down the streets of Manhattan.

Then all hell broke loose. Airborne planes were contacted and grounded. The two that did not respond were headed to Washington D.C. The passengers of hijacked United Airlines Flight 93 heroically caused their aircraft to crash in a rural Pennsylvania field. Hijacked American Airlines Flight 77 was rerouted by the terrorists to a tragic path toward the Pentagon. Minutes later it impacted the western side of the building, and 125 Pentagon workers plus 64 on the airplane died as a result.

Citizens from more than 90 countries died that day from these acts of terror, innocent men, women, and children from across the globe.

Stories of heroes displaying extraordinary acts of valor were the order of the day.

President Bush addressed the American people that evening:

"Today, our fellow citizens, our way of life, our very freedom came under attack in a series of deliberate and deadly terrorist acts... These acts of mass murder were intended to frighten our nation into chaos and retreat. But they have failed. Our country is strong. A great people has been moved to defend a great nation... America was targeted for attack because we're the brightest beacon for freedom and opportunity in the world. And no one will keep that light from shining."

September 11 was about a cowardly attack. September 12 was about the beginning of a focused response. That day, 22,000 people returned to a Pentagon building that was still burning, with smoke pouring forth. People streamed in with grim determination on their faces, ready to pick up the pieces. It was inspiring. I am reminded of the phrase... it is not what happens when you get knocked down that matters, it is how you respond and move forward when you get up that makes the difference.

The Pentagon repair team immediately adopted the slogan "Let's Roll," honoring the heroic words and actions of Todd Beamer on Flight 93 as he led the passengers to charge the terrorists. "Proud to be an American" stickers sprouted up everywhere.

President Bush came to the Pentagon that day to address the Joint Chiefs. Among his other messages, he looked at Chairman of the Joint Chiefs General Richard Myers, Chief of Naval Operations Admiral Vern Clark, Chief of Staff of the Army General Eric Shinseki, Chief of Staff of the Air Force General John Jumper, Commandant of the Marine Corps General James Jones, and Vice Chairman of the Joint Chiefs General Peter Pace, and said to each of them—one at a time—"Do not ever forget what happened yesterday." One of the meeting attendees said it felt like the beginning of the next chapter in our nation's history.

There had been no plan of action for how to deal with an attack originating from inside the country. Planning always had focused on combat operations overseas, with fortress America being secure.

September 11 was the ignition switch for greater efforts to secure our borders and increase focus on fighting terrorism. The world would never be the same. The impact of the airplanes is still felt today.

AXIS OF EVIL

It was evident that President Bush was prepared to take military action against countries that supported international terrorist groups. When he spoke to the American people in his State of the Union Address in January 2002, he stated, "The price of indifference would be catastrophic." He used the "Axis of Evil" moniker to describe Iran, Iraq and North Korea—countries that supported terrorists.

In the case of Iraq, the *economic* element of national power had been used for years as an instrument to entice compliance with United Nations imposed sanctions. This had resulted in limited success. In 2002, the *political* and *diplomatic* elements were rising in priority. The press wrote frequent articles about the roles of the Congress, State Department, and Defense Department in advising the president on options for moving forward. All elements of the government decision-making process were engaged, with the Department of Defense and the *military* instrument now receiving additional attention.

Several factions emerged within the administration. Secretary of State Colin Powell led a group consisting of Brent Scowcroft, James Baker, Norman Schwarzkopf, and others. They insisted that if an invasion of Iraq were to occur, it must take place in the context of an anti-terrorism coalition. This group reflected the interests of European leaders as well as Arab states. They did not oppose an invasion, but the coalition integrity was preeminent.

On the other side was the Secretary of Defense Donald Rumsfeld and Deputy Secretary of Defense Paul Wolfowitz. They were convinced that the evolution in warfighting capabilities would allow an attack on Iraq without relying on either European or regional coalition partners. They proposed the use of special operations forces to topple the terrorist-supporting Iraqi regime, without the need for utilizing massive ground and air forces or allies in the region.

National Security Advisor Condoleezza Rice indicated where the president stood:

"No one goes to the use of military force lightly, most especially this president who is deliberative, who, even when we were brutally attacked on 9/11, took his time in assembling a coalition, making sure we had a good military plan... And he will be deliberative here. He has not determined that the use of force is the best option."

Others clearly stated their positions:

Chairman of the Joint Chiefs of Staff General Richard Myers:

"The only thing I would say, if the president decides that military action is needed against Iraq, the U.S. armed forces and our allies will prevail."

The Chief of Naval Operations Admiral Vern Clark:

"The President of the United States said we are going to keep them on the run. The Commandant and I sent a letter to the secretary of defense that said, 'Your answer to that is the United States Navy and the United States Marine Corps. If you're going to keep them on the run, you've got to be out and about, and we are out and about'."

In the meantime, concerns were raised over the preparedness of the military services to execute a complex mission against a dug in adversary such as in Iraq. The "Peace Dividend" from the end of the Cold War had reduced the force significantly—by 40%. The Army had dropped from 750,000 to 460,000 Soldiers since 1991; the Navy moved from 450 to 315 ships, and aircraft carriers from 15 to 12; the Marine Corps had successfully preserved its size; while the Air Force was as small as it had been since its inception in 1949, with a fighter force average age per airframe of 20 years. Significant capability, and therefore responsibility, had been placed in the Reserves and National Guard in this interval. Questions were in the air as to the potential for a high number of casualties; whether U.S. armed forces were spread too thin based on the reduction and the continuing multiple commitments around with world; and most importantly would we be required to garrison forces in Iraq for years to come.

Plans for a possible attack on Iraq began materializing in 2002 and were groomed in early 2003. War planning efforts were led by the Central Command (CENTCOM) out of their Tampa, Florida headquarters. CENTCOM was responsible for U.S. military operations in the Middle East. General Tommy Franks was the commander, and he would run through many iterations of plans with Secretary Rumsfeld before the final plan was reviewed and approved by President Bush.

Coalition maritime forces would support both the land and air efforts in the overall campaign plan, called 1003V. Coalition ships would patrol the waterways around the Arabian Peninsula—from the Red Sea, through the Bab-el-Mandeb Strait, to the Northern Arabian Sea and the Gulf of Oman, through the Strait of Hormuz, and ultimately the Arabian Gulf—such that troops and logistics could flow unencumbered into the fight. Additionally, naval aircraft would provide the preponderance of air support in the first days of major hostilities *because they did not have to get permission from host nations* but could fly directly into the fight from international waters.

Plans for the overall Global War on Terrorism evolved to deal with the Axis of Evil. Task Forces would be created. The mettle of every Soldier, Sailor, Airman, Marine, and Coastguardsman would be tested. Now, serving as a strike group commander, I would lead a deployment to carry on the military's engagement in the war on terror in the Arabian Gulf in the spring of 2003.

GENESIS OF FORTUNE FAVORS BOLDNESS

A May 2014 article in *Proceedings* magazine by Lieutenant Commander Christopher Nelson entitled "Where Have All the Naval Memoirs Gone?" correctly suggests a dearth of writings from Navy leaders over the last several decades, from which the current and future generations can benefit. "...someday a young officer is going to turn to the bookshelves and wonder what challenges the U.S. Navy faced in the early 21st Century, and all he or she will see will be gaping holes where there should be bowing shelves." Junior personnel have made it clear to me that they want to know what happened, why certain decisions were made, what was the thought process, and what can they learn from the operations in 2003. It is now July 4, and I want to respond to their requests for information.

In Edmund Morgan's *American Heroes, Profiles of Men and Women Who Shaped Early America*, he writes about a wide variety of people who made a difference, with the common thread being their *leadership*. He focuses on the lesser known players in our history, who in their own way, contributed greatly. Similarly, here I tell the story of the brave service men and women who quietly led in the engine rooms, on the flight decks, in the combat centers, in rigid-hulled inflatable boats in the middle of the night, in the air, and on the ground in Southern Iraq.

The story of the U.S. Navy exploits in the Arabian Gulf in 2003 was well known across the Atlantic by our closest ally. In 2004, the Navy staff received a notice from the British Embassy in Washington, D.C. informing that Vice Admiral Tim Keating (the Navy Component Commander in the Gulf during Operation Iraqi Freedom) and I had been endorsed to receive the award of *The Most Honorable Order of the Bath* and the *Most Excellent Order of the British Empire* respectively. These are Honorary Orders of Knighthood, bestowed by Her Majesty the Queen, Elizabeth II, who formally approved the awards on 25 January 2005.

Yet heroics of the U.S. Navy, while initially well covered by the embedded press, were not as well known by the American people. There had been a conscious effort by the leadership to downplay Navy successes in the interest of "Jointness." The Army and Marine Corps were slugging it out on the ground, and the Air Force was frustrated by Saudi Arabian flying restrictions. Thus, chances to take photos of three or four carriers operating together in the Arabian Gulf did not occur, and other public affairs opportunities to highlight Navy successes were minimized.

Naval operations played a pivotal role in creating conditions for the initial success of the land and air campaigns. A force of 147 ships operated in the theater. Many of these ships were part of the coalition, while others independently supported operations.

This book tells the story of events carried out by sailors of many nations in the waters of the Arabian Gulf in the spring of 2003:

- How Navy SEALs opened the war effort by capturing 41 Iraqi soldiers on the major oil terminals in the Northern Arabian Gulf—after learning from United Nations Oil for Food representatives that the Iraqis had orders to blow up these platforms. Today more than 90% of the economy of Iraq is derived from the oil that flows through those terminals.
- How 802 Tomahawk missiles were fired from ships and submarines in the Arabian Gulf and the Red Sea—with superb execution and flawless precision—to pave the way for our forces by knocking out radar sites, aircraft and airfields, and a wide variety of other critical command and control facilities.
- How heroic aviators flew off the decks of three aircraft carriers in the Arabian Gulf (two others operated from the Mediterranean) 24-hours-a-day in all types of weather—challenging their skills honed over years of training—to provide air cover for Soldiers and Marines as they headed north to take Baghdad.
- How young men and women patrolled the waters at the mouth of the Northern Arabian Gulf in rigid-hull inflatable boats 24-hours-a-day—capturing three tugs and a barge with 86 mines destined for the middle of the Gulf—saving countless lives and preventing the destruction of ships.
- How coalition mine countermeasures ships and helicopters cleared hundreds of miles of waterspace, creating a swept channel that allowed the U.K. ship RFA *Sir Galahad* (L 3005) to transport humanitarian aid into Iraq.
- How Sailors and Marines performed extraordinarily during every mission.

This is their story. I will do my best to tell the tale of how collectively naval leadership created the environment where they could succeed.

8

This is *not* meant to be an authoritative resource. It is my recollections from the deck of *Constellation*. If the book is remiss in any fashion, the mistake is solely mine, and for that, I take full responsibility. Fortunately, I have used my notes, daily activity briefings I provided to the embedded press, and the press accounts from news outlets broadcasting around the world. Additionally, many shipmates who were in the fight in the Gulf at the time, including from Australia, Kuwait, and the United Kingdom, have stepped forward to provide firsthand perspectives on events.

My goal is to place you on the deck of *Constellation,* in the air with pilots as they flew missions into the night over Iraq, with the brave Sailors who plied the waters of the Northern Arabian Gulf, and ashore in Umm Qasr as naval forces moved into Iraq. Along the way, I provide personal background and leadership lessons; lessons I continue to offer today to rising admirals and generals in courses around the world sponsored by the Naval War College. I also pass these lessons along to deploying strike group commanders as they head overseas to stand the watch and execute the National Military Strategy, and to officers assigned to fleet staffs. (These lessons will be noted in italics throughout the book.)

I write this story for those Sailors, Marines, and Coastguardsmen who served in the Arabian Gulf in this timeframe, to recount their stories. It is for veterans of all times and services, as they truly appreciate the challenges highlighted in coordinating operations across a wide theater with thousands of participants from many nations. It is for the American people, such that they can appreciate the sacrifices of their young heroes who stood the watch to protect their security. It is a leadership book, with an emphasis on lessons to help those who follow in our footsteps. And it is a great adventure story that deserves the light of day.

Military organizations are rich with acronym usage. I've provided a comprehensive glossary of terms at the end of the book as a navigational aid.

Finally, there are four Appendices:

A. **Blessed**: My background growing up in Vermont.

B. **Mentors and Early Leadership Lessons:** The talented people who helped mold my leadership style.

C. **Letters from Commanders:** Senior officer correspondence to the *Constellation* team.

D. **Daily Press Briefings:** A chronological detail of daily events.

Please take the time to read these as they are central to my goal of passing along lessons from my experience and those of others. I hope you enjoy the book and come away with a better appreciation of the events of that time, and the people who *made a difference.*

NON SIBI SED PATRIAE

NOT FOR SELF, BUT COUNTRY

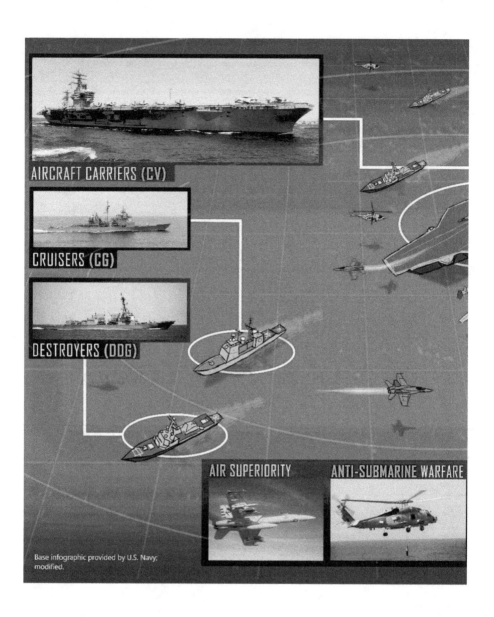

AIRCRAFT CARRIERS (CV)

CRUISERS (CG)

DESTROYERS (DDG)

AIR SUPERIORITY

ANTI-SUBMARINE WARFARE

Base infographic provided by U.S. Navy; modified.

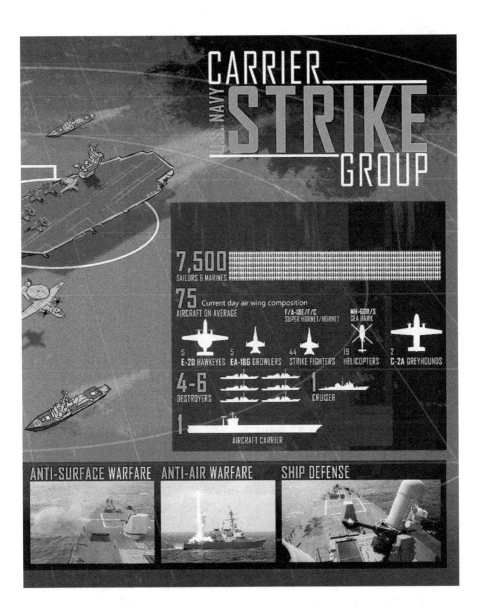

U.S. NAVY CARRIER STRIKE GROUP

7,500 SAILORS & MARINES

75 AIRCRAFT ON AVERAGE

Current day air wing composition

		F/A-18E/F/C SUPER HORNET/HORNET	MH-60R/S SEA HAWK	
5 E-2D HAWKEYES	5 EA-18G GROWLERS	44 STRIKE FIGHTERS	19 HELICOPTERS	2 C-2A GREYHOUNDS

4-6 DESTROYERS

1 CRUISER

1 AIRCRAFT CARRIER

ANTI-SURFACE WARFARE · ANTI-AIR WARFARE · SHIP DEFENSE

CHAPTER 1 | CRUISER-DESTROYER GROUP 1

"It is not the critic who counts, nor the man who points out where the strong man stumbled, or where the doer of deeds could have done them better. The credit belongs to the man in the arena whose face is marred by dust and sweat and blood, who strives valiantly, who errs, and who comes up short again and again, who knows the great enthusiasms, the great devotions, and spends himself in a worthy cause. The man who at best knows the triumph of high achievements and who at worst, if he fails, fails while daring greatly, so that his place will never be with those timid souls who never knew victory or defeat."

—President Theodore Roosevelt

Cruiser-Destroyer Group 1 (CCDG–1) was established in 1973. Its motto, *Fortune Favors Boldness,* was appropriate for Sailors going into battle. Fortuna was the goddess of fortune and the personification of luck, and the motto is a derivation of a Latin proverb that has been used historically in the military. In 1993, the group staff permanently embarked in its flagship, the aircraft carrier USS *Constellation,* homeported in San Diego, California.

I took command of CCDG-1 on 18 June 2002. It was a beautiful San Diego day, and the *Constellation* crew put forth a class act on the flight deck for the change of command ceremony. It was the beginning of a wonderful relationship with the ship. Commander 3rd Fleet, Vice Admiral Michael Bucchi, was aboard as the guest speaker.

The change of command ceremony, as the event program stated:

> "... is a time-honored tradition that formally restates to the Officers and Sailors the continuity of the authority of command. Although the ceremony is not prescribed specifically by U.S. Navy Regulations, it is a unique naval tradition. Custom has established the ceremony be formal and impressive, designed to strengthen the respect for authority which is vital to any military organization.

The heart of the ceremony is the formal reading of official orders by the relieving officer and the officer to be relieved. Command then passes upon utterance by the relieved officer, 'I stand relieved!' This simple procedure signifies the transfer of total responsibility, authority, and accountability from one individual to another... The ceremony reflects the commitment, responsibility, and dedication of free men and women proudly serving their country."

By tradition, the incoming officer at a change of command should keep the remarks short. I abided by that unwritten rule, drafting my remarks the night before on a yellow legal pad. I did have something to say to my new staff, to the assembled leadership of the strike group, and to the Sailors and their families. I ended my remarks by stating, "We will go in harm's way, and we will make America proud." That short sentence captured the essence of what was to follow over the next year.

A few days later, I provided a hint of what was to come in an interview with the *Constellation* daily newspaper, *Starscope*:

"I'm here to provide vision on where the strike group should go in its training and ensure readiness to operate in harm's way... I'm here to establish priorities of mission accomplishment and fleet readiness, which includes quality of life issues... I believe the strike group may very well have a vital role to play during its next deployment. Whether taking part in Operation Southern Watch or dealing more directly with Iraq, I see our involvement in future events to be significant."

CONSTELLATION STRIKE GROUP

CCDG-1 consisted of the admiral and his staff. The mission of the group was "to plan for and exercise operational and tactical command of the air, surface, and submarine forces at sea, in a multi-threat environment, in the pursuit of national objectives."

- Ships were assigned to the group as they prepared for training and operations overseas.
- The carrier was the centerpiece, and the group took the name of that ship.
- In this case, it was the *Constellation* Strike Group, and it consisted of approximately 7,500 Sailors and Marines.

In 2002, the following ships and aircraft squadrons were assigned to the group:

USS *CONSTELLATION* (CV 64)

The name *Constellation* is one of the most famous in U.S. Naval history. This name was held in high esteem by the Congress in 1794, as it represented the ring of stars on the new American flag. A wooden-hulled frigate, it was the first ship to be commissioned in the U.S. Navy; the first to put to sea; and the first to engage, defeat, and capture an enemy vessel.

The latest iteration of *Constellation* was an aircraft carrier commissioned in 1961 and refurbished with a major overhaul in the early 1990s. An aircraft carrier, like the "*Connie*," is a small town. It requires many services to support a multitude of needs. There is a desalinization plant that makes fresh water, a bank, post office, laundry, television studio and photo lab, convenience stores, chapel, library, machine shop, hospital, print shop, bakery, restaurants, and weather bureau. The statistics below give you an idea of the dimensions of this behemoth.

CONSTELLATION STATISTICS

BUILDER	NEW YORK NAVAL SHIPYARD
KEEL LAID	SEPT. 14, 1957
LAUNCHED	OCT. 8, 1960
COMMISSIONED	OCT. 27, 1961
TOTAL COST	$400 MILLION
PROPULSION SYSTEM	8 STEAM BOILERS
MAIN ENGINES	4 STEAM TURBINE ENGINES
SPEED	MORE THAN 30 KNOTS (35 MPH)
LENGTH OF FLIGHT DECK	1,079 FEET

WIDTH OF FLIGHT DECK.. 270 FEET
AREA OF FLIGHT DECK... 4.1 ACRES
HEIGHT FROM KEEL TO MAST... 17 STORIES
COMPARTMENTS AND SPACES.. MORE THAN 3,000
ANCHORS... 2 (EACH WEIGHS 30 TONS)
WEIGHT OF ANCHOR CHAIN LINKS..................................... 365 POUNDS EACH
COMBAT DISPLACEMENT WEIGHT... 88,000 TONS
PROPELLERS............................ 4, EACH 21FT. IN DIAMETER AND 44,000 LBS
WEIGHT OF RUDDERS... 200,000 POUNDS EACH
SIZE OF AIR WING...................................... 72 TACTICAL AIRCRAFT
AIRCRAFT ELEVATORS... 4
CATAPULTS... 4, STEAM-DRIVEN
ARRESTING GEAR CABLES.. 4 STEEL CABLES
CREW.. SHIP: 2,900, AIR WING: 2,480
DAILY CAPACITY OF WATER DISTILLING PLANTS..................... 400,000 GALLONS
MEALS SERVED PER DAY... MORE THAN 18,000

This part of America's treasure was nicknamed *America's Flagship* by President Ronald Reagan on August 20, 1981. The president reached back in history to 1797 when the U.S. frigate *Constellation* was called America's Flagship.

However impressive statistically, a ship is a mere display without its crew. President Reagan addressed the crew when he visited and said, "Let friend and foe alike know that America has the muscle to back up its words, and ships like this and men like you are that muscle."

The Sailors and Marines who bring this ship to life come from all parts of America and represent all races and creeds. They are young, with the average age of the crew at 20.5 years. Many of the Sailors who worked on the 4.1-acre flight deck in the middle of the night in the war were at their senior proms the previous year.

Everyone who has the honor to step foot on a U.S. carrier is impressed. "Letterman's Top Ten Cool Things About Living on an Aircraft Carrier" include: "It combines all the excitement of going on a cruise with the fun of living at the airport, and there's no more pleasant wake-up call than the roar of an F/A-18 Super Hornet."

CARRIER AIR WING 2 (CVW–2)

Joining *Constellation* was Carrier Air Wing 2 (CVW–2). Their motto was *For Liberty, We Fight,* and the original wing was established on 1 May 1945. The air wing's 2,480 airmen and 72 aircraft constituted the primary offensive and defensive weapons of the carrier. They worked with the ship's crew to create the ballet known as carrier flight operations. Maintainers, pilots, crews, and a host of other specialists came together to ensure the health and readiness of the air striking arm of the group. CVW-2 dominated the airspace surrounding the ship and projected power ashore. The air wing consisted of the ten squadrons noted below with their commanding officers:

- VF-2 "Bounty Hunters"—10 F-14D Tomcats (fighter)— Commander Andrew Whitson and Commander Douglas Denneny
- VFA-137 "Kestrels"—12 F/A-18C Hornets (fighter/attack)— Commander David Dober and Commander Walt Stammer
- VFA-151 "Vigilantes"—12 F/A-18C (fighter/attack)– Commander Mark Hubbard
- VFMA-323 "Death Rattlers"—12 F/A-18C (fighter/attack)— Lieutenant Colonel Gary Thomas
- VAW-116 "Sun Kings"—4 E-2C (early warning and battle management)—Commander Kevin Andersen
- VS-38 "Red Griffins"—8 S-3 (refueling and electronic warfare)—Commander Steve Kelly and Commander William Hart
- VAQ-131 "Lancers"—4 EA-6B (electronic warfare and jamming)—Commander John Lockler and Commander John Geragotelis
- HS-2 "Golden Falcons"—4 H-60 (multi-mission helicopter)— Commander Stephen Vissers
- HSL-47 "Saberhawks"—4 H-60 (multi-mission helicopter)— Lieutenant Commander Shawn Malone, officer in charge

- VRC-30 "Providers"/ "Ruffnecks"—2 C-2A (delivery of supplies and passengers)—Lieutenant Commander Jeffrey Alves, officer in charge

DESTROYER SQUADRON 7 (CDS 7)

The Destroyer Squadron 7 (CDS 7) staff was also embarked aboard *Constellation*. The commodore was the immediate superior in command of five ships in the strike group that focused on surface and subsurface warfare. The ships and their commanding officers were:

- USS *Valley Forge* (CG 50) (cruiser)—Commander Pat Rabun
- USS *Milius* (DDG 69) (guided missile destroyer)—Commander Jeffrey Harley and Commander Trey Mitchell
- USS *Higgins* (DDG 76) (guided missile destroyer)—Commander Michael Gilday
- USS *Thach* (FFG 43) (frigate)—Commander Bill Sheehan and Commander James Loeblein
- USS *Kincaid* (DD 965)/USS *Fletcher* (DD 992) (destroyers)—both were a part of the team at various points—participating in the Navy Sea Swap program where crews would rotate to different ships

Two additional ships coordinated their movements with CDS 7:

- USS *Bunker Hill* (CG 52) (cruiser)—Captain Faris Farwell, was our Air Defense Command ship
- USS *Rainier* (AOE 7) (fast combat support ship)—Captain Rodeo Pinson, was our replenishment ship. They were *always* there, ready and able to provide whatever was required for food (awesome cookies!), fuel, and ammunition.

STRIKE GROUP LEADERSHIP

REAR ADMIRAL BARRY COSTELLO

I attended the College of the Holy Cross with a Navy ROTC scholarship. Following graduation, I served in at-sea and shore assignments that prepared me to command Cruiser-Destroyer Group 1. I had sailed with strike groups as a destroyer squadron operations office (CDS 5) on USS *Ranger* (CV 61) and as destroyer squadron commander (CDS 23) on USS *Nimitz* (CVN 68), often operating in the North Arabian Gulf. In these assignments, I gained invaluable experience working with the group commander and his staff, the carrier commanding officer, and the air wing commander. During my assignment as the operations officer at 3rd Fleet, I learned the ins and outs of fleet staff operations. My assignments on the Joint Staff and at Navy legislative affairs gave me an appreciation of how information flowed in the Pentagon and on Capitol Hill. These tours of duty provided me with a solid foundation from which to lead at this critical juncture of our history.

Some leaders try to handpick the people who will be the key players in their organization. Sometimes this works out well, but often it is a failed strategy. *I believe you should play the cards you are dealt, give your people a positive environment and every opportunity to succeed, mentor them, and if they do not rise to the challenge—then make a change.* This is the philosophy I executed with all my commanders, and it worked for my team. My warfare commanders consisted of the following leaders:

CAPTAIN JOHN MILLER

Commanded *Constellation* and was the Information Warfare Commander (IWC) for the strike group. He was a naval flight officer specializing in weapons and sensor employment in the aircraft and began his career in the F-14 community. He spent time in Washington, D.C. as a White House Fellow in the George H.W. Bush administration. His at-sea career focused on the Arabian Gulf region, whether flying F-14s or commanding USS *Dubuque* (LPD 8) and USS *Juneau* (LPD 10). Therefore, he was the perfect naval officer to command *Constellation* for the 2002–2003 deployment. He was the total package of warrior ethos, organizational excellence, and people skills. When I first met him at a National Security Administration briefing in Fort Meade, Maryland, I immediately noted his positive attitude and obvious competence. My first impression was that he would play a critical role as one of my advisors on the challenges that lay ahead. That assessment proved to be right on the mark. Commander Miller was fortunate to have two superb assistants in executive officer Captain David Maloney and Command Master Chief Mark Hayes (*who made his first overseas deployment on Constellation 26 years earlier*).

CAPTAIN MARK FOX

Commanded CVW-2. He was a pilot extraordinaire, having shot down an Iraqi MiG in Operation Desert Storm. He commanded the first F/A-18E/F Super Hornet Squadron, VFA-122. Additionally, he served in the White House Military Office, and at Supreme Headquarters Allied Powers Europe in Belgium. He was a superb leader, and he set a professional tone throughout the air wing. I recall him coming to me with a squadron leadership challenge early on in our relationship. He presented the issue clearly, explained his thought process, defined options, and detailed the action he was about to take. He wanted to inform me of the action, looking for my input and perspective should I desire to engage. His thinking was spot on correct, and I indicated my concurrence. Captain Michael Geron was the deputy air wing commander, and the command master chief was Peter Flores. These leaders played pivotal roles in developing the air wing team.

COMMODORE MARK BALMERT

The leader of CDS 7. He was the Sea Combat Commander (SCC), directing the ships and submarines assigned to the group. Commodore Balmert grew up in the Navy destroyer community, commanding the USS *Chandler* (DDG 996). He was well versed in the intricacies of dealing with the submarine threat and utilized every asset in the San Diego area to support the training of his teams. He was also responsible for escort operations, and this duty would take on great significance during our time in the Arabian Gulf. This would include the military escort of hundreds of ships from the Suez Canal to the Bab-el-Mandeb Strait off Yemen to the Strait of Hormuz bordered by Iran and Oman.

CAPTAIN FARIS FARWELL

Commanded the cruiser USS *Bunker Hill* (CG 52) and served as the Air Defense Commander (ADC), utilizing assets from the ships and air wing to protect the force from any air threats. He deployed to the western Pacific and Arabian Gulf many times during his career. His previous command of USS *Reuben James* (FFG 57) prepared him for this major command assignment. His challenges were compounded by the reality that of the top four commanders, he was the only one not based aboard *Constellation* (some might say this would be a blessing, but connectivity with the leadership is imperative to ensure one is in step and understands Commander's Intent). He recognized this as an area where he needed to concentrate and succeeded in staying connected. He was a great leader who took on the tough task of working ship and air wing assets together to protect the force.

CAPTAIN DON HEPFER

My chief of staff. He provided critical continuity through the transition of leadership. He did a fantastic job of running the staff, dealing with day-to-day administrative and personnel issues. He kept the schedule functioning smoothly, which allowed me to focus on planning at the operational level of warfare. Captain Hepfer was also an experienced advisor regarding operations. I valued his opinion, wise judgment, and loyalty.

———

A key leadership principle I developed early in my USS *Elliot* command tour in 1992 was *to create an environment where your people can succeed.* It became very clear to me that the *Elliot* team had all the elements to be highly successful. *My role was to provide them with the necessary tools, strategic guidance, and an atmosphere where success was a given when we all worked together.* Once that was achieved—I got out of the way and let my team run. They exceeded my every expectation and worked hard not to let the "old man" down. *In this positive environment, people want to come to work, and there is an opportunity for them to use their imagination and initiative to make things better.* I teach this concept today to admirals, generals, and business leaders. Seems obvious, but it is the rare organization that truly succeeds in achieving this dynamic. I used this concept in every command, including 3rd Fleet—it works.

Now, in 2002, I employed this principle. This leadership team would train together for the next five months and create the environment for the 7,500 Sailors and Marines to succeed in combat. Secretary of Defense Rumsfeld said, "You go to war with the army you have, not the army you might want or wish to have at a later time." I could not have wished for a better group of Sailors and Marines to carry out our mission. They were exactly the right team, in the right place, at the right time.

CHAPTER 2 | PRE-DEPLOYMENT TRAINING

"Winning is habit forming, and it occurs because of a team effort with concise goals, clear expectations, and detailed planning... You are the leaders of the group. This is your time. Seize the moment. Step forward to lead your crews to continue the positive momentum we have established..."

—Rear Admiral Barry Costello, USN
Commander, Cruiser-Destroyer Group 1

PRIORITIES

My first weeks in command focused on visiting each of the ships in the strike group to look the leadership in the eye and gauge their capabilities. The June to October 2002 training timeframe would be important to ensure we were ready for deployment. With that in mind, I listened to their concerns and challenges. It was also an opportunity to address the crew and pass along my *Commander's Priorities*. On each visit, I spent time with the commanding officer and the command master chief (senior enlisted advisor). Then I spoke to the officers in their dining area, the chiefs in their meeting room, and the crew on the flight deck. It was clear that the Sailors "had their lights on" and were a talented group who would rise to any challenge. I talked to these audiences about the upcoming deployment in November, their role in getting ready, and my priorities for them.

The issue of *priorities* has been a part of my mantra since 1990 when I received them in my welcome to the Joint Staff in the Pentagon (my first time in the building). I was then assigned to the J7, Joint Doctrine and Interoperability Directorate, as a new commander. Part of my check-in included an audience with Major General Mac Armstrong, U.S. Air Force, the Deputy J7. Up to this point in my career, I had no direct interaction with admirals or generals; this visit was precedent setting for me. I readied myself with potential questions and answers. When I walked into his office, I had a pen in hand, ready to take many notes. I was prepared to write down key elements of National Strategy or Chairman of the Joint Chiefs General Colin Powell's Vision for the Force.

It was just another check-in for General Armstrong, but for me, it opened new vistas. He began by welcoming me and said that he would tell me about *his* priorities; and since I worked in his organization, they would become *mine*. He talked of priorities in a manner that I had never heard.

He began with the first priority, *"Take care of yourself."* By this, he did not mean to be selfish, but rather develop myself mentally, morally, and physically.

- Read good books, editorial pages, and journals he said. Be well versed in the issues of the day and engage in intelligent conversation outside of military topics.
- Practice whatever religion or faith you believed in, as that foundation will come in handy during trying times. It is a part of your being and should not be ignored.
- Stay in shape by making time each day for some physical activity. Put it in as an integral part of the schedule, *not* as an after-thought.

The second priority was to *"Take care of your family."*

- Moms and dads would not be with us forever. Find time to spend with them; tell them you love them, and how you understand that without their sacrifices you would not have been able to succeed.
- Kids grow up quickly. Make sure you are at that important soccer game even on a workday. If you need to make up the time on the weekend, so be it.
- Do not take your spouse for granted. Ensure they know the pivotal role they play, and more importantly the fact that you appreciate it.
- Take leave (vacation time). The military provides it so that you can spend time with your family. It is *not* a sign of dedication to have 60+ days of leave saved on the books.

The third priority was to *"Execute the job on the Joint Staff."* It was not third because it was unimportant. On the contrary, the role of the Joint Staff was increasing dramatically. The part I would play in the initial formulation of Joint Doctrine would be groundbreaking.

General Armstrong explained that he *did not lose* people because they did not work hard... most military officers are type "A" personalities (very competitive, high work involvement). But he *did lose* people because they did not take care of the first two priorities. One could not properly focus on the job in support of the team effort unless the first two priorities were "squared away." If they were, the officer had every opportunity to reach full potential. If not, there was no chance, no matter how many hours were put into the job.

That is my memory of the interview, 27 years ago. I had not written a thing in my notebook... but I remembered every word. As I walked out of the general's office, I knew my perspective would never be the same. His philosophy was so very simple, yet so deep and inspirational. *Treat people like adults, encourage them, place their welfare and that of their family first and they will exceed your wildest expectations.* Why had I never heard this before? What a concept. *Every* person who has worked for me since that day, no matter what rank, has received this guidance. I can attest to the fact that organizations succeed with these ideas as their guiding principles.

PREPARING FOR BATTLE

Early in my command assignment, I spoke to all officers in the air wing. Captain Fox had his team assembled in the Naval Air Force Pacific auditorium at the Naval Air Station North Island. My first words were, "We are going to war... every time you prepare for a mission and launch off the deck of *Constellation,* treat it as a wartime flight." The silence was deafening, as the import of my words set in. The look on the faces of the audience told what they were thinking—this is a surface warfare officer (vice aviator) who has either lost his mind... or maybe knows something we do not know... a 50/50 chance of either possibility!

There was a method to my message and delivery. I truly believed that the *Constellation* Strike Group deployment window of November 2002 to May 2003 would be the optimal time for a strike against Iraq if

26

the other Instruments of National Power failed to produce an acceptable outcome to the current stalemate. The United Nations process of weapons inspections was plodding forward at a slow rate, and I felt the administration did not have endless patience. Also, I had deployed to the Arabian Gulf many times over the past 28 years and knew firsthand that winter was a significantly better time to launch an attack than during the oppressively hot summer. Thus, I wanted my team to be on a mental wartime footing from the beginning of our training exercises, or workups. There was no time to lose—lives would be at stake.

Workups are wonderful opportunities. They are like training camp in sports. You get a chance to see players in action, observe their strengths and evaluate how to address their weaknesses. There are trainers ashore and at sea. The idea is to train ashore first, working on basics and integrating skill sets, and then go to sea to test out the training aboard ships—with all the "Murphy's" (adage that states that "anything that can go wrong, will go wrong") available to test the crew's ability to adjust. Workups are observed and assessed by a team of experienced officers whose job is to identify deficiencies, such that the group can benefit from these events and be better prepared to operate in the forward areas.

The Navy is currently emphasizing synthetic training where skills are tested in a simulated environment. This is good, *but* there is still a need to get underway and test skill sets and systems within the reality of the unknown variables that occur only at sea.

As a part of my preparation for the *Constellation* Strike Group training, I visited the carrier USS *Abraham Lincoln* (CVN 72) in May 2002 to observe Rear Admiral John Kelly and his staff during a pre-deployment exercise. I saw the interaction with Rear Admiral Ham Talent's team of assessors (he was Commander Carrier Group 1 (CCG-1)—a shore-based training staff for strike groups).

I also had the opportunity to fly on to USS *Coronado* (AGF 11), flagship for 3rd Fleet, to observe the training during the same period. It was a perfect opportunity to learn. I took detailed notes and asked many questions while trying to be unobtrusive, realizing that the *Constellation* Strike Group would be jumping through the same hoops four months later.

The one thing that stood out was how the perceptions of reality on the 3rd Fleet staff versus those on the *Lincoln* Strike Group staff differed dramatically. It was as if the two organizations had different sets of facts. This reality was not fatal to success, and the *Lincoln* Strike Group did well. However, *I saw that frequent, near constant, communication with higher headquarters as to perceptions and intentions was imperative.* This lesson stayed with me throughout training, during the transit to the Gulf, and during the combat operations. Lives were saved in combat because of effective communications with commander 5th Fleet in Bahrain and the Combined Air Operations Center (CAOC) in Saudi Arabia during the war.

TRAINING ASHORE

In our early workups, the strike group team went to Tactical Training Group Pacific (TTGP) for a five day in port warfare commanders training session where sophisticated simulators mimic ship and aircraft movements. It involved being presented with warfighting scenarios; conducting planning and creating options for action; presenting these options in a brief to commander 3rd Fleet with a recommended course of action and appropriate rationale noting pros and cons of each option; and finally, executing the selected option in a wargame. It was an important week for everyone to get to know how to work together and to discuss a range of operational issues.

One issue that always arises in training is the interpretation of the Rules of Engagement (ROE). Simply stated, ROE are the guidelines handed down by the Chairman of the Joint Chiefs that address when and where someone can discharge a weapon. ROE are challenging to fully comprehend and are normally parsed by the local Judge Advocate General (JAG—lawyer). The ROE have been the subject of volumes of analysis and years of debate. This issue is highlighted before and during every conflict.

The JAG, Lieutenant Commander Errol Henriques, gave his spiel on ROE to the assembled leadership. This led to a healthy discussion of terms such as "hostile intent" and "hostile action." How can one determine intent? What constitutes hostile action? It takes work to appreciate subtleties, stay within the law, and understand the differences. The give-and-take became more animated as they argued different scenarios—*just what I wanted*. The audience was restless. The officers had appropriately pushed back to minimize restrictions on their movements and actions. The group needed to get this conversation out of their system early, before going to sea together, and long before going into combat.

I let the discussion continue for a while and then stepped to the front to quell the building tempest. I told them that I appreciated the give-and-take. The JAG had done his job to school us on the fine points of ROE. Now it was my turn. I boiled down this discussion of the ROE for them and provide my Commander's Intent: *"You will not take the first hit*—that's it. Do your homework and know the situation before you launch/engage. If you feel that the enemy has demonstrated hostile intent, or you have seen a hostile action—do your job and engage. *Do not hesitate, or you will lose.* Use sound judgment and common sense, and I will back you."

As a junior officer, I heard a similar sentiment from Vice Admiral Henry Mustin while I attended Surface Warfare Department Head School in Newport, Rhode Island and adopted it as my own philosophy. *I wanted to have thinking captains, pilots, and tactical action officers, but could not afford to have these talented people overanalyzing a situation that could lead to the loss of American lives. We would not be trigger happy. We would be well schooled in our environment, use intelligence wisely, and destroy anyone who threatened the force.*

The training week at TTGP culminated with a wargame scenario that placed the *Constellation* Strike Group in the South China Sea. The intelligence built up to address a situation where one of the contested islands in that part of the world became the focus of naval forces.

- Captain Farwell, as the ADC, was tasked to provide me with situational awareness of our environment by keeping track of the air traffic and maintaining aircraft airborne.
- Commodore Balmert, as the SCC, worked to ensure we discovered anyone approaching the island we were tasked to secure by maintaining awareness of all ships and submarines

approaching the force, as well as the appropriate disposition of our ships, helicopters, and surveillance aircraft.

- Captain Fox supported both efforts with his air wing.
- Captain Miller kept *Constellation* in position, while also carrying out his role as the IWC, using the airwaves to advertise our peaceful intentions while attempting to determine intentions of other forces with the help of our intelligence team.

The TTGP training team threw as many variables into the equation as possible, attempting to overwhelm decision makers. The warfare commanders anticipated future actions, which caused the TTGP staff frustration as their "surprises" were either discovered early or handled efficiently. There were many *firsts* on the plus side, and several lessons learned which would benefit us in our upcoming at-sea exercises.

This training gave me my first opportunity to evaluate the talent of my staff in the watchstanding arena. *Standing watch is both an art and a science.* Watchstanders must ensure the commander is informed as required, ensure the orders of the commander are carried out and be able to lead the watch team in the command center. Additionally, the watchstander needs to be able to reach throughout the force at a moment's notice to get critical information, to redirect the effort of deployed forces, or to recommend launch of additional assets. It takes an individual with stamina because the hours are long and the pace is often furious. It takes good judgment because the person needs to be able to prioritize the focus of the effort.

There is no rulebook to direct who stands the Flag (admiral's) watch. I have always sought out those whom I could trust without regard to their job designation. The rank of the individual did not matter to me. I needed to be able to go about the business of operating the force, to stay connected with higher headquarters as well as subordinates, and to plan for future events—confident that my watch team was keeping the force moving in accordance with my direction or letting me know of any required deviation.

Many officers rotated through the watch to get experience; however, once we sailed west, I settled on the teams that I would retain throughout the deployment, including during the heart of the warfighting. I would rely on four "horses" to lead the admiral's watch.

The morning watch (0600–1200) would be directed by Lieutenant Commander Jay Cavalieri, a meteorologist by trade, assisted by Lieutenant Kitty Ketter, an S-3 naval flight officer. Both were well versed in surface warfare and air wing issues, and they were effective in supporting the first launches of the day.

Lieutenant Commander Rich Theil, my radar link coordination officer, took the afternoon shift (1200–1800). He was a driving force behind keeping the radar picture up-to-date. His voice was well recognized throughout the force. Your ship did not want to be called on the carpet by Rich—as you knew he was right and had tried to sort things out informally before a "blast" over the voice circuit.

The evening watch (1800–2400) was directed by Commander Brick Conners. Brick was the senior aviation expert on my staff. He was an F/A-18 pilot and had an outstanding appreciation of the challenges of operating aircraft from the carrier deck. I relied heavily on his counsel, and he never let me down.

Lieutenant Jake Jacobs assisted Brick. Jake was my aide and came from the P-3 community. The aide does not normally stand watch, being fully employed taking care of the admiral's schedule. However, I saw enormous potential in this officer and decided that his talents would be best utilized learning strike group operations versus being solely focused on supporting my movements. He exhibited extraordinarily good judgment, and despite his relatively junior rank, had an uncanny ability to interface with senior officers and get things done.

The night watch (0000–0600) was led by Commander Mark Colby and Commander Al Desmaris, two strong players who would get us through the early hours. These were two experienced officers, and therefore I could sleep with confidence—critical, as I needed the rest to remain clear-headed to make good decisions.

I learned things later from others that I did not appreciate at the time. In a 2017 conversation with Jay Cavalieri, he related his memory of sailing for the Gulf after our Singapore port visit. As I signed out the watch bill (paper that designates all personnel to stand watch) for this final leg of the transit to the 5th Fleet operating area, he asked when I was going to shift to senior captains for the watch. I told him that the team was set, and he would play an integral part in teeing up our day for success. I thought I had made this commitment clear earlier, but apparently, some thought that I would shift into wartime mode. *This was an example of my need to be very precise regarding my intentions.* Jay recalled his sense of... wow, he is really going to stick with us junior players. I'd better continue to play at the varsity level because this is it for the duration of the deployment.

9/11/2001 ANNIVERSARY

On the first anniversary of September 11, Secretary of Defense Rumsfeld sent a message to the military:

"Today, Americans everywhere are pausing to remember September 11 of last year—a day forever etched in our minds and hearts.

While the dimensions of the tragedy were profound to be sure, so too was the outpouring of patriotism that united our people. Heroes arose among us who rescued the wounded, comforted the dying, and went to war to defend the freedoms Americans hold dear.

You can be proud of what has been accomplished thus far... but notwithstanding the many accomplishments, we are still closer to the beginning of this war than to its end. Victory will take patience and courage. But we will prevail. We will prevail because our cause is just—and our nation is blessed with the greatest armed force on the face of the earth.

Thank you for all you have done, and continue to do, for our country and the world."

At 0846, bells rang in firehouses and churches across the country. The strains of Mozart's Requiem were heard in at least 21 different time zones, including in 24 countries. Splinters of the destroyed buildings were on display at memorial sites in Nevada, Tennessee, Ohio, and Wyoming. The day was marked by candlelight vigils and prayer services in thousands of American communities, each commemorating the day in their own solemn way.

Aboard *Constellation*, Sailors gathered in the ship's forward hangar bay to remember and honor the men and women who sacrificed their lives for freedom on that fateful day.

Commander Robert McClanahan, the ship's chaplain, gave a respectful and heartfelt invocation.

Commodore Balmert spoke about events leading up to 9/11/01 on *Constellation* and ended his remarks as follows:

> "On the first observance of Patriot's Day, let us not forget our freedom has enemies. That is why we so proudly serve this nation."

Following Commodore Balmert's remarks, Captain Miller focused on the present:

> "We are stronger today than we were a year ago— stronger as a nation; stronger as a Navy; stronger as a crew... We are stronger now because the heinous acts of that day serve to remind us of how precious our lives, relationships, and freedoms are. We are stronger on *Constellation* because we know what the consequences of not being ready might be."

My concluding remarks focused on the future. I quoted President Bush:

> "We cannot defend America and our friends by hoping for the best... The only path to safety is a path of action."

TRAINING AT SEA

We continued our training off the coast of southern California into October, including two at-sea periods of major significance before deployment. These are called Composite Training Underway Exercise (COMPTUEX) and Joint Task Force Exercise (JTFEX). These exercises are designed to get the group prepared for operations in the forward theaters of 7th Fleet (western Pacific/Indian Ocean) and 5th Fleet (Arabian Gulf).

Carrier Group 1 would observe, educate, and grade the events, with a focus on staff reactions. This was an important mission set. I met with Rear Admiral Talent early in the training window and established my goals.

I made several things clear from the start. First, we would not have any staff meetings without his representative present. There would be no secret meetings to figure out how to outsmart the trainers. My staff made the mistake of having one meeting without a trainer present. I immediately shut down the meeting until Rear Admiral Talent's representative arrived. I only had to do that once—the message was clear.

The second thing I emphasized was that I was not concerned about grades for the various events, or any competition in this regard with strike groups that had passed this way before us. Rather, I wanted Rear Admiral Talent and his team to be brutally frank with us and not sugar-coat our weaknesses—lean in and make recommendations based on their observation of other groups' best practices and *prepare us for war*. I would rather score in the '70s and '80s while learning with different watch teams than score 100 while only playing my starters and not reaping the full benefit of the training. I wanted us to be fully prepared when we headed west for deployment. Even with that approach, the strike group achieved a high score. Rear Admiral Talent and his people did a superb job, and the success of our efforts during the war was a testament to their professionalism.

As we moved forward toward deployment, all aspects of strike group operations were coming together nicely, except the ability to act as a Launch Area Coordinator (LAC) for the planning and execution of Tomahawk missile missions. The Tomahawk Land Attack Missile

(TLAM) is a pilotless, long-range, all-weather submarine or ship-launched land attack cruise missile. The missile was designed to be a highly survivable weapon, used against pre-programmed land targets by flying low-altitude, contour-following missions. Tomahawk is powered by a high-efficiency turbojet engine using high-density fuel. The range of the missile is classified. However, it is unclassified to say that it is more than 1,000 statute miles.

There are two variants of Tomahawk cruise missiles. Both are distinguished by their warhead. TLAM-C has a conventional warhead. TLAM-D has a conventional submunitions (dispense bomblets) warhead, and another payload launched against power grid type targets.

The missile is 18 feet long with a nearly 9-foot wingspan. It generally flies at subsonic speed (381–571 mph). The missile uses inertial guidance from launch point to the target with Inertial Navigation System (INS), Terrain Contour Matching (TERCOM) position updates, Digital Scene-Matching Area Correlator (DSMAC) to increase terminal accuracy in the target area, and a Global Positioning System (GPS).

The assigned team had little background in the Tomahawk weapon system and therefore was unable to lead in the intricacies of timing multiple missile launches for simultaneous arrival on land targets. This had the potential to be a major issue, with significant implications.

Lieutenant Commander Dino Pietrantoni checked on to the staff just before deployment. He was a born leader, who effectively used levity to ease the tension of the moment. *And*—was a Tomahawk expert! Nirvana. Immediately our evaluations by training teams went through the roof. "Best ever" was a common phrase. This critical piece of our readiness was finally in place.

The COMPTUEX was a three-week window in which the strike group completes required gun, torpedo, and missile firings for qualification. These exercises provide multiple opportunities to interact with air, surface and submarine force opposition in an intermediate level of sophistication. The strike group had previously worked on individual ship and unit skills; now all ships came together for the first time to work as an entire force.

The carrier left port with a clear flight deck because the pilots of the air wing had been honing their skills elsewhere, being unable to operate off the deck of a carrier pierside. They had flown to their home bases earlier after completing preliminary at-sea qualifications off the carrier flight deck. They then went to Fallon, Nevada for training at the Naval Strike Warfare Center. There they conducted mock dogfights, executed precision strike training, and studied the lessons learned from prior events. Each flight received a replay with a realistic no-holds-barred analysis of the tactics employed by the crews—with *goods* and *others*. These performance critiques can dampen the ego of even the most skilled pilots and prove to be excellent training at the highest level.

The rest of the ships sortie (join up) at the designated position off the waters of Southern California. The air wing flies onto the carrier at sea. Communications circuits are checked and always present challenges. Engineers ensure engines, pumps, and evaporators are working as designed. Weaponeers conduct last minute checks on their control consoles. Operators tune radars for peak performance and ensure the ship is in the proper position within the group. The supply department checks food stores for the at-sea period. The ships are humming along, preparing for the myriad of tasks that will come their way.

This same cycle occurs in preparation for JTFEX, which is a 12-day graduate-level exercise with the added complexity of operating with assets from the other services (joint) and other countries (combined). Normally these exercises are separated by several weeks, allowing the players to step back, take a critical look at the COMPTUEX execution, and incorporate lessons learned into the planning for JTFEX. In our case, we worked with 3rd Fleet to merge the timing of these events. Considering the logistical challenges of flying the air wing off as the carrier remained in port and then back on the carrier a few weeks later coupled with the fact that we were deploying earlier than the normal rotation, we requested that the events be separated by only a weekend. This allowed the air wing to stay on the carrier, and the ships and crews to retain their focus and edge as they became immersed in the more advanced JTFEX scenario.

JTFEX has its own buildup of intelligence to support a complex scenario. World tensions are heightened. There are a wide variety of role players who represent regional nations and their navies. There are potential threats in the air, on the surface, undersea, and in cyberspace. Proficiency in each of these domains would be tested. Captain Farwell on *Bunker Hill* worked closely with Captain Fox to set up the air defense of the force. Commodore Balmert prepped for surface and submarine warfare, and Captain Miller readied for interaction in the information warfare arena.

The force was probed by various threats. Reaction times, as well as knowledge of the ROE, were tested. Tensions ran high. The group had to make a transit through a narrow strait (similar to the Strait of Hormuz in the Arabian Gulf). Decisions were required as to a day or night movement through the strait, flying helicopters or not, positioning submarines, and dealing with small boats that crossed our path. These potential real-world events had been discussed, but now it was time to determine if the guidance had permeated through the various ship commands and reached the watchstanders who might be the key people required to make immediate decisions to protect the ship or to strike a near or far target.

The training was very realistic. The crews really got into the action. Restraint was the initial guidance, with the right of self-defense always present. As the world situation deteriorated, the leadership was required to reassess the force posture, and ultimately hostilities commenced in all domains. We had several early wins in training, which set a positive tone.

RESPONSIBILITY FOR WEAPONS LAUNCH

We had successfully carried out hundreds of flights during our COMPTUEX and JTFEX exercises. Safety was paramount in all written and verbal guidance as we continued to jump through the pre-deployment hoops at sea. Life was good. The evaluators from 3rd Fleet and their surrogates from CCG-1 were pleased with the group's attention to detail. We were in the *red zone* to use a football analogy, closing in on the successful completion of the JTFEX. Only two days remained, with one last day of strikes.

In my earlier assignment as the operations officer (N3) at 3rd Fleet (1994–1996), I experienced many at-sea exercises of deploying strike groups. The 3rd Fleet reserve detachment would serve as the Joint Force Air Component Commander (JFACC) for this exercise. This group consisted of senior reserve officers with vast experience in all things aviation. They had many deployments to forward operating locations such as the Air Force Operations Center in Saudi Arabia. They had also run many of the air scenarios for strike group graduation exercises.

Thus, the scene was set for the team of professionals from the JFACC to interact with the experts from the air wing. They would work together to plan and execute the daily Air Tasking Order (ATO) as well as any emergent tasking. There is no more sophisticated training in the world. Thousands of people are involved in the movement of aircraft and weaponeering (deciding what weapons go on which aircraft and the actual crews to place bombs on targets).

My background and experience at 3rd Fleet taught me that very few things execute as planned, as circumstances change in a fluid environment. Planning is a critical element of the process, and the value of that effort is the thought that is involved. But once the dynamic environment of operations takes over, it is up to the aviators (in this case) to carry the plan forward or adjust to the situation at hand.

It is a tried and true reality that mistakes generally occur when people are tired. This would be no exception. We were coming to the end of two exhausting training periods. I interviewed Commander Walt Stammer in 2017. He was the executive officer of the VFA-137 "Kestrels" in 2002. His perspective is summarized here.

> Part of the air wing certification was a long-range strike. This strike had been planned for several weeks but had been weathered out because the required civilian Omega contract tanker could not launch in the harsh conditions. The strike planners in the air wing aboard *Constellation* and the JFACC team at 3rd Fleet had ample opportunity to view photographs of the "target" at Nellis Air Force Base. They questioned the Nellis controllers via email, to confirm coordinates and to verify that this target was, in

fact, a strike target—to be attacked by real weapons. Questions arose, as this target looked to be a very new and pristine structure, as opposed to the typical hulks on any range. They received an affirmative answer from Nellis controllers via email.

On that fateful day, many aircraft were striking various targets. One of these targets was the long-range strike mission to Nellis Air Force Base (approximately 450 miles) for an F/A-18 laser-guided training round (LGTR) (no explosives, but kinetic energy from the round). The group of four fighters made their way north from the waters off Southern California. On the way, they received fuel from the waiting Omega tanker.

The aircraft approached the target, recognized that it was a *very new* trailer ("...the Air Force has lots of money; on Navy ranges targets are normally burned-out hulks of buildings or vehicles"). The crew made the final reports as required, and then launched their LGTR. The round entered one side, passed through the trailer, and exited the other side... of a trailer that was NOT a target for this exercise.

Fortunately, and miraculously, no one was injured. The strike occurred after work hours, and the trailer, normally manned by range personnel, was empty.

An investigation ensued. Bottom line: it should never have happened. Yes, the team did inquire as to the appropriateness of this target via email. But something was seriously wrong with this "target" and *direct voice communication* with a supervisor at Nellis would have been appropriate based on the early indications and concerns that something was amiss. The gut feeling was that there was something wrong, and that intuition should have been pursued further. *This was a good lesson.* We learned from it, and it helped us as we later launched live weapons in support of the advance of coalition ground forces through southern Iraq in March and April. The wartime guidance provided was: *launch* if sure; but to *not launch* if there was *any* question.

I am grateful for Commander Stammer's firsthand account of this incident. He flew to Nellis that day, though he was not the pilot who dropped the LGTR.

The "so what" is for each strike group going through training to go many extra miles to "trust but verify." Even with my prior 3rd Fleet exercise experience, and numerous verbal and written cautions to pay close attention to detail when dropping weapons—it still happened. *At the end of the day, it comes down to the individual Sailor or Marine, like any other organization, being trained to make the right decision regardless of all the guidelines put into place by higher authority.*

"MAN OVERBOARD—THIS IS NOT A DRILL"

Operations at sea are inherently dangerous. Safety is paramount. There are moving parts, rough seas, and multiple occasions for accidents. This is true on any ship. However, the deck of an aircraft carrier during night flight operations is a special case.

The noise is deafening. Aircraft are positioned, launched, and recovered with minimal lighting. Blast deflectors are erected, and pilots rev up their engines. Aircraft are launched off the front of the ship by four steam-driven catapults, accelerating from 0 to 150 miles per hour in two seconds. At the back end of the flight deck, there are four arresting wires that cross the deck that catch returning aircraft as pilots drop a hook, decelerating the aircraft from 150 miles per hour to a complete stop in that same two-second interval. The process is termed *cat* (catapult) and *trap* (recover on deck).

For anyone who has experienced a cat and trap, it is a life-changing experience that your mind, body, and spirit never forget. There is a rush of adrenaline as you sit attached to the catapult awaiting the launch. Similarly, that same rush occurs as your returning aircraft approaches the deck—a deck that looks like the size of a postage stamp, possibly rocking at the same time as you gauge your angle of descent. Naval aviators (Navy and Marine) are the only people in the world who can perform this feat.

On Saturday, 19 October 2002, *Constellation* was conducting night flight operations in the waters off San Diego 100 miles from the coast. The flight deck crew consisted of hundreds of Sailors. They ranged from veterans with years of experience on the deck to those who had recently reported aboard with no experience. New personnel are assigned a veteran "buddy" who guides them through the evolutions taking place on the flight deck and ensures their safety as aircraft are moved into position for launch and recovery.

However, on this night that safety procedure broke down. Shortly after midnight Airman Michael Harris of VFA-151 entered the flight deck from the starboard catwalk (right side ladderway) between elevators one and two. He inadvertently walked behind an EA-6B Prowler jet aircraft just as the pilot was revving up its engines. Airman Harris was immediately blown over the side of the ship by the engine's blast of energy.

The rest of the story is an amazing struggle for survival. The night was moonless; the sea was pitch-black. *Constellation* responded immediately to the man overboard. The bridge and radar teams marked the spot in the ocean as precisely as possible where Airman Harris had entered the water and began maneuvering the ship to return to that position. The ship continued to travel a considerable distance before the effect of the rudder kicked in. Then the ship traced its track in the opposite direction. The strike group ceased all operations to focus on the rescue effort.

Bunker Hill, Valley Forge, and *Kinkaid* left their assigned stations to join the search. Helicopters scanned the sea for any sign of Airman Harris. Despite these efforts, there was no contact.

The life vest Airman Harris wore was equipped with a strobe light, whistle, and dye pack. The lack of a strobe light signal was puzzling. Was he unconscious? Had he somehow submerged? Was he alive? The water temperature was 62 degrees Fahrenheit. The medical team advised that the estimated survival time in these waters was four and a half hours.

The search continued throughout the night. The vastness of the sea is hard to visualize and truly difficult to appreciate until a situation such as this arises. The analogy of finding a needle in a haystack in the dark would be appropriate. But it was clear that we would not quit the search until this Sailor was found—period.

Tides, winds, and currents were factored into the search pattern. Higher headquarters was kept informed. Finally, at 0700 Sunday I called Vice Admiral Bucchi at his home and provided him with a report on the history of the event, current status, and my intention to continue the search. He appreciated the call, concurred with the plan, and asked to be kept informed as developments occurred.

By this time hope was fading as the Sailor had been in the water for seven hours. However, at 0720, a green patch of water was spotted by a helicopter crew. It was Harris' green dye pack that he had saved until daybreak that caught the eye of the crew. This team stayed close to Airman Harris.

As it turned out, the impact with the water, after a fall from 60 feet from the flight deck, caused the strobe light to be inoperable. This answered the question of why no strobe light was seen. Harris was initially unconscious after he hit the water, and when he awoke, he realized he was in a fight for his life. He was alone, on a pitch-black night, in the chilly waters of the Pacific Ocean. He was armed only with his training, physical readiness, and faith. The odds were very long against his survival...but survive he did!

The *Constellation* newspaper *Starscope* provided full coverage of the event. They reported that a helicopter from *Constellation* was on the scene with the helicopter from *Bunker Hill* and came to Airman Harris' rescue. As they neared the position, the Search-and-Rescue (SAR) swimmers went into action. The helicopter maneuvered into position, and one of the swimmers jumped into the water while the second member of the team manned the hoist. "We were prepared to face the worst, but when we saw his hands waving at us, we knew he was alive," said AW2 John Wittrock, a SAR swimmer for the HS-2 Golden Falcons. AW2 Jake Ohlson was the SAR swimmer who pulled Harris from the water. "When I got to him, I asked him how he was doing, and he said he was cold but OK."

The *Constellation* medical team evaluated Airman Harris and had him flown to Balboa Medical Center, San Diego for further assessment. He received medical treatment to support his kidneys and other internal organs that were impacted by his extended stay in salt water. Lieutenant Jeff Greene, a physician assistant on board, said, "He did everything right out there."

Later Airman Harris was flown to rejoin his teammates as *Constellation* entered the Arabian Gulf. This was an incredible story of a young American Sailor saved by keeping his wits about him in a life-threatening situation—now reunited with his crew—*much wiser for the experience.*

Because of this incident, Navy leadership dispatched a team to redesign the flight deck vests, and today there is a GPS chip in each vest that will send a signal back to the ship, indicating the exact position of someone who had the misfortune of falling overboard. The system is called "Man Overboard Indicator" (MOBI), and it incorporates a radio transmitter that broadcasts an emergency signal when immersed in salt water.

———

The *Constellation* Strike Group successfully completed advanced training. COMPTUEX and JTFEX exercises provided many opportunities to test procedures in all warfare disciplines. The team came together to make appropriate adjustments and moved forward with renewed confidence in their ability to deal with any eventuality they would face on deployment. The Tomahawk missile and maritime escort aspects of the training were especially beneficial. It was time to head west on deployment to 7th and 5th Fleets.

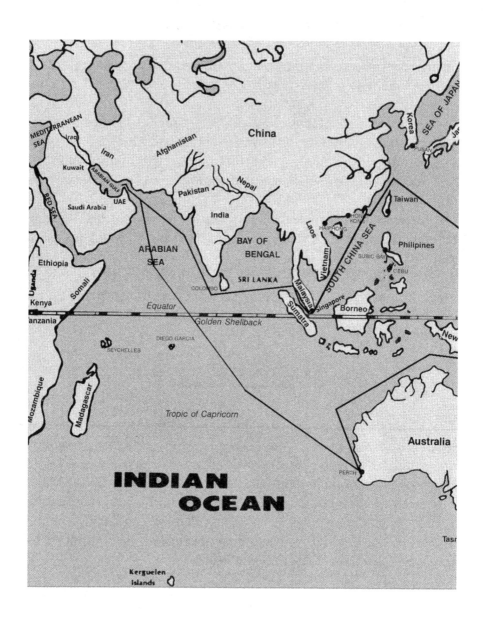

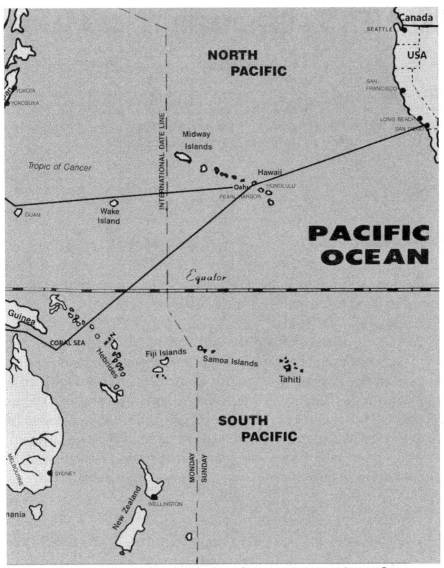

TRANSIT ROUTE OF THE *CONSTELLATION* STRIKE GROUP TO AND FROM THE ARABIAN GULF.

CHAPTER 3 | DEPLOYMENT TO THE ARABIAN GULF

"Citizens are mighty proud that the Constellation Strike Group is out here on the point, ready for call for fire. We are going to bring our asymmetric strengths to bear—which are speed, precision, and overwhelming force—if we go to war with Iraq, this world is going to see a new level of expertise."

—Admiral Vern Clark, USN
Chief of Naval Operations

On Saturday, 2 November 2002, *Constellation* Strike Group headed west from San Diego. This would be *Constellation's* 21st and final deployment. A banner reading "Okay, Let's Roll" hung from the fantail. Captain Miller told the gathered press, "The president told us a year ago to be ready, and we're ready."

Families gathered on the pier for a tearful wave goodbye, knowing their loved ones would be gone for more than six months, and possibly up to a year. For some of the crew, this would be their first deployment. For others, it would be one in a long series of departures on deployments in support of our nation. In either case, it was a difficult and emotional day, as much would happen on both ends while families were separated. Our goal was to return with everyone, but there were no guarantees while operating in the dangerous environment of the Arabian Gulf.

PEOPLE

I have talked about the leadership team. Here I want to highlight the excellence of our Sailors of all ranks and responsibilities. I chose two of many stories to display the competence that permeated this team.

The first was written by Seaman Journalist Jacob Joy, from the *Constellation* team, about Chief Warrant Officer Harold Hall.

> "When Sailors use the term 'salty,' they are talking about seasoned Sailors who have been there and done that. The ones who have spent years on the water... who have been to the ends of the earth and back, learning the Navy

inside out, and remained true to the creed they recited way back in boot camp. The ones who've missed countless birthdays and anniversaries, gone without the comforts most people take for granted, and continue to put their necks out on the line, all for their country.

Chief Warrant Officer Harold Hall, otherwise known as 'Cowboy,' is salt... this is his 17th deployment... and he has 26 years of naval service so far... His motto: 'I don't believe in bad days.'

Cowboy grew up in Dallas... 'I'm the same guy everywhere I go... if you stay positive and focused, it affects everyone around you. People feed on that. Sailors have got to stay positive. Our whole lifestyle is based on positive action and motivation. We set the standard for the rest of the country to emulate... Never let anyone break your spirit... I have the heart of a champion. Winning is an all-the-time-thing to me.'

Cowboy has a lot of pride in his division and in his spaces... He is a straight shooter, with high standards."

That snippet is indicative of one of many leaders who made it their goal to make a positive difference every day.

The next story involves two of our junior Sailors. It is a story written by Otto Kreisher of *Copley News*, one of our embedded reporters for an extended period from March to June 2003. He searched for the human side of stories and visited with many of the hardworking junior Sailors during his time on *Constellation*. He wrote the following:

"Where they work is a mix of Dante's Inferno, with crushing heat and flickering flames, and an early Industrial Age nightmare of pipes, valves, gears, wheels, gauges, tubes, and massive spinning turbines. But Matthew Sembach and Daniel Collinson don't seem to mind. 'I enjoy it,' Sembach said. 'I just like working with machinery.' Collinson had a similar sentiment.

Both Sailors are machinist's mates third class and 24 years old. They work in different parts of the *Constellation*'s engineering spaces, the massive caverns deep within the hull of the ship that hold the eight huge boilers, eight main turbines, six electrical generators and a bewildering array of other machinery.

Although the glamour on an aircraft carrier may be with the warplanes up on the flight deck, virtually everything that makes this 1,000-foot-long floating city of 5,000 people function starts in the engineering space.

'All the guys up there only want to fly their aircraft, but they're not leaving the flight deck without us,' Sembach said. 'Unless we're pushing the ship through the water in the right direction, they're not going anywhere.' He is a fireroom supervisor in Main Machinery Room 3... each of these rooms has two massive boilers that produce steam at 1,200 pounds of pressure, which drives large turbines and a giant transmission to turn one of the four big screw propellers. The boilers also supply the steam that powers the four catapults to launch aircraft, provides laundry service, generates all the ship's electricity and distills the sea's salty brine into potable water.

Sembach said his job is 'to make sure that our boilers are operating correctly'... in addition to gleaning information from gauges, Sembach said, 'I listen to the plant. I can tell when something changes.'

The temperature in the plant can range from 100 to 140 degrees. In reference to the heat Collinson said, 'That was pretty bad.' He worked his way up to his current job monitoring the health of his generator. A key responsibility, he said, is making sure enough sea water runs through the system to keep the generator cool. Collinson said he also supervises three younger Sailors working in his area. 'It's a lot of responsibility every day,' he said. 'It has its days, like any job, but it keeps me busy. I feel good about what I'm doing, and I'm learning something new every day.'"

There are thousands of other individual stories. Each one would parallel the commitment noted in these two examples of the many dedicated Sailors that make our Navy great.

BATTLE RHYTHM

For the next seven months, the *Constellation* Strike Group team would operate 24 hours a day. It was imperative to establish the most effective manner to conduct the business of operations throughout the organization by setting a battle rhythm. By this, I mean structuring the "rhythm" of daily briefings, meetings, meals, aircraft operations, and a wide variety of other events—some daily and planned well in advance, while others arose on short notice and must be accommodated into the cycle.

The basic premise of the battle rhythm is to provide opportunities for the staff to meet throughout the day to plan, to have ample opportunity to receive commander's guidance early and often, and to have windows of time for "decision briefs." Every group has its own rhythm, but the principles are the same. You do not totally "own" your battle rhythm, as it must account for the battle rhythm of higher headquarters. That said, our leadership team put together a template from which we could deviate as required. It held us in good stead throughout combat operations.

In my case, I do my best work early in the morning. Thus, I decided that the morning meeting of the staff and senior officers would begin at 0800 in the war room, a conference room where leadership and other officers would gather to discuss events of the day in a classified environment. Historically I had seen this occur at 0900, but it often caused leaders to be stuck in a meeting with the admiral and his team throughout the morning. I wanted to see the leadership (carrier commanding officer, carrier air group commander, destroyer squadron commander, and cruiser commanding officer (or representative)) first thing in the morning, provide my guidance, and then release them back to their organizations at 0900 so that they could be productive for the rest of the morning. I wanted them to *disseminate the content of our gathering to their people, an important effort to ensure the entire team was aligned with the commander's intentions for the day.*

The first time we gathered in this manner, one of my staff officers indicated that he would come and get me when everyone was ready to begin the meeting. I told him that would be unnecessary because I would be sitting at the head of the table at 0800 and we would begin immediately—regardless of who was present. As the brief proceeded, it was clear that the staff effort to package the information (intelligence, operations, logistics, and other subjects) needed work. I arose from my seat at 0859. The briefer (those who stand up in front and present information on the issues of the day) said that the session was not over. I disagreed, stating that the meeting would end at 0900 every day, so learn how to more efficiently package the information.

The next day, people were in their seats at 0800 for the beginning of the meeting, confident that they could plan their day after 0900. There was a genuine appreciation that I was giving them back time for their own use. It was not 100% happiness, as briefers had to prep an hour earlier than normal. However, I attempted to mitigate this by communicating that complex PowerPoint slides were not desired. Keep it simple and tee up the discussion—that was the key to a successful session.

The day was filled with planning discussions, and air and ship operations. I had an *open-door* policy and made it clear that I was interested in *working with planners early and often. This concept is now called "Design," where the commander provides input at the front-end to support planning efforts from the beginning and assists planners in directing their focus.* This maximizes the probability that the end-product coming to the commander hits the mark.

There is a necessity to achieve "balance" with proper rest, diet, and exercise, and to incorporate this into the battle rhythm. Fatigue is a primary cause of poor decision-making and negative command climate. I learned this reality from my time as a destroyer squadron commander on deployment—where I made mistakes that I could trace back to fatigue. I was determined to achieve a balance that would keep exhaustion at bay. This might seem obvious, *but* I have seen very poor execution of operations and poor leadership by well-meaning, hardworking leaders who burned themselves out and caused unintentional and unnecessary havoc with their staffs. We were preparing for war, and many lives would be at stake. My solution, with a day that started at 0500 and ended at midnight, was to *take a rest* from 1145–1300 every day. This provided a battery charge for me in the middle of the day. My aide was the gate guard during this window, ensuring no one disturbed the "old man" unless it was urgent.

To make sure I heard the voices of the strike group Sailors, I would periodically take a helicopter ride to visit the other ships, listen to the crews, and provide them direct insight as to my thinking for the deployment. As any leader will tell you, these interactions with the ships' crews are energizing, and I received valuable feedback from the junior Sailors as to how things were going, while answering their penetrating questions.

Dinner was at 1800. I was taught by Captain George Miller (USS *Whipple* (FF 1062) in 1983, where I served as his weapons officer), that meals were *not* a time to talk about work. I have known officers who avoided meals so that they would not have to interact with the admiral as he played 20 questions or "stump the dummy." There was no way I would allow that to happen in our Flag Mess (dining area for the admiral's staff and senior officers). Either sports or the news of the day was the primary subject of discussion. It was a *no threat* environment. Additionally, I ensured it was less formal than the past. Sliders (hamburgers) were more than acceptable. I found out later in discussions with junior officers that the resulting cost decrease in their monthly mess bill was much appreciated.

After dinner, I scheduled one more opportunity to meet with my senior leaders (1900–2000), to briefly review the day's operations and discuss actions that were to occur throughout the night. This was less structured than the morning gathering, and it provided them a chance to get things in front of me before nightfall, as well as for me to provide my guidance for evening operations.

I really liked this forum, as it allowed me (like the morning session) to put out my guidance for all the leadership to hear, as opposed to providing it in one-on-one sessions. An Achilles heel of organizations of this size is lack of cross-domain (air, surface, subsurface and cyber) information flow. As an example, the air wing could be totally focused on an action that might be in contradiction with something the air defense commander, surface/subsurface warfare commander, or the carrier commanding officer had in mind. That lack of communications and resulting conflict can be disastrous to the *harmony* that is necessary for success. It is the responsibility of the commander to ensure this does not occur, and that open lines of communication are maintained. Issues must be well vetted by all affected organizations before they come to the commander. *The commander ensures the environment is such that subordinate commanders will come without hesitation to provide priorities and review decisions that are coordinated across multiple domains.* The morning and evening meetings provided such a forum where all could be heard, and where my decisions were made in the open to foster the necessary harmony.

A sign appropriately hung in our conference room stating: "No Fighting in the War Room!"

CONSTELLATION FIRE

A fire on a carrier has the potential for catastrophic consequences. As we approached Hawaii, *Constellation* had a fire in an engineering space at 2020 on 8 November. It was caused by a fuel oil leak in Four Main Machinery Room. This is one of four cavernous rooms below the main decks that house the boilers and engines that power the ship, also known as "main spaces." The size and complexity of pipes and machinery in these rooms is impossible to imagine. Suffice to say that it takes a crew of professionals to manage the interaction between the steam, electrical and mechanical systems.

The fire alarm was sounded throughout the ship. Training lessons quickly kicked in; the ship's crew went to their general quarters positions (where the crew goes to their battle stations, and the ship is segmented by closing hatches to prevent flooding or fire movement). Ventilation was secured to the affected area as a step to prevent the spread of the fire. Sailors on the scene took their initial actions. The Damage Control Assistant (DCA) determined when/whether to release halon gas, a fire retardant. The commanding officer was on the ship's bridge receiving reports from the executive officer and providing him guidance—being careful to defer to those on the scene whose training had prepared them for such an emergency.

In the meantime, I was querying my watch officer on what he knew and if he had received reports from the ship. It was quiet and tense. My staff did not want to be pressing an already overloaded internal communication system; however, it was appropriate to keep the Flag (embarked admiral and staff) informed in such an emergency. Minutes pass by very slowly when you are trying to stay informed; frankly, it is an uncomfortable position. Reports were immediately sent to higher headquarters per the instructions in these cases. It is critical to get ahead of the flood of questions from on high, by early and often outreaches— preferably by voice, to provide an opportunity for two-way dialog versus a prolonged stream of back and forth email or "chats" (texts).

Early partial reports with a promise of additional information as it becomes available are significantly more important than a time-late comprehensive report. I reached out early to Admiral Doran at Pacific Fleet, Vice Admiral Bucchi at 3rd Fleet, and Vice Admiral Mike Malone the commander of Naval Air Forces. Very quickly everyone in the Navy hierarchy knew that *Constellation* had a fire. For a ship headed to a potential war zone—this was *not* good news.

The firefighters did their job superbly. The initial actions to isolate the fuel leak were successful, and measures put in place to deal with the fire were effective. After several hours, the ship stood down from general quarters, and all gear was restored. There was a collective sigh of relief when it was reported that there were no serious injuries.

The next morning Captain Miller offered me a tour of the fire area, and I invited Rear Admiral John Greenert to come along. Rear Admiral

Greenert, a submariner by trade, had flown from Hawaii to the carrier to enhance his awareness of strike group operations. After the fire, he had been tasked by Admiral Doran to provide an assessment that would determine how long the carrier would need to stop in Hawaii for repairs. When we arrived on the scene in the engine room, we saw a combination of fatigue and satisfaction on the firefighting crews' faces. They meticulously explained the source of the leak, the initial actions to minimize the flow, the recognition of the danger, the resultant call for general quarters to alert all hands to the imminent danger to the ship, and how they rallied the appropriate teams to fight the fire. Their actions—engrained by months of training—resulted in very minimal damage to lagging (insulation) around a pump casing.

After evaluating the situation, I recharacterized the *main space fire* as a *fire in a main space* to provide the outside audience, appropriately concerned after seeing the initial reports, a better sense that the impact was minimal. Additionally, I took the opportunity to praise the heroic actions of the engineers and firefighters.

Rear Admiral Greenert called Admiral Doran and advised that he had "eyes on" the situation and confirmed that there would be no need for the *Constellation* to pull into Pearl Harbor for repairs. I'm guessing there was a sense of both amazement and relief at the Pacific Fleet Headquarters. This was not the role Rear Admiral Greenert had seen himself in when he flew out from Hawaii for his engagement with strike group operations, but I was certainly glad he was there and will forever appreciate his calm professionalism.

Once the initial post-fire touches to higher headquarters were complete, I called Admiral Mike Mullen, vice chief of naval operations. The situation had clarified at that point, and I wanted Admiral Mullen to hear the update directly from me. My memory was that I caught him at a Navy football game, and he was scheduled to leave shortly for a meeting with Secretary Rumsfeld. He was most appreciative of the update, passed along his "well done" to the *Constellation* crew for their quick actions, and was now armed with the latest information from the scene to brief the secretary. I had worked closely with Secretary Rumsfeld in my previous assignment on the Joint Staff and knew he would have a barrage of questions for the Navy staff regarding the who/what/when/why of the *Constellation* fire. I wanted Admiral Mullen to be prepared with the answers.

This entire process was an early example of the concept of *"Feed the Beast."* By that I mean it is the responsibility of the junior commander and his staff to provide timely information to the higher headquarters as events unfold, both verbally and in written reports. This seems logical but is rarely accomplished to the degree required for success. One can never communicate too frequently, provide too many details, or provide too many commander's assessments of the situation. The more you feed relevant information up the chain of command the better. If the staff is good at providing frequent, timely reports, the higher-level staff who is getting questioned by their superiors will tend to back off sending information requests, appreciating and confident that they are getting the information as fast and as accurately as possible.

Additionally, I stress to our upcoming Navy leaders the importance of having and maintaining a current contact list and staying connected with your superiors, your counterparts in other organizations (other services, or countries, staffs), and your juniors that carry out orders. In a crisis, there is zero time to research whom one should contact and how to reach them.

Captain Miller sent a *"Constellation* Main Space Fire (MSF) Roll Up" to Vice Admiral Malone on 14 November. In his typically forthright manner, he began the report with two items that on their face were not good:

> The first was the view that the fire had been caused by personnel error. It was too early to determine whether the error was the "result of a well-intentioned, but seriously misguided actions of one Sailor, or more deeply rooted in our organization." The second was that two Sailors, who had not checked in with the Top Watch and were not on watch, were in the #4 Boiler Room repair space—a space that only exits into the 4 Main Machinery Room (location of the fire). Since they had not checked in, they were not accounted for when the space was evacuated, and halon discharged. They established

communications with Damage Control Central, remained in the space for over an hour, and fortunately did not get injured.

The fuel leak had begun at 2020. The leak was called away to space watchstanders and Damage Control Central. A chief warrant officer (CWO) working on another job in the space responded immediately with an Aqueous Film-Forming Foam (AFFF) hose, putting fire extinguishing agent on the leak, a nearby fire pump, and the watchstander who was working on the bonnet valve (he was fuel soaked as he used his body to deflect the fuel away from the hot fire pump surfaces into the bilge). AFFF bilge sprinkling was also immediately activated to establish a vapor seal.

Despite the efforts of the CWO, the fuel flashed into a Class Bravo fire (flammable liquids). He extinguished the fire, but it quickly re-flashed, and the space was ordered evacuated in accordance with the Main Space Fire Doctrine. Halon was discharged at approximately 2026. At 2045, the captain ordered a team to re-enter the space to rescue the two Sailors previously mentioned. This decision was made after conferring with the chief engineer and the damage control team.

The space was "brutally hot," due to the negative ventilation and hot equipment in the space. A full hour would pass before the *Constellation* team was able to determine that the fire was out, the vapor seal was intact, and the rescue complete.

Captain Miller followed his "others" with ten "goods" that I list here for the benefit of future Navy firefighters:

1. The response to the leak was fast and followed doctrine. The majority of the hazard was flushed over the side before the fire could spread, and the personnel evacuated quickly when the fuel ignited into a fire.
2. Medical teams responded immediately setting up multiple stations to care for heat stress victims.
3. Isolation and boundaries were quickly set, giving the ship early control of the situation as the halon was able to be discharged before the fire got out of control.
4. The Chief Engineer and the Main Propulsion Assistant kept one shaft turning to ensure the attached lube oil pump lubricated the engine and locked another shaft. Both actions prevented more serious damages.
5. The Air Operations Officer coordinated a successful recovery while communicating with Hickam Air Force Base (nearest landing field if required) and Damage Control Central.
6. Supply immediately responded with ice, water, and fruit for the firefighters—critical so that they could re-enter the space.
7. Over 1000 Sailors responded to assist in multiple ways to the main effort.
8. The DCA took charge of the entire evolution, and his cool demeanor and adherence to doctrine were critical to success.
9. One strike group ship closed and was standing by to assist with additional firefighting equipment and supplies, while the rest remained clear.
10. The Engineering Officer of the Watch maintained control of the entire engineering plant, successfully managing a wide variety of tasks that were critical to minimizing damage.

Captain Miller summarized his thoughts with:

"The Main Space Fire Doctrine works, as does halon; the space will be hotter than you think; you cannot have too many teams, and practice is imperative. Watchstanders commented after the fact that the fire was just like the drills!"

Vice Admiral Malone was appreciative of the timely feedback and fired off a Bravo Zulu (well done) message to the captain and his team.

"The time and sweat spent perfecting your damage control efforts during preparation for your deployment were clearly evident in the crew's swift response and superb performance... Please pass my personal congratulations to the entire *Constellation* team and in particular to the brave men and women of the damage control teams for their professionalism and courage in preempting a potential disaster."

This entire event tested the mettle of the crew, and they met or exceeded every expectation. Their reactions would be an early indication of the outstanding performance that would characterize future operations throughout the deployment. I could attempt to call out individuals who were leaders of the rapid response to the fire, the CWO whose quick reactions saved lives, the medical teams who were at the ready, and the damage control organization... BUT they would defer to the TEAM effort because that was their ethos, of which I was very proud.

TRAIN AS WE WOULD FIGHT

The first major training opportunity after deploying from San Diego would be in the waters surrounding Hawaii. Commodore Balmert and his team would face several submarines coming out of Pearl Harbor. This type of interaction is typical as groups leave the west coast and provides one of the final occasions to test out systems and command and control arrangements. The Undersea Warfare Training Exercise (USWEX) was very complex. Commander, Submarine Force, U.S. Pacific Fleet (SubPac) would provide the subs for the engagement, and

Commander Task Force 12 (CTF 12), one of their subordinate organizations, would plan and monitor the exercise. That was the idea.

That said, I had been burned several years earlier by the CTF 12 watch team when I was the commodore for the *Nimitz* Battle Group. We had perfectly executed a feint, wherein two destroyers radiated their sensors, and the carrier/remaining force went quiet by shutting down all radars and communications. The submarine fell for the ruse and the carrier steamed by without detection. That was until the submarine received a message from the staff back at Pearl Harbor directing it to run at flank speed to catch up to the carrier just before it exited the exercise box. This intrusion was not revealed until a week later, when the submarine captain told me he was totally faked out, and but for the "intelligence" from the ashore staff—he was out of the picture. I appreciated the captain's honesty, and never forgot that lesson.

As the planning progressed for this event, I made it clear to Commodore Balmert that he was *not* to drive the carrier through a Hawaiian Island strait where it would be a sitting duck for the submarines. We would certainly not do this in "real-world" wartime operations, and the training should mirror how we intended to fight (in a case where we needed to go through a strait, there would be ample precursor operations by surface, air, and underwater assets to ensure the environment was as safe as possible for the transit of a unit like a carrier). The Exercise Directive indicated we needed to be in an area at a certain time, inside the Hawaii operating areas. Commodore Balmert did a superb job of vectoring the carrier around the islands without detection while sending a few "greyhounds" (destroyers) through the strait to attack the submarines waiting in their ambush. Once we were in the exercise box, the anti-submarine warfare team succeeded in using speed, maneuver, and deception to keep the carrier safe from submarine attacks as the ship conducted sustained flight operations in support of air wing training.

SubPac was not pleased that I had directed the carrier movements around the waiting submarines at the choke point. I accepted the pushback without concern because my focus was on retaining a true warfighting mindset throughout the force and *train as we would fight.*

Maneuver and deception would play a significant role during our deployment.

HELICOPTER DECK LANDING QUALIFICATIONS

We had one final adventure as we trained in the Hawaiian operating areas. One of the *Constellation* based helicopters was conducting deck landing qualifications (DLQs), where the crew would fly to and land on the fantail (rear) of a destroyer. Nothing is routine about flying helicopters, but this evolution was standard practice. The weather was clear, and the seas were calm. The teams being qualified would take turns flying the helicopter, swapping out on deck. As day turned to dusk, and dusk to night, the visibility for the pilots and the lighting scheme on the ship changed.

During this night operation, one of the pilots got confused and set the helicopter down short of the stern of the destroyer, in the ocean. The crewman in the rear of the helicopter stated that his first indication that there was a problem was when he saw and felt salt water coming into the helicopter... that was not good! It was only through the heroic action of the co-pilot applying power and immediately lifting the helicopter that a larger disaster did not occur. The co-pilot successfully set the aircraft down on the fantail of the ship. The crew was certainly emotionally shaken by this "adventure," and the condition of the helicopter's electronics was an unknown.

The officer in charge of the helicopter squadron aboard *Constellation* proposed several options to Captain Fox and me. These included flying the aircraft from the destroyer fantail back to *Constellation* that night, the next day, or with a different crew. However, we neither had the time nor the expertise to do the appropriate assessment of the status of the aircraft's material condition based on the saltwater intrusion. After all options were presented by the air wing commander and his team, I made the decision to send the ship to Pearl Harbor as we passed by and have the helicopter craned off for further inspection. There was no reason to attempt the "fly off" and put any of our people or the aircraft at risk. *This was NOT an example of "risk-averse," but rather a risk assessment that properly balanced the pros and cons of each alternative, and arrived at a logical, prudent answer.*

This incident revealed a weakness in the pilot screening process. In this case, there was a very affable lieutenant in the pilot seat who failed at a critical moment to bring the helicopter aboard in a nighttime landing situation. The good news was that no one got hurt. The other good news was that we discovered that this pilot lacked the confidence to succeed... better to discover this now rather than later in the wartime situation to which we were headed. A review of his record indicated several borderline performances, leading indicators of potential future issues. This incident solidified his own conviction that he was not cut out for this type of flying. He did not fly again on the deployment but contributed to the administrative and planning areas.

VETERANS DAY

As we departed the Hawaiian operating areas, we paused to recognize Veterans Day. Messages from American leadership were published in *Starscope*. Included in the newspaper was an article entitled: "What Does it Mean to be American."

> "You probably missed it in the rush of news last week, but there was actually a report that someone in Pakistan had published in a newspaper an offer of a reward to anyone who killed an American, any American. So, an Australian dentist wrote the following to let everyone know what an American is so they would know when they found one.
>
> **An American is** English, or French, or Italian, Irish, German, Spanish, Polish, Russian, or Greek. An American may also be Canadian, Cuban, Mexican, African, Indian, Chinese, Japanese, Australian, Iranian, Asian, or Arab, or Pakistani, or Afghan. An American may also be a Cherokee, Osage, Blackfoot, Navajo, Apache, or one of the many other tribes known as native Americans. They may have trouble with the language, but that does not change their love of their country.

<u>An American is</u> Christian, or he could be Jewish, or Buddhist, or Muslim. In fact, there are more Muslims in America than in Afghanistan. The only difference is that in America they are free to worship as each of them chooses.

<u>An American is</u> also free to believe in no religion. For that, he will only answer to God, not to the government, or to armed thugs claiming to speak for the government and for God.

<u>An American is</u> from the most prosperous land in the history of the world. The root of that prosperity can be found in the Declaration of Independence, which recognizes that God-given right of each man and woman in the pursuit of happiness.

<u>An American is</u> generous. Americans have helped out just about every other nation in the world in their time of need. When Afghanistan was overrun by the Soviet army 20 years ago, Americans came with arms and supplies to enable the people to win back their country. As of the morning of September 11, Americans had given more than any nation to the poor in Afghanistan.

Americans welcome the best, the best products, the best books, the best music, the best food, the best athletes. But they also welcome the least. The national symbol of America, The Statue of Liberty, welcomes your tired and your poor, the wretched refuse of your teeming shores, the homeless, tempest-tossed. These are in fact the people who built America.

Some of them were working in the Twin Towers the morning of September 11, earning a better life for their families. I've been told that the World Trade Center victims were from at least 30 other countries, cultures, and first languages, including those who aided and abetted the terrorists.

So, you can try to kill an American if you must. Hitler did. So did General Tojo, and Stalin, and Mao Tse-Tung, and every other blood-thirsty tyrant in the history of the world. But, in doing so, you would be just killing yourself. Because Americans are not a particular people from a particular place. They are the embodiment of the human spirit of freedom. Everyone who holds to that spirit, everywhere, is an American."

Thus, it was with this kind of support that *America's Flagship* and the group headed west from the Hawaiian operating areas.

BLUE WATER FLIGHT OPERATIONS

The Pacific is the largest water mass in the world, covering more than 30% of the earth's surface. It spans 64.26 million square miles. Distances are hard to comprehend for those who have not spent time riding the waves, and even for those who have, the vastness continues to amaze.

While traversing these waters, opposing objectives can come into play from the surface warfare and aviation community mindsets. This is not a bad thing, but rather a reflection of years of training with different priorities.

Surface warriors are focused on staying either *on* or preferably *ahead* of the Position of Intended Movement (PIM) (direction/speed of your course to the next destination). Their goal is to get to the next port while conducting some anti-air, anti-submarine, and anti-surface warfare training en route. The cruisers and destroyers can go 32 knots but typically transit at 16 knots for fuel conservation. Trying to catch up when behind PIM is difficult. Excessive speed in high sea states is to be avoided because of the potential damage to sonar domes and other shipboard equipment (a factor that does not affect a ship the size of the carrier to the same degree).

Aviators are trying to capture every opportunity to fly. This often means that the carrier must travel in the opposite direction of PIM to create enough wind over the deck for safe flight operations.

This healthy tension between the two communities can cause the strike group commander to referee to ensure the transit time is used to its best advantage while preparing for operations in the forward fleet areas.

During certain portions of the transit, there are what we call "divert fields," such that if a pilot could not make it back aboard the carrier for any reason, there was an option to send him to a shore-based field. In this case, Guam would be an example of the islands that dot the Pacific, with facilities and a runway to support flight operations. However, there are times in the transit that no such option exists. These are called *blue water* operations. During pre-deployment training, the air wing and carrier receive a blue water certification indicating that they have trained together and achieved a high level of proficiency in successfully getting their aircraft and pilots aboard safely, without the need for a divert field.

While conducting blue water operations one evening the sea state, wind and weather worsened, and the forecast was not good. CVW-2 had trained for this as they might face these conditions in transit to the Arabian Gulf. The issue arose whether to press forward with flight operations in this situation.

I called in Captains Miller and Fox to discuss options. What was their professional opinion? We discussed the pros and cons. What was the risk-benefit calculus? Would the experience gained offset the potential loss of crews/aircraft? Could we justify the risk as a benefit to air wing readiness dealing with harsh conditions during blue water operations with no divert fields available? This could not be a "manhood" issue, but rather an unemotional analysis of alternatives. Ultimately, we decided to cancel the rest of the flight plan for that evening. There would be times in the future when a different calculus would come into play to support "operational necessity" to fly in harm's way... this night did not fit that criterion.

I was blessed with the finest carrier commanding officer and air wing commander in the Navy. I trusted them and relied on their judgment. In turn, I believe they recognized that I could stand back and look at situations with a degree of experience and objectivity. This would set the tone for the rest of the deployment—with them, and with Commodore Balmert and Captain Farwell, where we found it advantageous to gather together on a regular basis for exchanges of ideas and viewpoints for the benefit of the entire strike group.

COMMUNICATING INTENT

The transit provided a perfect time to think and write. Up to that point, we had been working around the clock doing the necessary training and pre-deployment preps to ensure a successful departure. Time to think and write was at a premium. However, once we headed west, the requirements from the San Diego homeport waterfront were left behind, and the opportunity was there to look ahead. During this period, I published three *Commander's Guidance* messages that were intended to set the tone for the transit and our preliminary operations in the Arabian Gulf. They included my vision of the threat environment, our operations plans, and my overarching mission guidance. This would allow commanders to be aligned with my thinking and act confidently on their own without further direction if communications were severed. I looked forward to discussing this guidance with the team to ensure my intentions were clear.

The commodore "got it," and ensured each ship had digested the messages and had passed the admiral's intent to each of their crew. They were written for the Sailors at all levels of responsibility; I wanted to let them know what I was thinking and my expectations. However, as I passed through several of the air wing ready rooms on the carrier where the aircrews would hang out, I received a quick dose of reality. When I asked the junior officers what they thought of my guidance, they gave me quizzical looks. What was I referring to? I told them in more detail of my messages, and they replied that "we do not read message traffic." This was another good data point for me, early on, to appreciate that I would need to go to extraordinary measures to communicate directly with the commanding officers and crews of the air wing squadrons.

The learning point is that leadership cannot take anything for granted as to the actual dissemination of intent. Leadership communication by walking around was sometimes the best and only way to get your message out to those on the point.

SAILORS AS AMBASSADORS

On 14 November, our transit west took the group across the International Date Line. This is the dividing line where ships move from 3rd Fleet to 7th Fleet control. The team was now in the area where they could be called on for either humanitarian assistance or combat action at a moment's notice. The training of the past year would now come into play. Training never stops, but now the focus was on putting the lessons learned during the San Diego workups into action.

Our next stops were Hong Kong (22–26 November 2002) and Singapore (1–6 December 2002) for well-deserved port visits for Sailors and Marines who serve as forward ambassadors of America. The importance of these visits cannot be overstated. Young people join the sea services with images in their minds of "seeing the world." This is one of the reasons that inspire enlistments from 18-year-old youngsters from Washington to Florida, from California to Maine—and all states in between. This is their opportunity to break from the confines of their home territory and explore worlds only seen on TV, in pictures or on the Internet.

The weather off Asia worsened as we headed west from Hawaii past Guam. Our port visit to Hong Kong was in jeopardy.

I had experienced this situation in 1995 when I deployed on *Nimitz* as the destroyer squadron commander. During that transit, we were directed by the Navy weather predicters to stay at sea in the lee of Taiwan until a fierce storm passed from northwest to southeast. This delay would cut our port visit from four to two days at best. I suggested an alternate safe passage routing to the strike group commander, Rear Admiral Bien. We requested clearance from 7th Fleet to sail northwest, then turn south and ride *with the storm* through the Taiwan Strait as we approached Hong Kong.

The strait is an international waterway that is politically sensitive due to its position between mainland China and Taiwan. Getting approval from higher headquarters would be a bit of a gamble. However, the request *was* approved. We surfed into port without incident, successfully preserving the four-day visit much to the happiness of 7,500 eager Sailors and Marines, and many spouses who had flown to Hong Kong.

Several months later, in March 1996, we returned from the Arabian Gulf to Taiwan in response to China's missile launches to the north and south of Taiwan, as they attempted to influence the upcoming election. This was referred to by *Time* magazine and other news articles as *Nimitz* returning to Taiwan after its *show of force transit* months earlier! It was thought that the earlier transit *must* have been forwarded to the White House and President Clinton would have given the final blessing (versus someone on the 7th Fleet staff). No amount of information could convince the press that the earlier transit was simply for weather avoidance, even though Rear Admiral Bien was interviewed and indicated the innocence of our routing.

That experience came in handy in 2002. I approached the weather issue in the same manner, with the same successful transit from north to south into Hong Kong. The initial chagrin by the crew was replaced with gratefulness that the old man had been through this before and had an acceptable solution. I sent out a "Taiwan Strait Mindset" message to all commanding officers:

> "We will not fly... I do not intend to react to an overflight of the strike group by the PRC (*China*) in the strait... We will transit the strait in Form 1... our fight is not here with China. We are en route to a port call in their country. There is no intelligence indicating any threat to the strike group. My intention is to remain cool if anything flies toward or approaches the strike group. I expect you to do the same."

With that as a backdrop, we anchored in Hong Kong Harbor on time, ready to visit with our hosts.

A successful port visit by ships is the expectation of the fleet commander, who lives in the region 365 days a year. This success is measured by positive interaction with the local populace, including participating in several projects to assist schools and aid agencies, *and*— an incident-free stay. Anything less, and the group will receive a bad reputation that will be tough to overcome for the rest of the deployment. All the "goods" you do operationally will be marred by one unsatisfactory port visit.

I'd like to pass along some considerations for future deployers as they prepare for their first overseas port visit:

> Detailed planning is required—for *every* aspect of the visit. As leadership pursues this attention to detail, there might be pushback from veteran Sailors and Marines. "We've done this before, no need to micromanage." But,

in fact, there *is* a reason. For example, in 7th Fleet, there is often a curfew imposed because of some past misbehavior by *individuals*. I stress the word *individuals* because the majority of people on liberty overseas are model ambassadors and I was constantly proud of them. Unfortunately, it takes only a few to cause a problem for thousands.

In Hong Kong, there is a place—Fenwick Pier—where the liberty boats from the anchored ships all converge to disembark and embark the crews going back and forth. Having this central location is good in some respects. However, significant senior leader engagement/planning is required to preclude incidents. If liberty is to expire on the pier at midnight—guess what—thousands of people, fueled by alcohol, arrive at 2359. Mix that with the fact that there are men and women from different ships gathered together, and bad things could occur.

Bottom line: senior leadership across the group needs to be on watch, and be engaged, or that great at-sea performance will be forgotten in the aftermath of a liberty incident.

Our next stop was in Singapore. On the way, we executed a planned engagement with four ships and a submarine from the Singapore Navy with a goal of increasing mutual understanding and interoperability. The interaction included the Singapore Navy directing a U.S. Navy SH-60F helicopter, and exchanges of intelligence officers.

The Singapore Navy "punches above its weight." By that, I mean that despite the small size of this country and its small navy, it is equipped with the latest and best technology, and the officers and crews are well trained on how to use their equipment. The service members are highly educated, and in group settings with coalition partners, it is *always* the Singaporean officers who stand out by the depth of thought that goes into their commentary.

As in Hong Kong, the port visit in Singapore provided a welcome opportunity for young Sailors and Marines to get off the ships for well-deserved rest and adventure. Tours were arranged to introduce the team to the culture of the land. Cameras captured sights to be shared either via email or in person upon return to homeport. Shopping opportunities were fantastic, with a multitude of wares available from local merchants. This provided great entertainment for the Sailors and Marines who found treasures to take home to their families and friends.

TRANSIT TO 5TH FLEET (ARABIAN GULF)

Resupplied and rested, it was time to get back to the serious business of preparing to relieve the *Lincoln* Strike Group of their responsibility as Commander, Task Force 50 (CTF 50), which plans and conducts strike operations in the 5th Fleet area of operations. We flew a contingent ahead to *Lincoln* and to 5th Fleet headquarters and received liaison officers from each of these staffs who would ride *Constellation* from Singapore to the Arabian Gulf. These officers provided updates on what was happening *now* in the Gulf—appreciating that we had departed San Diego six weeks earlier. There is a great deal of written guidance as to how business is conducted in the Gulf, but with each new commander the interpretation varies slightly, and that is okay. One simply needs to understand that reality and redouble efforts to find "ground truth" as it exists in real time.

The liaison officer methodology is critical to success. We sent our best, brightest and most experienced officers to Lincoln, to 5th Fleet headquarters, and to the Combined Air Operations Center (CAOC) as operations ramped up, and they were invaluable. By sending superstars you lose talented players from your ship and their current job, but the return on investment is huge because these people act as your personal liaison to the leadership of the receiving command and provide timely feedback as to what is going on in that headquarters and how you can maximize your effectiveness. The schoolhouse solution is to send your very best, and it is correct. In the same regard, gather the liaison officers sent to your command and ensure they are fully employed and have access to all levels of your organization and planning teams.

INDIAN NAVY INTERACTION AND STRAIT OF HORMUZ TRANSIT

It was my job to consider the political sensitivities of the time. Where were we in the world? What was the threat? What was our mission? I needed to keep the strike group focused.

On the way to the Gulf, we transited past India. I was familiar with the Indian navy and had hosted the Indian chief of naval operations before our departure from San Diego. He was a true gentleman, an able professional, and a dedicated warfighter. As we exited the Strait of Malacca from east to west and entered the Indian Ocean, we were approached by an Indian long-range surveillance aircraft, the TU-142 Bear. This is a huge Russian-built bomber aircraft with the ability to fly for long distances. It was a great opportunity for our air defense team to exercise reporting, identifying, and intercepting using air wing fighters.

As we continued west, we interacted with an Indian destroyer interested in taking a close look at our group. This provided the sea combat commander an opportunity to deploy surface surveillance initiatives.

Rounding the tip of India, and heading north, we executed a scheduled exercise with two Indian submarines, one Kilo class (a diesel-electric attack submarine made in Russia) and one Type 209 (a diesel-electric attack submarine made in Germany). This was one of the best training opportunities for our anti-submarine forces, matching tactics against very capable submarines and their professional crews. There was deep water off their coast and sea room to permit full play by air, surface and subsurface platforms. Since the U.S. Navy does not possess diesel submarines, but the rest of the world has hundreds, the training value of these interactions cannot be overstated. We have continued to evolve these exercises over the last decade to the benefit of both navies.

The strike group pressed on, transiting through the Strait of Hormuz, passing through the dangerous waters bordering Iran and Oman. My guidance was that we would transit during the day overtly, with no desire to interact with the Iranians. Our pass down from the *Lincoln* team was that the Iranian navy, with their frigate size ships, had been professional in their encounters—as opposed to a separate group called the Iranian Revolutionary Guard Corps navy who was equipped with small attack craft that harassed passing ships from other countries.

I told the team—we are possibly going to war with Iraq... not Iran. I desired to remain focused on completing our successful transit to the Gulf and to begin the turnover with *Lincoln* without any distractions.

One such distraction came in the form of an Iranian P-3 surveillance aircraft fly-by to take pictures. This was a regular occurrence on transits close to Iran. I was not interested in interacting with this aircraft and directed our air wing and air defense commander not to attempt any intercept. Let them take their pictures... we were headed north to take position to fly in support of 5th Fleet priorities in Iraq.

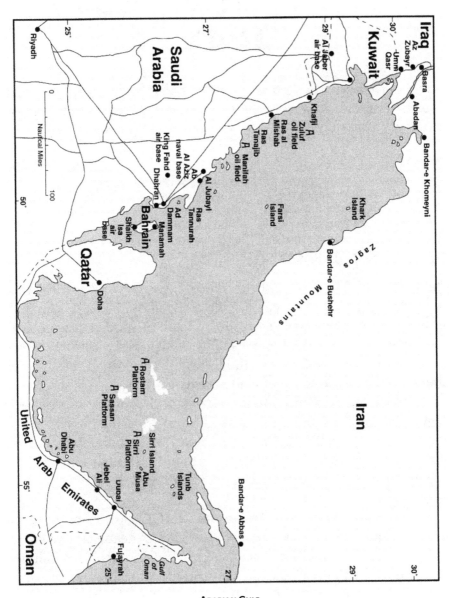

ARABIAN GULF

73

CHAPTER 4 | ON STATION—READY FOR TASKING

"Tina Turner was wrong when she said we don't need another hero. America today needs heroes and heroines, and I'm looking at America's heroes and heroines right now... Write your chapter in American history... Make your claim to be the 'Greatest Generation'... Depend on your faith as you go forward."

—Rear Admiral Barry Black, USN,
Chief of Chaplains, Aboard Constellation, January 17, 2003

COMMANDER TASK FORCE 50

The team arrived in the Gulf. The turnover with the *Lincoln* strike group on 17 December 2002 went seamlessly. Rear Admiral John Kelly ensured his force provided us with every detail we needed to come up to speed quickly in the area of responsibility (AOR), minimizing any hiccup working with the CAOC or the 5th Fleet staff. The advance preparation provided by liaison exchanges paid huge dividends.

Lincoln departed en route to Australia for required work on their flight deck and for some well-deserved liberty. Sensing the impending operations over the horizon, I suggested to Rear Admiral Kelly that we would look forward to his return in a few months. I recollect that he said something to the effect of "no way, we are headed back to the west coast."

I was now Commander Task Force 50 (CTF 50), responsible for strike operations at sea in support of Vice Admiral Keating (commander 5th Fleet and commander Naval Forces Central Command) in Bahrain. Also, I took on the responsibility of working with Commodore John Peterson, commander of Destroyer Squadron 50, who was designated CTF 55, responsible for surface operations and Maritime Interception Operations (MIO).

We started work on details of coalition communications. One of the interesting issues early on was that of access to the U.S. Secret Internet Protocol Router Network (SIPRNET) by the U.K. force. Sharing access to this U.S. communications system had been discussed over the years but had not been finalized. However, when we entered the Gulf, the *Lincoln* strike group staff indicated that clearance had been received, and we were "good to go" with the U.K. access (Australian access in the works). This would make coordination markedly easier, because the alternative, Combined Enterprise Regional Information Exchange (CENTRIX) was a cumbersome system that was not as user-friendly. Once we officially relieved as CTF 50, I mentioned this success to the 5th Fleet staff and received a speedy answer that it had *not* been granted to either U.K. or Australian forces. This was disappointing, as I thought I had heard that President Bush wanted the transparency to occur immediately.

Faced with this inadequacy, and the reality that coalition communications would need to be conducted over CENTRIX, I took a pulse of the U.S. and coalition force and determined quickly that some units had CENTRIX systems, and others did not. Of those who did... some equipment worked, and some personnel knew how to use it. The situation was bleak. Out of curiosity, when I was in the 5th Fleet headquarters for a planning session, I went into their command center and asked where their CENTRIX terminal was and who was manning it. The watchstanders grew quiet. One finally offered that is was in a separate back room (essentially a closet) and was not manned. That visual spoke volumes.

I reached back to Admiral Doran at Pacific Fleet and asked if he had any technicians who could help unravel this challenge. The next thing I knew, an individual named Bob Stephenson appeared in the Gulf. He was from the N6 (command, control, communications, computers, and intelligence: C4I) shop at Pacific Fleet. He came with expertise and CENTRIX sets to install on ships that needed them. Over the span of a week, he touched every U.S./U.K./Australian ship in the Gulf and reported back to me that the units were all functioning, that training had been conducted, and that he was headed back to Hawaii. I thanked him profusely and made several lighthearted remarks. Bob did not react. I asked him if everything was okay because he seemed unable to crack a smile. He simply replied that he was "from the submarine community" and that was that! I have had the pleasure of working with Mr.

Stephenson since he performed his magic in the Gulf, and he is a true professional in every sense of the word.

As CTF 50, my staff and the leadership of the strike group dug in to better connect with other staffs. This included numerous trips to Bahrain to coordinate with the 5th Fleet staff, and to Saudi Arabia to the U.S. Air Force led CAOC located at Prince Sultan Air Base.

Staffs worked tirelessly to be the bridges with CENTCOM Forward in Qatar (a country who had authorized the U.S. to build a headquarters facility as a command center to control U.S. military operations in the region), the Air Component Commander (Lieutenant General Michael Moseley, U.S. Air Force) in Saudi Arabia, the Ground Component Commander (Lieutenant General David McKiernan, U.S. Army) in Kuwait, Marine Forces Central Command (Lieutenant General Earl Hailston, U.S. Marine Corps) in Bahrain, and coalition force leadership throughout the region.

We spent December getting reacclimated and flying in support of Operation Southern Watch (OSW), enforcing the no-fly zone over southern Iraq that was put in place in 1991 to prevent Saddam Hussein from using military airpower against the Iraqi people. This effort supported United Nations (U.N.) Security Council resolutions 687 (Gulf War cease-fire), 688 (population protection) and 949 (Iraqi military withdrawal). Interaction with Iraqi forces had increased in both frequency and intensity. As Captain Fox put it:

> "Reactions to increasing Iraqi efforts to down coalition aircraft were sharp and decisive. Conducting a 'Response Option' (RO) attack on our third day of operations in the Gulf, Carrier Air Wing 2 (CVW-2) delivered more ordnance, hit more aim points and destroyed more Iraqi targets in one strike than we had during the entire 2001 deployment."

The work was dangerous. Iraqi military forces fired over 400 times on coalition aircraft enforcing this zone in 2002 alone. In December 2002, Iraqi aircraft successfully shot down an unmanned surveillance drone over southern Iraq, indicating a growing proficiency in their ability to identify and target airborne contacts.

We were only a few months away from potential major combat operations, and there was much to do in preparation at the 5th Fleet headquarters in Bahrain. Vice Admiral Keating was constantly engaged with his counterparts. This was both because his leadership style was such that he fully appreciated the power of shared communications and intentions, *and* because General Tommy Franks, commander CENTCOM, made it very clear to his three-star leadership in the Army, Navy, Air Force and Marine Corps—you'd better get along and solve issues at your level—the option of bringing them to the CENTCOM staff might not achieve the desired result.

By this, he meant that issues are best solved at the lowest level. Once they rise to a higher staff, other considerations might come into play, other staff members might become decision makers without the prerequisite background, and a different direction might emerge, one that none of the lower level commanders desired. Bottom line: negotiate it out at your level, or you may have to live with a decision that is less optimal. Component commanders understood this reality and worked together in support of the overall mission.

The 5th Fleet staff leadership was superb to work with, and they ensured that we were fully "read in" on all ongoing planning. Commodore Balmert and Captains Miller, Fox, and Farwell went to work delving into the details of planning, providing their counsel as to what would be the optimal method of employing the capabilities of the strike group. This engagement proved to be critical as we moved toward combat. Their credibility caused higher headquarter staffs to have confidence in their judgment, and to know that they would push information up the chain of command—keeping everyone informed of current events and intentions for future operations.

As a point of irony, while we were at sea in the Arabian Gulf preparing for the potential conflict, the *Constellation* hosted the Decommissioning Work Definition Conference with representatives from U.S. Pacific Fleet; Naval Air Forces; Puget Sound Naval Shipyard; Naval Inactive Ship Maintenance Office; and Superintendent of Shipbuilding, San Diego. Here was a crew getting ready to go into major combat operations, and they were hosting the gathering to plan the decommission of this 41-year-old ship on 7 August 2003! The executive officer, Commander Maloney said, "We have to take everything that's not attached to this ship, put it back in a warehouse, transfer those items back to the Navy, and then transfer the crew." It was a necessary step, but the timing was ironic.

MEDICAL ISSUES AND READINESS

Two medical issues had the potential to derail or have a significant impact on operational readiness. Leadership and medical teams had to become very proactive to address these issues.

The first was a cruiser crew with a spreading case of whooping cough. The timing could not have been worse. The ship could become combat ineffective. However, through great leadership of the commanding officer and his medical team—supported by the medical facilities ashore—the ship continued on mission and executed many significant taskings.

The second issue was that of vaccinations for anthrax and smallpox. Iraq had used chemical weapons against Iran during the 1980–1988 Iran-Iraq war and gassed its own citizens in 1988, killing thousands of innocent Kurdish men, women, and children. The intelligence community believed that if the coalition launched an attack, Saddam would realize his days were numbered, and he would use his deadliest weapons. The possibility of Iraq using anthrax or smallpox viruses against coalition personnel was anticipated.

In 1997, the Clinton administration initiated the Anthrax Vaccine Immunization Program (AVIP) under which active duty U.S. service personnel were to be immunized if serving in certain danger zones. Controversy ensued since vaccination was mandatory and a perception developed that the vaccine was unsafe. It sometimes caused serious side effects, such as considerable local and general reactogenicity (erythema, induration, soreness, and fever).

Smallpox historically killed 30 percent of its victims. The highly contagious virus, for which there is no known treatment, also could be a powerful weapon. Routine vaccination in the U.S. ended in 1972, making the population highly vulnerable to attack. But the vaccine, made from a live virus, was also dangerous. Health experts estimated that one or two of every million people vaccinated for the first time would die, and about 15 others would suffer life-threatening side effects.

When we departed for deployment, the consensus across the force was that these vaccinations would not be an issue for those at sea. The government was focused on getting all military forces that would be on the ground in the Iraq vicinity vaccinated as these forces could potentially be in a hazard area if a biological attack was launched by Iraq. The Navy would be miles away out in the Gulf. However, just before Christmas, the U.S. Fleet Forces Command (a Navy leadership organization under the CNO) issued a directive that naval forces at sea would be required to receive the vaccine. This was very controversial, as rumors swirled as to the potential negative effects of the vaccinations. Some Sailors and Marines were digging in their heels, refusing to get the shots. This issue had the potential of dividing the crews. Leadership received the shots first, and after that demonstration, the resistance slowed... but did not die.

I sent a message to the commanding officers of all the ships under my command on 7 January 2003:

"Captains,

I want to provide commander's guidance regarding the anthrax and smallpox vaccination programs. I have held off to let the dust settle on the overall Navy policy during this turbulent time. The last thing I want is to whipsaw people around on this issue.

We are on the verge of war. It is important to all of us that we are ready to execute our mission 24/7. *Constellation* Strike Group will be in the Gulf for the fight over the next several months. The vaccination program is intended to assist our combat readiness.

I want to minimize the distraction this program may have on the group. I have directed the medical team to work with all ships to make the vaccinations available to our Sailors. I rely on your best judgment in administering the program in your commands. The medical community advises to spread out the shots within a command over time so that you do not experience a drop in readiness due to any side effects that might occur.

My goal is to not create a situation where Sailors' careers are potentially terminated, or disciplinary measures are imposed because of this program. My goal is to follow the CNO's guidance of providing an education program on the benefits of the shots, including safety and readiness. Provide relevant information in a non-confrontational manner and allow time for reluctant Sailors to make a reasoned decision concerning their participation. Ensure all Sailors who desire the shot are provided with the opportunity, before getting proactive with those who are reluctant. Time is our ally in this process.

If you run into a challenge, let's discuss it before you go too far down a path of action. Sailors are too valuable to lose over this, and I rely on your leadership to keep this program in the box. Most people left with us on this deployment feeling they would not be required to get either shot. Take a measured approach.

Use your best judgment and keep me posted."

Figure it out and go slowly. Eventually, the storm passed due to good leadership at the deck plate level, and all Sailors and Marines chose to receive the vaccinations.

SENIOR LEADER VISITS

Visits by senior leaders have the potential to boost crew morale. It is true that Sailors are required to scrub the ship a bit more in preparation for these visits. But great ships have cleanliness as a day-to-day prerequisite, and these were great ships.

GENERAL RICHARD MYERS, CHAIRMAN OF THE JOINT CHIEFS OF STAFF

It was Christmas time. We were pleasantly surprised to receive a visit from a United Service Organizations (USO) supported entourage on 22 December. General Richard Myers, Chairman of the Joint Chiefs of Staff in the Pentagon, led this group.

Raised in Kansas, General Myers earned a mechanical engineering degree from Kansas State. He joined the Air Force in 1965 and flew F-4 Phantom fighter jets in combat over North Vietnam. He later headed the United States Space Command and was the vice chairman of the joint chiefs before being selected by President Bush to be the chairman of the Joint Chiefs in 2001.

The chairman was a true people person. I had the pleasure of working closely with him in the aftermath of 9/11 and got to see him in a wide variety of situations dealing with the secretary of defense and his staff, the service chiefs, and the combatant commanders. *In every case, he maintained a calm demeanor, led by example, and worked with all concerned to craft solutions. He listened, learned, and led from the front. If something was successful, he was quick to shower praise on the responsible people. If something was poorly received by higher authority, he immediately took responsibility, shielding his juniors from any flak.* To say I respected him greatly would be an understatement.

The chairman brought along his wonderful administrative assistant Mary Turner. She was one of the quiet, understated heroes of the Pentagon. Mary represented a group of dedicated people who maintained continuity of action through the periodic changing of the military leadership. She understood the need for people to see the chairman and worked her magic to ensure meetings occurred while protecting him from a 24-hour-a-day schedule.

This entourage included Roger "Rocket" Clemens of Red Sox and Yankee fame, and Drew Carey, a well-known TV personality and comedian.

We assembled the crew in the hangar bay to see our guests. The enthusiasm of the team was contagious. I introduced Chairman Myers— who I think it fair to say—was blown away by the energized reception from the crew. He responded in kind:

> "I can tell from the energy of this crowd, you know what it's all about. You know the impact that this ship has on world events cannot be underestimated. You're a powerful force to be reckoned with, and the reason is not the great machinery around us. It's not the great aircraft around us. It's you—Sailors and Marines—that make this go. Thank you. I am proud of what you do... proud to be on your winning team!"

After his remarks of thanks for the sacrifices of the Sailors and Marines aboard, he introduced Roger. It was clear that Roger was very touched by the scene. He spoke with emotion as the crew wildly clapped their approval.

> "Just being able to come out here in person, from all the way back home, and say thank you for what you do and who you are, is a great privilege. It is the experience of a lifetime. What I do compared to you is very, very small. I've been playing major league baseball for 20 years. I've had the opportunity to win a lot of awards, pitch in some really big games and world series and this definitely tops all of that: talking to you all."

He told the story of his 9/11 experience when he was in New York City and was scheduled to be on the mound in Yankee Stadium that night. He saw the devastation as the Twin Towers of the World Trade Center fell. After a week of canceled games, he took the mound in Chicago and saw his manager Joe Torre crying as the National Anthem was played, the first time they had heard it since 9/11. It was a powerful moment. The next week they returned to play at Yankee Stadium, and

Roger had the opportunity to shake hands with many heroic firemen and Port Authority personnel who were being honored at the game.

Drew Carey then took center stage. Drew's first joke was a bit off color. The crew went wild. I decided this would be an appropriate time for me to usher Chairman Myers out the back of the hangar bay to go meet Sailors strategically stationed around the ship.

After Drew fired up the crowd, the Rocket launched baseballs out to the adoring fans. What could possibly go wrong? High-speed baseballs being fired around multimillion-dollar aircraft, with Sailors and Marines eager to dive to retrieve one of these once-in-a-lifetime mementos! Fortunately, no one was injured. One F/A-18 was renamed "Rocket 1" in a briefing to me about a wing maintenance issue. I'm sure that was just a coincidence...

The morale boost was immediate and long-lasting. The USO does a superb job of arranging such visits to the forces on the front lines. I have been on both ends of these visits (previously accompanying Secretary Cohen and his entourage, including Carole King, to the Gulf over the holidays in 1999). I can say with surety that the performers come away amazed by the spirit and patriotic fervor of all they meet. They are forever changed after one of these tours.

Christmas held a surprise for Damage Controlman 2nd Class Paul Allen when he received a personal phone call from President Bush. Due to his outstanding work, Petty Officer Allen had been selected by the *Constellation* leadership to chat with the Commander in Chief. Pretty heady stuff for a young Sailor!

ADMIRAL VERN CLARK, CHIEF OF NAVAL OPERATIONS

Admiral Vern Clark visited on 17 January 2003 and addressed the crew in the hangar bay. His college degree was from Evangel College, a small church-affiliated school in Missouri. After completing Navy Officer Candidate School in 1968, he served for four years before leaving to pursue other interests. In this interim, he earned a Master of Business Administration, a rare skillset in the military that would prove invaluable during his time in command of the Navy. A year later, he returned with the belief that he could improve the Navy he left behind. He served at every level of command (in the Navy and the Joint arena), ultimately being tapped to lead the Navy as chief of naval operations (CNO), a first for a non-U.S. Naval Academy graduate with broken service (having stepped out for one year). CNO ensured his leadership team of admirals was taught finance and used business models to focus their time on priorities, including evaluating the product of their efforts.

Admiral Clark spoke at some length to the crew and expressed his heartfelt pride in the Sailors and Marines on the point. He spoke as if delivering remarks from the pulpit, and the audience hung on his every word.

CNO could see that *his* team was ready. His leadership in directing investments into readiness accounts over the past few years was now paying dividends. His business acumen helped ensure ships were properly manned with the right skillsets. Weapons were available in ample quantities, and they were GPS-guided, a game changer. Fuel was on hand. The impact was immediate and dramatic. The morale of the crews received a boost as they performed their jobs and kept their equipment in a high state of readiness. When asked a question regarding the timing of our homecoming, he replied:

> "I want you to get home on time... but if the nation needs you here, there is no hesitation on my part to keep you here as long as required by the mission."

Senior leaders are energized by interaction with junior enlisted. Appreciating that reality and understanding that they had flown many hours to be with the force, we arranged stops along the way for the CNO and other senior leader visitors to preside over reenlistment ceremonies and to award warfare devices, recognizing that a Sailor had passed an extensive qualification test in either aviation or surface warfare skills.

CHIEF OF NAVAL OPERATIONS

3 0 JAN 2003

Dear Admiral Costello,

Just a quick note of thanks for hosting my visit. Barry, I've made many, many ship visits wearing a number of different hats and I've seen plenty of visits from the other side as a host. To a man, our travel party walked away from our visit impressed. The pride and professionalism demonstrated by the Sailors and Marines of the CONBATGRU was truly inspirational. The feeling in the hangar bay was electric. That feeling doesn't come down from the stage, it was conveyed up to us from that fantastic group of Sailors in the audience.

The spirit of the entire CONNIE Battle Group team was infectious and is a direct reflection of your leadership.

Keep up the exceptional work.

Warm regards,

VERN CLARK
Admiral, U.S. Navy

LIEUTENANT GENERAL JOHN ABIZAID, DEPUTY COMMANDER, CENTRAL COMMAND

Lieutenant General John Abizaid, then the deputy commander of CENTCOM, flew to *Constellation* on 21 February 2003 to spend time with Sailors, to get a sense of conditions at sea, and to discuss the way forward with the strike group leadership. He was the right-hand man for General Franks, who had specifically selected him for the position. I worked for General Abizaid in 2001 as one of his deputy directors on the Joint Staff when he served as the J5—director for Strategic Plans and Policy and knew firsthand his leadership style.

Lieutenant General Abizaid was a superb, understated leader, who was respected by all who were fortunate to work under his command. He was a 1973 graduate of West Point and saw combat in Grenada. He later studied at Harvard and the University of Jordan in Amman. General Abizaid had a Master's degree in Middle Eastern studies, a command of Arabic, experience in Jordan and northern Iraq, and an Arab-American background (his grandparents emigrated from Lebanon). He was a student of the Middle East who appreciated the subtle cultural differences that dotted the map. His fluency in Farsi, one of the languages of the area, came in handy as local leaders would slip into their native tongues to share perspectives not meant for the ears of an American or coalition leader.

Like General Myers, Lieutenant General Abizaid asked me what we needed. My answer was the same. Sailors and Marines were trained and ready. The ships were in great material condition. We were prepared for any tasking. We had three clear challenges:

The *first* was the potential for mines to be deployed by the Iraqis. Intelligence reports indicated the Iraqi arsenal contained thousands of these ship killers. Our maritime interception operations teams had the waterways bottled up and inspected every ship thoroughly to ensure nothing slipped into the Gulf waters. Unlike Operation Desert Storm in 1990, we would ensure that we controlled the waters in the northern part of the Gulf. My request: to be given authority very early to take out the identified mine storage facilities before mines could be deployed at sea to threaten coalition ships. The general indicated that he would be supportive of this request as priorities were determined in the targeting process.

The *second* challenge I discussed was the threat of attack on our warships. There was a threat of an enemy aircraft taking off from a southern Iraq airstrip acting as a suicide attacker against the coalition warships pressed up close to the coast. The other threat from the Al Faw Peninsula was the CSSC-3/Seersucker coastal defense surface-to-surface cruise missile that could reach out to sea and attack our ships operating in the Northern Arabian Gulf (30-57-mile range). Intelligence assessments indicated that there were missiles on the peninsula. In this case, while concerned, I felt confident in our air defense posture and readiness to mitigate this threat.

The *third* challenge was associated with the two major oil terminals located off the Iraqi coast. The Iraqis had shown a propensity to blow up their oil production facilities ashore. It did not take much imagination to consider the possibility of the illogical self-destructive action of the Iraqi's to blow up these terminals at sea, which would result in the flow of vast amounts of oil into the Gulf waters. This would hamper coalition maritime effectiveness and create an environmental disaster, one that I did not want to be placed in charge of cleaning up. My consistent mantra was to allow us to seize these assets—*now*, to preclude any misbehavior by the Iraqis. We had practiced with our SEAL teammates and could strike at a moment's notice. Unfortunately, there was one catch. The pumping station that flowed oil to these terminals, a critical element of thoroughly seizing the package, was on the Al Faw Peninsula, Iraqi soil. Therefore, by capturing the oil terminals, we would effectively be starting the ground war. I argued the case that this minor intrusion onto the peninsula would not be significant. The leadership noted my argument but were not prepared to allow this mission to proceed—at least not yet. However, that did not deter me from *continuing to plant seeds regarding the importance of action to secure these vital assets early in the coming conflict.*

Each of these leaders infused energy. Each of them exuded a quiet confidence. I felt very blessed to have these leaders up the chain of command, knowing that they would do everything in their power to support our efforts, while *not* trying to micromanage from afar.

CHAPTER 5 | PLANNING ACROSS THE THEATER

"The basic requirement of decentralized operations in general war is a pre-planned response in accordance with commonly understood doctrine. Lord Nelson did not win at Trafalgar because he had a great plan... He won because his subordinate commanders thoroughly understood that plan and their place in it well in advance of planned execution. You must be prepared to take action when certain conditions are met; you cannot anticipate minute-by-minute guidance."

—Vice Admiral Henry Mustin, USN 1986

COMBATANT COMMANDS

A fact that is not fully appreciated by the American public is that the chiefs of the services (Army, Navy, Air Force, Marines, and Coast Guard) do not "fight" the force. The Goldwater-Nichols Act of 1986 placed responsibility for the fight in the hands of the *geographic* combatant commands to coordinate with the area countries:

- European Command: EUCOM (Europe)
- Central Command: CENTCOM (Middle East)
- Southern Command: SOUTHCOM (Latin America)
- Indo-Pacific Command: INDOPAC (Indo-Pacific)
- Northern Command: NORTHCOM (U.S., Mexico, and Canada) (established in 2002)
- Africa Command: AFRICOM (Africa) (established in 2007)

For completeness, the *functional* combatant commanders include:

- Transportation Command: TRANSCOM
- Special Operations Command: SOCOM
- Cyber Command: CYBERCOM (established in 2009)

- Strategic Command: STRATCOM (responsible for the nation's nuclear arsenal and more)
  - Space Command: SPACECOM (established in 1985, merged with Strategic Command in 2002; reestablished as a sub-unified combatant command under Strategic Command by the National Defense Authorization Act for FY 2019)

Combatant commands constitute a headquarters element with military units permanently assigned to it. They operate with component commands—one for each of the U.S. armed services, along with a joint special operations component and several subordinate joint task forces.

The chiefs of the services (Joint Chiefs) principal role is the manning, training, and equipping of the force. This is outlined in Title 10 of the United States Code, which provides the legal basis for the roles, missions, and organizations of each of the services as well as the Department of Defense. General Franks, combatant commander, CENTCOM, had a keen awareness of this distinction of roles and missions between the combatant commanders and the Joint Chiefs and bristled when he felt the Joint Chiefs were getting too involved in planning the war effort. His disdain for the Chiefs was very public, as he would refer to the body as "Title 10 motherfuckers."

GENERAL FRANKS AND COMPONENT COMMANDERS

General Tommy Franks was born in Oklahoma, raised in Texas and attended the same high school as First Lady Laura Bush. He joined the U.S. Army as an enlisted man in 1965. He was singled out for his leadership, attended Officer Candidate School, and was commissioned as a second lieutenant in 1967. He served as an assistant division commander during Operation Desert Storm, gaining experience that would help him lead CENTCOM from 2000 to 2003.

General Franks was developing his leadership team. He made it clear that he wanted to hear all positions on the various challenges facing the force. Get everything out in the open. He insisted that his components from the maritime, air and land forces get along harmoniously. He would not stand for any backstabbing.

The component commanders were varsity players and understood it was in their best interest to present well-thought-out coordinated plans to General Franks for his consideration and a subsequent briefing to Secretary Rumsfeld and the president. The component commanders were:

Maritime: As previously noted, Vice Admiral Tim Keating, 5th Fleet, was the naval component commander.

Air: Lieutenant General Michael Moseley was the air component commander. He was a fighter pilot, who had previously served as combat director for Joint Task Force Southwest Asia. He assigned Air Force Major General Dan Leaf to act as a liaison to the land component, placing this two-star general in the Army headquarters to ensure a smooth flow of communications and to knit the two organizations in the most effective manner. Additionally, Rear Admiral David Nichols, as deputy air component commander, and Captain William Gortney, who led the naval amphibious liaison element, would reside in the air component headquarters. These very experienced and highly respected naval aviators would prove critical to the effective tasking of air assets from all services and coalition partners.

Land: Lieutenant General David McKiernan, commander 3rd Army/Army Forces Central Command, was the land component commander. He had experience in Operation Desert Storm and was recently the operations officer (G3) for the U.S. Army. Also included in land forces were the Marines with Lieutenant General Earl Hailston as the Marine component in Bahrain; and Lieutenant General James Conway, commander I Marine Expeditionary Force on the Kuwait/Iraq border with the assault force.

Coalition leaders successfully integrated their capable forces into these organizations. Working together in various combined exercises over the past decade would now pay significant dividends.

RECRAFTING STRIKE GROUPS TO MEET WARFIGHTING DEMANDS

As we entered January 2003, the surge of news articles on the pending operations escalated. There was ample discussion regarding the timing of any attack on Iraq, the reliance on a U.N. Security Council Resolution, *and* the availability of U.S. and allied aircraft carriers.

The U.S. Navy maintained a fleet of 12 aircraft carriers: six on the Atlantic coast, five on the Pacific coast, and one forward deployed to Japan. USS *Harry S. Truman* (CVN 75) arrived in the Mediterranean in November, and USS *Constellation* was on watch in the Gulf in December. The firepower of the two carriers would have supported the first potential window to launch a major strike on Iraq. However, this did not occur as the U.N. situation had not fully run its course, and other forces were required by the war plan that continued to evolve and mature.

A review of carrier availability indicated that two Atlantic based carriers (USS *Dwight D. Eisenhower* (CVN 69) and USS *Enterprise* (CVN 65)) were undergoing extensive overhauls and would not be ready for deployment soon. Two others were in the initial stages of training. USS *Theodore Roosevelt* (CVN 71) returned from deployment in March 2002 and would be the most likely ship to join USS *Truman* in the Mediterranean if required to support a major operation.

In the Pacific, the picture was different. USS *Lincoln* headed back to the Gulf from Australia in January. USS *Carl Vinson* (CVN 70) had recently finished a major maintenance period and was entering its training phase. USS *John C. Stennis* (CVN 74) could be ready for deployment as required in early 2003. Additionally, USS *Kitty Hawk* (CV 63), based in Japan, could reach the Gulf in February 2003. USS *Nimitz* could support Gulf operations in April 2003.

In the U.K., the light aircraft carrier HMS *Ark Royal* (R07) was ready to deploy, while HMS *Invincible* (R05) and HMS *Illustrious* (R06) were undergoing maintenance. This was also the case for the French carrier FS *Charles de Gaulle* (R91)—in maintenance.

Marine Expeditionary Unit (MEU) availability was also a consideration. A MEU is comprised of 2,200 Marines commanded by a colonel. There were seven U.S. MEUs. Three were based at Camp Pendleton, California. Three were based on the east coast at Camp Lejeune, North Carolina. The final one was based in Okinawa, Japan. They are expeditionary quick reaction forces composed of a reinforced Marine infantry battalion as a ground combat element, a composite medium tiltrotor squadron as the aviation combat element, a combat logistics battalion providing the logistics combat element, and a company-size command element as the headquarters group. As is always the case, the Marine Corps was ready to support operations with a mix of their forces. One MEU was in theater, and three more could be ready in early 2003. These smaller units would join the airlifted Marine team, and the force would ultimately number 87,000 U.S. and Royal Marines in theater supporting the fight, with I Marine Expeditionary Force in command.

Admiral Clark worked closely with the Commandant of the Marine Corps General James Jones. They provided options to General Franks as he presented his plans to Secretary Rumsfeld.

General Jones was raised in Paris and was fluent in French. He received an International Relations degree from Georgetown in 1966, and then joined the Marines through Officer Candidate School. He served as a platoon leader in Vietnam. Through his career, he served in a variety of positions in command as well as a military aide to the secretary of defense.

As a part of a discussion between Secretary Rumsfeld and Admiral Clark, there was a sense of frustration by Rumsfeld: "If I have 12 carriers, why can I only use three at a time?" There is a rotation policy that accounts for three carriers forward deployed, three in transit to/from theater, three in training and three in deep maintenance. That rotation paradigm served the Navy well for decades, maintaining ships, upgrading their systems, and providing rotation opportunities for the 7,500 Sailors involved in strike group operations (2,900 ships company on the carrier, 2,500 with the embarked air wing, and 2,100 on the remaining ships in the group).

CNO Clark worked hard with the staff to figure out how to maximize the contribution of the Navy to the possible conflict. One of the early initiatives was to rename the 12 carrier *battle* groups to carrier *strike* groups. The 12 amphibious readiness groups (with big-deck amphibious ships as the centerpieces) were up-gunned with cruisers and submarines and recrafted as *expeditionary strike groups*. This recognized the shift of focus of naval forces from the traditional *blue water* expertise for war at sea to an emphasis on supporting the ground forces by *striking* targets ashore. Thus, with a stroke of the pen, the Navy multiplied its strike force by two, from 12 to 24 groups. The next move was to adjust schedules so that instead of only having the normal rotational three carriers available, deployments would be lengthened for those already in theater, and preparations for deployment would be expedited for those next to go.

The "Powell Doctrine" (named after the Chairman of the Joint Chiefs General Colin Powell) was to use overwhelming force to guarantee victory in Operation Desert Storm in 1990. The idea was to go in big and end the fighting quickly. In that conflict, six carriers were requested from the Navy.

However, this was a different era. Despite his push for more flexibility from the Navy, Secretary Rumsfeld had reviewed the Iraqi war plan and was determined to fight this war with a lighter more lethal force. He felt that the Iraqi military would be routed, and the Iraqi people would welcome the coalition forces.

Based on the moves with the carrier schedules, the CNO offered a total of eight carriers to support the war effort. General Franks appreciated the Navy flexibility. He checked with Lieutenant General Moseley and Vice Admiral Keating to determine what number of carriers and strike fighters would suffice to execute the plan. There was agreement that five carriers (with 250 Navy/Marine Corps fighter aircraft), with three in the Arabian Gulf and two in the Mediterranean, would be the right number.

The result of these initiatives meant that in the Arabian Gulf the *Lincoln* Strike Group's deployment went from six to 10 months; the *Constellation* Strike Group was there in December and was extended to seven months; and the *Kitty Hawk* Strike Group (Rear Admiral Matthew Moffit) surged on an unscheduled deployment from Japan where it was forward deployed.

Backfilling *Kitty Hawk* in the Pacific was the *Vinson* Strike Group (Rear Admiral Marty Channik), whose stateside training was abridged, appreciating that its role would be as a ready response asset as opposed to "in the fight." Rear Admiral Channik lobbied hard to get his team to the Gulf but ended up remaining in the Pacific. *Nimitz* Strike Group (Rear Admiral Samuel Locklear) arrived in the Gulf in April after major air support to the ground war from sea had ceased.

In the Mediterranean, the *Truman* (Rear Admiral John Stufflebeem) and *Roosevelt* (Rear Admiral John Harvey) strike groups operated together under the 6th Fleet Commander, Vice Admiral Scott Fry. They were *in support of* Vice Admiral Keating, as the CENTCOM naval component commander.

The Expeditionary Strike Group (ESG) and Marine Expeditionary Unit (MEU) schedules were likewise adjusted for best effect. This meant that three to four ESGs and the MEUs that were embarked would be ready to go as early as December 2002.

This effort to support the forward commander could have negative repercussions over the long-haul regarding maintenance schedules and future big-deck ship rotations. That reality was fully appreciated, and CNO tasked several groups to study the challenges presented by the new organizational concepts and provide recommendations going forward. This became the foundation for the Fleet Readiness Plan, which would be executed by the Navy to ensure the ability to provide the president with options for future force utilization around the globe.

SECRETARY OF STATE COLIN POWELL

Secretary Powell had a critical role to play. He was central to crafting the coalition that would face Iraq. The 2003 war would be different than Operation Desert Storm (when he was the Chairman of the Joint Chiefs). That war had the stated goal of restoring the status quo ante in the region. The 2003 conflict would redefine the region as Syria and Saudi Arabia would be encircled by U.S. military forces, and Iran would be partially surrounded.

European support for the effort was fractured, with France and Germany leading the opposition. U.S. diplomats pushed a line of thinking that these two countries did not speak for Europe. Russia and China vowed to block U.N. draft resolutions authorizing war on Iraq. Other countries felt that the U.S. would go ahead, with or without international support, so they considered their national interest postwar.

The Islamic world support would be critical to any diplomatic or military push against Iraq. The countries around Iraq would both influence the war and post-conflict regional structure. Six nations bordered Iraq: Kuwait, Saudi Arabia, Jordan, Syria, Turkey, and Iran. Only Kuwait was an ally of the U.S. Turkey was cooperative, but ultimately would not support overflights by aircraft or Tomahawk missiles or allow ground forces to transit across the country to the Northern Front, despite assumptions by planners that these access rights would be granted. Iran, Syria, and Jordan officially opposed the war. Saudi Arabia cooperated openly on many levels while opposing the war publicly.

These positions challenged Secretary Powell as he built the coalition. He had to deal with the perception of the U.S. as an imperial power attempting to redefine regional geopolitics for the long-term. The Arab countries were concerned about:

- The possibility of an extended U.S. and U.K. presence in the region.
- The U.S. would effectively have a base of operations from which to reach out and influence events in their countries.
- The belief that the U.S. would use Iraqi oil accounts to rebuild the country, effectively keeping the market price low.

In January 2003, Secretary Powell spoke at the World Economic Forum in Davos, Switzerland where 2,500 business leaders, international political leaders, economists, and journalists had gathered to discuss issues facing the world. Iraq was on everyone's minds, and there were many opponents to any war with Iraq. He said:

> "Americans did not go into the world in the 20th Century for self-aggrandizement, but rather for the liberation of others—asking of those others only a small piece of ground in which to bury our dead, who gave their lives for the freedom of men and women they never knew or met..."

Powell's diplomatic efforts resulted in a coalition that knit together multiple capabilities, with many country forces providing critical assets by 30 January. Eight European nations—the Czech Republic, Denmark,

Hungary, Italy, Poland, Portugal, Spain, and the United Kingdom—
jointly published a letter of support for the U.S. position on Iraq.

SECRETARY OF DEFENSE RUMSFELD AND GENERAL FRANKS

On October 17, 2002, Secretary Rumsfeld held a press briefing to
provide his thinking on the issues facing the country. At the briefing,
Rumsfeld described guidelines he promulgated upon taking office
regarding committing American military forces. As I read about the
briefing, two things he said caught my attention. The first was his
assertion that all elements of national power (diplomatic, informational,
military, economic) must be employed before, during, and after any
possible use of force. The second would be a foreshadowing of the
future: *"And remember that it's a great deal easier to get into
something than it is to get out of it."*

As 2002 moved forward, there was an interest by the secretary of
defense to review the plan for any potential military action in the Middle
East. He and his deputies, Stephen Cambone and Douglas Feith, desired
to drill down into the details. General Franks was summoned to the
Pentagon to provide an overview of the plan. The feedback that emerged
from the encounter was that it was an exhaustive session. This initial
meeting focused on "assumptions" that go into any plan. Assumptions
are pivotal in that they allow the planning process to go forward.
However, if the assumption turns out to be incorrect, it requires a relook
at the plan to see if it needs revision, and a "branch" plan created. Each
assumption was challenged by the secretary, and a "robust" discussion
ensued.

These interactions between Secretary Rumsfeld and his staff with
General Franks and his staff occurred right up to the commencement of
hostilities in March 2003 (and continued for the next several years).
Relationships between the groups were tense, and it took a great deal of
patience as the flood of "snowflakes" (handwritten questions from
Secretary Rumsfeld) were dispatched to the Joint Staff in the Pentagon,
and to CENTCOM in Tampa.

An unsung hero in this saga was Lieutenant General Abizaid. He
had previously served as the Director of the Joint Staff. In this role, he
had frequent and close interaction with Secretary Rumsfeld and his

senior staff. This proved invaluable, as his understanding of the foibles of the Department of Defense personalities allowed him to act as a shock absorber for the CENTCOM staff. He created an effective flow of communication that ensured queries from the Pentagon were answered promptly, while at the same time, the staff executed the war plan effectively consistent with President Bush's direction to *not* have Washington D.C. personalities direct or question every decision on the battlefield.

On 24 December 2002, Secretary Rumsfeld signed the first of the many deployment orders for the Army, sending 24,000 troops to Kuwait. By the end of February, he sent nearly 200,000 U.S. Army forces to the region including elements of the 3rd Infantry Division, 101st Air Assault Division, and 82nd Airborne Division.

By 1 March 2003, naval forces (the U.S., coalition, and others) in the CENTCOM area of responsibility had grown to 136 ships and 50,329 Sailors and Marines. The three carriers in the Gulf (and two in the Mediterranean) were complemented by six U.S. Navy big-deck amphibious assault ships. Here are some statistics about the assault ships:

- 850 feet long; with a crew of 960 Sailors
- Mission: to carry Marines to the fight; with up to 35 helicopters and eight AV-8B Harrier vertical launch aircraft fighter-bombers
- USS *Tarawa* (LHA 1), USS *Bataan* (LHD 5), USS *Bonhomme Richard* (LHD 6), USS *Boxer* (LHD 4), USS *Kearsarge* (LHD 3), and USS *Nassau* (LHA 4) transported an additional 60 Harriers

VICE ADMIRAL KEATING AND THE 5TH FLEET TEAM

Vice Admiral Keating took command of U.S. Naval Forces Central Command and 5th Fleet in February 2002. To say that he was qualified for this assignment would be an understatement. He graduated from the U.S. Naval Academy and was designated as a naval aviator. He had extensive experience flying off aircraft carriers—including combat operations in Operation Desert Storm. He had served with Joint Task Force Southwest Asia in Riyadh, Saudi Arabia, and had command of an air wing and a strike group. He served as the deputy director for operations on the Joint Staff and as the chief of plans, policy, and operations on the Navy staff.

The Navy has traditionally sent their best and brightest senior officers to the 5th Fleet staff in Bahrain. There is an appreciation that this forward fleet could be engaged in combat with very little notice. There might not be time to ramp up, and the staff would need to be ready to "fight tonight." Captain Harry Harris was the operations officer (N3). He was the key player that Vice Admiral Keating relied upon to coordinate all operations. This coordination required a very deft touch in staying connected with counterparts at the higher headquarters at CENTCOM, with the leadership of various coalition forces, and with other component headquarters (special operations, air, and land). It was a massive undertaking.

An example of this coordination occurred when General Franks was working with Secretary Rumsfeld to provide President Bush with options, noting the pros and cons of differing timelines. The staff polled the group commanders on the timing of future operations. The question was: "What would the impact be if combat operations happened in April or May as opposed to the anticipated March timeline?"

The response from the maritime force leaders was that they could support any timeline; however, the delay would push potential attack options into the stifling hot weather. The heat would impact aircraft readiness, would have a negative impact on Sailors patrolling the waters of the Gulf in open boats, and would hold a very ready force at bay— acceptable, but not optimal. This response was echoed by Lieutenant Generals Moseley, McKiernan, and Hailston to General Franks, adding that the heat would negatively affect coalition aircraft launching from land bases and impact the ground force.

CTF 50 AND CTF 55 COORDINATION

On 13 January 2003, I flew with several staff officers to the CAOC in Saudi Arabia to meet with Major General Buck Buchanan, U.S. Air Force, the deputy director of the center at the time. Our conversation covered a wide variety of subjects relevant to the upcoming operations. These included:

- Mine storage areas.
- Time-sensitive strikes.
- Airspace control.
- Liaison officers.
- Staff coordination.
- Divert fields for aircraft in severe weather.
- Dealing with gun emplacements on Al Faw Peninsula.
- Dealing with seersucker missiles.
- Dealing with Iraqi navy patrol boats.
- A-Day (air) and G-Day (ground) timing (time between these efforts was shrinking from 16 to 6 days for planning).
- Tanking from U.S. Air Force (refueling in the air).

The visit concluded with me asking him, "What can I do for you." His reply was to "stay connected, so together we can seize every opportunity to support the ground force." Our team's positive relationship with the Air Force would continue to grow over the next months.

On Sunday 26 January 2003, 10,000 miles from the Arabian Gulf, in San Diego, Super Bowl XXXVII was being played. On *Constellation*, it started at 0230 on Monday due to the 11-hour time zone difference. Fans of both the Tampa Bay Buccaneers and the Oakland Raiders filled the hangar bay to watch the contest on the big screen satellite feed. The supply department provided a feast of ribs and wings, and music helped create a festive atmosphere. Shania Twain performed at halftime, and the commercials included zebras refereeing a football game between horses. Tampa Bay won its first Super Bowl 48–21, sealing Jon Gruden's legacy as a great coach. It was a break in the action to remind the crew of their homeland, if only for a few hours.

President Bush delivered his State of the Union speech on 28 January, building a case for war against Iraq. He said, "A future lived at the mercy of terrible threats is no peace at all." America remained split on the issue. U.N. weapons inspectors continued to shuttle in and out of Iraq.

Vice Admiral Keating hosted a Commanders Conference on 29 January. He passed along the current thinking of General Franks. There was a clear indication of an acceptance of high-risk operations to get the job done. A comprehensive list of topics was addressed. Legality of issues would be considered, but there was no question that we would not be overly constrained. The topics discussed included:

- Clearing the Khor Abd Allah waterway of vessels or bottling them up.
- The timing of a gulf oil platforms operation.
- Tomahawk launch procedures.

Commander's guidance included: first, let 5th Fleet be the voice of the naval actions to the outside. Keep the emails to organizations outside of the fight to a minimum once the fighting begins.

Second, *Vice Admiral Keating would trust his commanders and stay out of the management of day-to-day operations.* There would *not* be a daily video teleconference (VTC). He encouraged us to feed information to his staff such that the calls directly to him would be unnecessary.

Vice Admiral Keating concluded by asking his team to *consider the unlikely, but possible: what if Saddam attacks south tomorrow? The timeline may not be of our choosing. The enemy does get a vote.* At the end of the meeting, Vice Admiral Keating directed the leaders to let him know their requirements for success.

As I speculated months earlier, Rear Admiral Kelly and his *Lincoln* Strike Group returned from Australia to the Arabian Gulf on 31 January. In their absence, we had continued to refine the war plan. This planning was shared with the *Lincoln* team in such a manner that there was a seamless shift of responsibility for CTF 50 back to Rear Admiral Kelly on 5 February. Vice Admiral Keating determined that since Rear Admiral Kelly was the senior admiral, he would be the overall lead at sea. I took over as CTF 55 and focused on surface operations.

There was plenty of work to do. The issue now was to determine the most effective warfighting organization. The *Lincoln* and *Constellation* Strike Groups would be joined by the *Kitty Hawk* team at the end of February. There would be little time to make final adjustments to the command structure.

Rear Admiral Kelly and I had a lengthy discussion regarding the division of responsibilities between CTF 50 and CTF 55. The doctrine for three carrier strike groups operating in proximity allowed for a variety of possible command arrangements. Each mission set required coordination to the highest degree. We decided to use simplicity as our guide.

Rear Admiral Kelly, as CTF 50, would command and coordinate the deployment of the air wings operating from the three carriers. This air power would consist of 149 strike aircraft (32 F-14, 104 F/A-18, and 13 EA-6B). Additionally, approximately 67 more aircraft would do the critical work of airborne early warning, tanking, and helicopter support. He would be the single point of contact in discussions with Lieutenant General Moseley and Rear Admiral Nichols in the CAOC.

Rear Admiral Kelly also took on the responsibility for the air defense of the force. This was a significant tasking and was achieved by creating sectors led by experienced cruiser captains. The air defense concerns were:

- Defense against the Iraqi air force, should they decide to venture south.
- Missiles from either surface patrol boats, aircraft or shore sites.
- Deconfliction with potential Iranian aircraft that chose to fly in the contested battlespace.
- U.S. Army Patriot missile defense batteries; close coordination would be critical as this represented the highest threat to coalition aircraft if there was a mistaken identification.

From the *Constellation* Strike Group, I would provide *Higgins* to act as *spotlight* to identify Iraqi missile launches and to work with Patriot batteries ashore. *Bunker Hill* would take on the duties of *Green Crown*, providing positive identification and advisory radar control of over 200 sorties per day, ensuring safe ship-to-shore and return-to-force of Amphibious Task Force assets. *Milius* would fill a critical operational void as the air tanker control ship, coordinating Northern Arabian Gulf rendezvous and airspace deconfliction for U.S. Navy and U.S. Air Force aircraft.

I would take responsibility for:

- Surface warfare picture from the Red Sea to the Gulf.
- Mine warfare efforts.
- Maritime interception operations.
- Information warfare.
- Support to Tomahawk launches from surface ships and submarines.
- Support to naval special warfare and amphibious operations.

The *Kitty Hawk* Strike Group departed Yokosuka, Japan on 12 February and entered the Arabian Gulf on 27 February. They quickly assimilated into the established organization. Rear Admiral Moffit flew to *Constellation* on 14 March, and we discussed his role as the alternate commander for several warfare missions. Our thinking was that since *Kitty Hawk* was the last to arrive on station, we would eventually shift major command responsibilities to Rear Admiral Moffit and his staff as they would be the last to leave.

By mid-March, there were 147 ships engaged in the operation. The waterspace was crowded (see cartoon lampooning a pilot from *Constellation* who landed on *Lincoln*). How do you figure out which ships fall into which command structures? This job was given to the destroyer squadron commanders and cruiser commanding officers. The bulk of the ships fell under CTG 55.1, Commodore Peterson, and CTG 55.2, Commodore Balmert. In some cases, the commodores were in command, while in other cases they were coordinators. The cruisers and some destroyers were assigned to CTF 50 for the air defense mission.

Leadership organized the flotilla and remained flexible. Taskings were published nightly. Most remained constant, while a few ships would shift organizations and mission sets depending on needs and agreements of the senior leadership.

Bottom line: *The three rear admirals at sea appreciated the talent of their subordinate commodores and captains, provided guidance, and empowered them to deploy the ships as necessary to achieve the objectives.*

"Well, 'Bloody'... I hope we learned our lesson about returning to the *Constellation* **when we're told to.**"

CTF 55 MISSION

The Navy uses task organizations to define mission structure and warfighting responsibility. A *fleet* is the largest Navy operational organization. In this case, 5th Fleet was commanded by Vice Admiral Keating. Next is a *task force*. In 5th Fleet, the task forces are all numbered beginning with a five indicating its mission. For example, Task Force 55 (TF 55) was responsible for missions noted below in the 5th Fleet area, commanded by Rear Admiral Costello (CTF 55). Next, come the *task groups*. These are subordinate organizations commanded in this case by captains who were responsible for more specific areas of operations such as mine warfare (TG 55.4) or escort interceptions (TG 55.2). Finally, *task units* are smaller organizations with a more narrowly defined set of responsibilities. In this case, Captain Jones assigned as CTU 55.1.1 was responsible for leading maritime interception operations in the Gulf.

The Task Force 55 mission was as follows:

> "CTF 55 will ensure freedom of navigation and protection of sea lines of communication in the 5th Fleet area of responsibility, allowing the full measure of U.S. and coalition combat power to support operations against Iraq.
>
> CTF 55 will conduct escort operations, mine countermeasure operations, maritime interception operations, sea combat operations, information warfare, and control the Shatt al-Arab and Khor Abd Allah waterways. CTF 55 will support Tomahawk strikes, humanitarian assistance, naval special warfare, and amphibious operations. These efforts will contribute to the rapid isolation and defeat of Iraq."

PLANNING CONSIDERATIONS

As the planning for operations continued to mature, many issues needed to be addressed. For example, my notes from 21 February contained the following questions and considerations:

- Plan for routing dhows (small cargo vessels) south from Umm Qasr?
- First vessel up the Khor Abd Allah waterway?
- Gunfire support from ships into Al Faw Peninsula supporting the ground advance?
- Prisoners of war handling? Football stadium in southern Iraq?
- Mine storage areas—status—plan for elimination?
- Red Sea plan for Tomahawk coordination?
- Shatt al-Arab waterway plan?
- 96 hours to secure Al Faw Peninsula—U.K. input?

- Royal Marine Commandos to secure Umm Qasr and Naval Base?
- Small boat identification?
- Leaflets?
- Marine mammal employment?
- USS *Higgins* stationing for both Tomahawk shooting as well as Iraqi missile launch warning platform?
- Support to CTF 150 (Commodore Girouard—Canada) and CTF 151 (Rear Admiral Veri—Italy)?
- Support to Captain Jones on HMAS *Kanimbla* for maritime interception operations in the Northern Arabian Gulf (NAG)?
- Weather impact on operations (visibility sometimes down to 200 feet in the NAG)?
- Coordination with Kuwaiti forces (Rear Admiral Al-Mulla)?
- Coordination with Gulf Cooperative Council (GCC) state navy assets?
- Stationing of U.K. ships in the Northern Arabian Gulf?
- Use of Coast Guard patrol boats (WPB) and U.S. Navy patrol craft (PC)?
- Coordination with amphibious forces under Rear Admiral Marsh?
- Coordination with naval special warfare team and HSV (high-speed vessel) *Joint Venture*?
- Coordination with land forces, especially U.S. Marines—I Marine Expeditionary Force?

This list provides insight into the complexity of coordinating tasks and the depth of planning required to ensure success.

CTF 55 Organization

The following organizational chart depicts the Task Force 55 team:

CTF 55
Commander Middle East Force

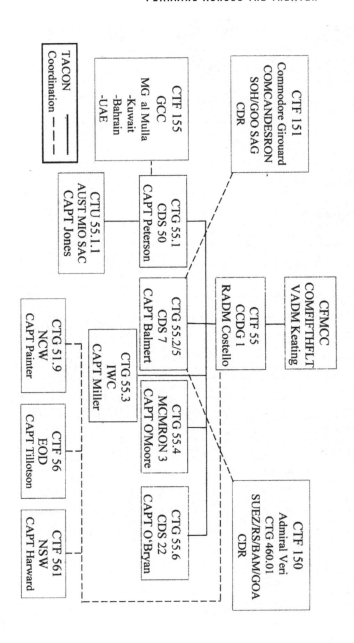

CTF 151
Commodore Girouard
COMCANDESRON
SOH/GOO SAG
CDR

CTF 155
GCC
MG al Mulla
-Kuwait
-Bahrain
-UAE

CTG 55.1
CDS 50
CAPT Peterson

CTU 55.1.1
AUST MIO SAC
CAPT Jones

CFMCC
COMFIFTHFLT
VADM Keating

CTF 55
CCDG 1
RADM Costello

CTG 55.2/5
CDS 7
CAPT Balmert

CTG 55.3
IWC
CAPT Miller

CTG 55.4
MCMRON 3
CAPT O'Moore

CTF 150
Admiral Veri
CTG 460.01
SUEZ/RS/BAM/GOA
CDR

CTG 55.6
CDS 22
CAPT O'Bryan

CTG 51.9
NCW
CAPT Painter

CTF 56
EOD
CAPT Tillotson

CTF 561
NSW
CAPT Harward

TACON ———
Coordination – – –

CHAPTER 6 | RELATIONSHIPS BETWEEN COMMANDERS

"The only thing worse than working with allies is working without them."

—*Winston Churchill*

COALITION LEADERSHIP

Coalition operations add an intricate dimension to planning and execution. They *can* be successfully managed to enhance the overall capability of the force.

For example, while working with a coalition force, differing interpretations of the ROE are addressed. Some see ROE as restricting activity while others see them as allowing action. Like many things, it is a matter of perspective. One way we addressed divergent views was by establishing a matrix that reflected who can do what, when, and within what constraints. Once this matrix was established, it became a force multiplier, where certain coalition partners could do things that others could not.

In addition to the ROE, each force received guidance from its home country military and political apparatus. Once again, this could be perceived as slowing the decision-making process in a coalition operation *or* be seen as a required step that is simply factored into the timing of the decision-making cycle. Being sensitive to this reality is a key quality of a successful leader.

Years of previous coalition operations in the Gulf paid huge dividends. Regularly updated matrices had been established, which provided clarity on capabilities and specific contributions from each country. Forces were familiar with the existing U.S. and coalition command structure and fit in seamlessly when they sailed into the region in 2003. We were blessed with outstanding leaders in the forces assigned from other countries. Some of the leaders and the forces are noted here.

UNITED KINGDOM

On 7 January 2003 Britain announced the deployment of the aircraft carrier HMS *Ark Royal* (R07) Task Force with 8,000 sailors. The Royal Navy force of ships included the big-deck amphibious ship HMS *Ocean* (LPH with 22 helicopters) and 28 others, including critical mine warfare ships to assist in clearing the waterways. Their destroyers and frigates would patrol the NAG and fire rounds into the Al Faw Peninsula (the southernmost point of Iraqi territory that protruded into the Northern Arabian Gulf) in support of the Royal Marines in their drive north in March. There were 45 aircraft as a part of this force. Two submarines, HMS *Splendid,* and HMS *Turbulent* would support a variety of missions, including firing Tomahawk missiles into Iraq.

Additionally, HMS *Cardiff* and HMS *Cumberland* participated in United Nations Security Council Resolution (UNSCR) MIO in the NAG and in the Gulf of Oman in support of Operation Enduring Freedom (OEF). In one operation, HMS *Cardiff* boarding teams searched and detained three vessels carrying $800,000 worth of smuggled Iraqi oil, effectively stopping the practice of oil smuggling via dhows (sailing and motorized vessels with long thin hulls used for centuries in the Middle East waters primarily to carry items like dates, oil, or batteries. Small dhows have a crew of 12 while larger dhow crews can number 30).

The U.K. provided Maritime Patrol Aircraft (MPA) for both the OEF mission in the Gulf of Oman and the UNSCR mission in the NAG. They also supported operations with the oiler HMS *Bayleaf*, which provided fuel services for coalition forces.

Rear Admiral David Snelson was the deputy to Vice Admiral Keating in Bahrain at 5th Fleet headquarters. The Royal Navy had volunteered to provide a senior officer to fulfill this role, and Rear Admiral Snelson was delegated authority commensurate with the position. He focused on all things coalition. He was the consummate professional who deserves a great deal of credit for creating harmony among the leaders of the participating countries—a factor critical to the success of the mission. He was reserved, forceful when required, and always thoughtful. He had the uncanny ability to sense when and where intervention was required.

I received several calls from him requesting coordination support over the course of the campaign. On one occasion, the "mission" was to sort out a disagreement between Brigadier General Jim Dutton (Royal Marine ground component commander) and Rear Admiral Clyde Marsh (U.S. amphibious force leader). Often these issues were turf battles among the staffs, but not always. I asked Rear Admiral Snelson to set up a lunch meeting on *Ark Royal* where I would meet with Brigadier General Dutton to sort through the issue (this might have included a beer, since the Royal Navy remained "enlightened" and had ample stores of beer aboard for daily consumption—whereas U.S. ships remained "dry").

Brigadier General Dutton laid out the issue, his position, the position of the U.S. amphibious commander (or at least what he had heard from the staff), and his recommendation. I responded that the recommended course of action seemed logical. I had more than enough information to go back to Rear Admiral Marsh and his Chief of Staff Captain Pam Markiewicz. Captain Markiewicz brokered a deal that was satisfactory to all parties.

A few weeks later we went through the same drill with lunch aboard *Ark Royal*. When I met Brigadier General Dutton, he looked me in the eye as we shook hands and said, "I really hate to see you because if we are meeting, it means that I have not been able to sort out a problem on my own!" Once again, the issue was vetted, I told him I would take care of it, and it was resolved.

Years later, I ran into Major General Dutton (having been promoted in the interval) as he spoke at a Joint Forces Command Capstone course in Norfolk, Virginia for senior officers while I was there as a facilitator. He spoke of coalition coordination and the friction between forces that needed to be addressed when taking the Al Faw Peninsula. He was working under the command of Lieutenant General Conway, U.S. Marine Corps, I Marine Expeditionary Force. However, he needed to work issues associated with the land-sea boundary along the Khor Abd Allah (KAA) waterway and Al Faw Peninsula. What were the ROE along the waterway? Was there a dividing line of responsibility between the amphibious commander and the land commander? What about special operations forces, patrol craft, and mine warfare forces operating in the waterway? How did the coalition forces fit into the overall command structure? Each of these and many other issues had required attention and persistence to achieve the desired harmony.

Rear Admiral Snelson remained a friend, and when I had an occasion several years later to act as a senior mentor for an exercise at the Royal Military College at Shrivenham, England, he invited me to stay at his London flat. He was then the Captain of the Port of London. While at his residence, I noticed a coffee table book of some size and magnitude, and out of curiosity, I explored it further. It was the story in text and pictures of the Royal Navy in the Gulf in 2003. I was fascinated, as it had action photos of sailors and marines conducting operations. The U.K. citizens were provided a wonderful capsule of their navy's exploits and heroics. They came, they saw, and they conquered—well done. The U.S. Navy had no book to compare with this masterpiece, and therefore our citizens are not nearly as well versed as their U.K. allies, regarding the success of the U.S. Navy and Marine Corps in 2003. That episode in London was one of the incidents that spurred me to action years later to tell this story.

The Royal Navy sailed with many unforgettable characters. One of them was Commodore (one-star rank in the Royal Navy), Jamie Miller. His flagship was *Ark Royal*. Shortly after his February arrival, I invited him to *Constellation* for a briefing on background, current situation, and vision for the conduct of combat operations, with an emphasis on my responsibility as CTF 55 and his role leading the U.K. maritime contingent. When he came aboard on 5 March, he brought an entourage that included a photographer and others to record the scene of his entrance and our meeting. I was a little taken aback by this, not fully appreciating the Royal Navy's approach to public affairs.

We engaged in polite introductory conversation, and then adjourned to the war room to provide him the briefing. I noted that the name tag on his uniform read "The General." This seemed a bit odd, as we have commodores and admirals in the Navy, but not generals. I chose not to inquire as to the backstory for this title. As we sat down at the table, I introduced Commodore Miller to my leadership team. The brief began with our intelligence officer providing a background for the discussion to follow. After a short interval, Commodore Miller took a small tin soldier from his pocket and placed it on the table. My team looked at me, and I signaled, "Do not even think of asking."

Eventually, Commodore Miller decided that it was time to tell us the story of the tin soldier and his own history. He told the story of his youth and his fascination with tin soldiers who were his childhood companions. Through his various navy commands, he would place these in obscure places around the ship and provide rewards to those who returned them to him, demonstrating that they had also been about the less traveled spaces of the ship, ensuring the spaces were clean and squared away. There is a story that one group got tired of this practice and returned the soldiers—melted down.

Commodore Miller was a very competent partner. He was also a wonderful host whenever I had the good fortune to visit him on his flagship. On one such day, I headed for a meeting aboard the *Ark Royal,* taking off as a passenger in one of our embarked helicopters. As the helicopter rose high above the flight deck, just before it transitioned to go over the water, there was a *very* loud mechanical thumping; the rotor transmission had suffered a major malfunction. *The helicopter literally fell out of the air and crashed hard onto the deck. It was a significant fall from altitude.*

If this had occurred seconds later, we would have been in the water of the Arabian Gulf. I would have reverted to my "dunker" training, remaining strapped in my seat as the helicopter settled into the water and then calmly exiting the submerged aircraft. This is not an easy concept to grasp, as the instinct is to get out of the sinking helicopter as soon as possible. However, years of research revealed that people died in helicopter accidents due to exiting early and getting hit by rotors continuing to spin.

I looked at my aide, Lieutenant Jacobs, and it was clear that there were no injuries to him or the pilots. Jake and I exited the wounded aircraft and walked toward the ready spare, a helicopter that was primed to go just in case there was a problem with the first one. I glanced up to the bridge of the ship and noted the concerned expression on Captain Miller's face. I could only imagine the discussion, as they witnessed the helicopter crashing on deck with the admiral aboard!

Not to be deterred from our mission, we entered the second helicopter. I kiddingly said to the pilots that while the crash was fun, I'd prefer not to repeat the adventure. Off we went.

After a lengthy period, I noted the engine noise changing, indicating we were approaching a ship to land on their flight deck. The crew below looked surprised to be receiving a visit from the admiral. We were approaching the wrong ship! After some communication, the helicopter crew realized their error and off we flew.

But the challenge remained. Where was *Ark Royal* in this Gulf full of ships, and how do we get there? Lieutenant Jacobs, ever vigilant, took charge of finding the path to the *Ark Royal* and vectored the pilot with a range and bearing. We finally arrived at the correct ship after several fly-bys of potential candidates.

The aircrew was understandably shaken by their inability to initially deliver me to the correct ship. They paid the consequence from their shipmates, as they were highlighted in the satirical air-plan cartoon the next day.

Years later at a Navy holiday party, I was sharing the story of my crash on deck in a lighthearted manner. There were many chuckles in the group, except for one officer who remained particularly quiet. When I finished, he announced to the group that he was the pilot of the helicopter that crashed on deck. I never knew it was him until then, years later. It certainly did not matter to me, but clearly, he recalled the incident as vividly (or more so) as I. We had a good laugh together.

AUSTRALIA

Captain Peter Jones led the Australian contingent and was the Maritime Interception Force commander, CTU 55.1.1, leading the UNSCR MIO mission in the Northern Arabian Gulf while coordinating the multinational effort. He relied on Commodore Peterson, CTG 55.1 and commander of Destroyer Squadron 50, to augment his force.

He used *HMAS Kanimbla* (L 51) (former LST) as his flagship. He positioned *Kanimbla* well to the north in the Arabian Gulf—in harm's way—to act as a mothership for the many Rigid-Hulled Inflatable Boat (RHIB) groups. Numerous crews and RHIBs provided by other ships in the force made it possible to provide 24-hour coverage of the mouth of the KAA.

Captain Jones deployed his force masterfully in all types of weather to deal successfully with nefarious dhow activity. He coordinated the rotation of RHIBs and looked out for the health and welfare of the crews who had to work in the stifling hot conditions. The professionalism of the young Sailors manning the RHIBs from the U.S., U.K., and Australian navies is a story unto itself. I was very proud of these Sailors, who worked day and night in the open sea with no fanfare or extra recognition.

The Australians also brought HMAS *Anzac* and HMAS *Darwin* to work the maritime interception operations (MIO) mission and contribute naval gunfire support to the Al Faw Peninsula operations, along with one maritime patrol aircraft and a diving team.

CANADA

Commodore Roger Girouard led the Canadian contingent, a team that had been engaged in MIO, escort duties, and general maritime surveillance in the Arabian Gulf for years supporting Operation Enduring Freedom (OEF), enforcing U.N. sanctions at sea against Iraq since 1991. HMCS *Montreal, Winnipeg, Regina,* and *Fredericton* were the Canadian navy ships supporting these coalition operations in 2003.

The Canadian government had determined that they would not support a military operation against Iraq. When the Canadian navy arrived in theater, the question arose, how could they assist while remaining within their national guidance? Commodore Girouard visited me on *Constellation* in early January 2003, and we discussed options. He dearly wanted to support a potential combat mission, and his sailors did not want to be left on the sidelines to watch the action. This fell into the category of figuring out how to work together within the constraints of national governmental orders and direction, both the letter and spirit of the law.

Ultimately, together we determined that since Canada fully supported the UNSCR MIO mission (OEF), his force would be best deployed in supporting that endeavor. Thus, he became the OEF MIO commander, leading the mission in the Strait of Hormuz, Gulf of Oman,

Makran Coast, and Karachi, Pakistan operating areas. His designation was CTF 151, and he coordinated efforts with Commodore Balmert (CTG 55.2/5). Commodore Girouard also coordinated all surface escort operations through the Strait of Hormuz.

This assignment was consistent with Canadian national guidance. The result was that it freed up several of my surface ships for other missions—effectively augmenting our force. This could best be described as a win-win solution.

The *Canada Free Press* ran an editorial on 14 April bemoaning Commodore Girouard's position, caught between supporting the Operation Iraqi Freedom coalition forces and a government that remained neutral in this fight. They quoted retired Lieutenant Commander John Buckingham:

> "Can you imagine the loss of credibility he will suffer as the commander of a multinational force? Can you imagine the impact on the morale of the men and women under his command? His position has been rendered untenable by the contradictions enunciated as policy by a dysfunctional government."

I could imagine... and we worked together to ensure he did *not* lose credibility, and that the morale of his sailors remained high, performing an important mission.

Leaders can almost always figure out a way to work together to maximize the effectiveness of their forces while staying consistent with country guidance/policy. Figure it out—be creative!

ITALY

Rear Admiral Rinaldo Veri from the Italian navy became Commander Task Force 150 as well as Commander Task Group 460.01 (a NATO designation) while embarked in INS *Mimbelli* (D 561). He was the OEF MIO commander for the Suez, Red Sea, Bab-el-Mandeb Strait (between Yemen and Somalia), and the Gulf of Aden. He also coordinated efforts with Commodore Balmert, and successfully executed a very important mission of ensuring safety in these important waterways.

An example of our correspondence follows:

From: Costello, Barry M. RADM
Sent: Monday, February 17, 2003 2:54 PM

Subject: Msg for RADM Veri

Rear Admiral Veri,
I want to formally welcome you to the theater of operations, and send
my appreciation for the fine job you and your staff are doing in the
Horn of Africa region.
There are many communications challenges associated with our current
operations. LOCE and inmarsat seem to be the best avenues to connect at
this time.
The escort mission, in support of the global war on terrorism, has
taken on heightened importance. Your leadership in the Bab el Mandeb
strait has been superb. This is a haven for known terrorist activity,
and it is imperative we effectively escort shipping in this area to
prevent suicide attacks.
Commodore Balmert is my leader for overall escort coordination, from
the Suez to the Bab el Mandeb to the Strait of Hormuz to the Arabian
Gulf. He coordinates with a number of leaders to ensure a smooth
transition of shipping between each choke point. Your role is
significant. If there is any issue you want to bring to my attention,
any concern on your part, please do not hesitate to bring it to my
attention. Just send me a note via LOCE or give me a call.
I enjoyed reading your biography. You are blessed to have three
children. The phrasing of your sports interest ('he prefers to
practice') is very humble! Maybe one day we will have an opportunity to
meet and have a game of tennis, followed by a good glass of wine. Until
then, all the best, barry costello, RADM/USN, CCDG-1, CTF 55.

Rear Admiral Costello,

I wish to thank you for your considered words and praise. We have been here a relatively short time, but our learning curve has made it feel a lifetime already. We here are in complete agreement that our operations are important and necessary. An effective and unified coalition is the cornerstone of the war on global terrorism.

It is a pleasure to work with Commodore Balmert's team. He has been very Supportive and has also shown considerable concern for our ability to operate successfully. We continue to improve our interoperability between all units, and Commodore Balmert has been a significant contributor to our integration of American units into Task Force 150. The key component to successful operations here is indeed the homogeneous mixture of coalition forces operating with the same goals and desires of success in mind. The synergistic effect of the six nations in cooperation here in the Horn of Africa has been tremendous. I strive to maintain the level of success of my Spanish predecessor, and hope to leave this continuing legacy to my German relief.

The nature of the escort business drives our operations here. But, even though significant resources are swallowed by this monster, we are still able to continue with our interdiction efforts at the same time. The flexibility and professional dedication of the units are paramount. I draw attention to the exemplary short notice boarding recently completed by USS Briscoe while she was enroute to an escort assignment, and also to the quick response of USS Fletcher supporting the special tasking given to protect ships transiting off the coast of Yemen. The willingness of your Captains and their crews to tackle assigned tasks has been both commendable, and a blessing. Our goal is the complete and thorough coverage of escort responsibilities while also achieving the fullest possible impact of interdiction operations throughout TF 150's assignedAOR.

I will not hesitate to communicate any concerns of mine to you, and I thank you for this opportunity. I am appreciative of your willingness to assist. At this time we areproceeding forward nicely. We are making daily improvements in connectivity, and correspondingly command andcontrol.

It is generous of you to overestimate my skills on the tennis court, however I beg of you to reserve judgment until the day we may meet over the net. It is, of course, alsoimportant not to rush to an opinion on these matters until after relaxing over a nice bottle of wine(italian of course!).

Warmest regards,

Rinaldo Veri
RADM, Italian Navy

KUWAIT

The Kuwaiti military had been waiting for the time when a coalition force would move against Iraq. There were long memories of the atrocities committed by the Iraqis when they overran Kuwait in 1990 and occupied the country until Operation Desert Storm unseated them from the Kingdom.

Major General Ahmed Al-Mulla was a highly qualified leader as chief of the Kuwaiti navy for seven years. He was a graduate of the Royal Navy College in Dartmouth, England, and the U.S. Naval Staff College. He had achieved his at-sea qualifications with the Royal Australian Navy and Royal Malaysian Navy. He spent many years cultivating positive relationships with each commander of 5th Fleet in Bahrain.

Major General Al-Mulla grew his force in proficiency and had a burning desire to participate in any activity against Iraq in the Gulf and especially in the KAA waterway that separated the two countries. He came to *Constellation* to meet with me on several occasions, assuring me of his navy's support for any CTF 55 operation.

Major General Al-Mulla was designated commander of Task Force 155, leading a group of ships from Kuwait, Bahrain, and the United Arab Emirates (UAE). He embarked in the UAE frigate *Al Emarat*, and commanded eight ships from this flagship, with the mission to support coalition contingency operations against Iraq, focused on the defense of Kuwait. Commodore Peterson would meet with him daily to plan out the taskings for his force, which was operating in the busy waters of the Northern Arabian Gulf.

Besides being a superb operator and a visionary for the Kuwaiti navy, Major General Al-Mulla was a leading force in ensuring the seamless movement of U.S. forces throughout the Kingdom of Kuwait.

20 February 2003

From: MG Ahmed Y. Al-Mulla
      Chief of Kuwait Naval Forces
      Mohamed Al Ahmed Naval Base
      Ras Al Jilea'a, Kuwait

To: RADM Barry M. Costello
      COMCRUDESGRU-1
      Aboard the USS CONSTELLATION
      The Arabian Gulf

Dear Admiral Costello,

On behalf of the Kuwait Naval Force's officers and men, I extend my appreciation to your officers and sailors for my recent visit to "America's Flagship" the USS CONSTELLATION. You have much to be proud of, as the entire crew was extremely courteous, candid, and professional.

The relationship between our two nations has continued to grow stronger every day as we work to strengthen our resolve in deterring aggression in the region. Your officers, sailors and marines are working hard alongside my officers and men to improve infrastructure, capabilities, communications, and coalition combat operations.

As we continue our preparations for any eventuality in the region, I am confident in our mutual cooperation in the defense of the State of Kuwait and look forward to our service together. I wish you and your command the best in all your endeavors. You and your staff are welcome any time to visit Kuwait Naval Base – my door is always open.

"TOGETHER FOREVER"

Sincerely,

Other countries that contributed naval assets to either Operation Enduring Freedom or Operation Iraqi Freedom: Denmark, Greece, Japan (76 million gallons of F-76 fuel), Netherlands, New Zealand, Poland, and Spain.

Bottom line: For OEF, the *Canadian* navy under Rear Admiral Girouard was the sector commander in the Gulf of Oman with six partner nations, and the *Italian* navy under Rear Admiral Veri was the sector commander in the Bab-el-Mandeb area with six partners. Major General Al-Mulla successfully coordinated a *Gulf Naval Force* in defense of Kuwait. The *Australian* navy under Captain Jones commanded the Northern Arabian Gulf MIO in *both OEF and Operation Iraqi Freedom (OIF)* with five partner nations. The *U.K.* forces fit seamlessly into the overall structure of both operations due to the outstanding prior coordination by Rear Admiral Snelson.

All five of these officers were superb leaders, and their efforts were critical to providing security in the region in 2003. They used a variety of communications networks and Internet protocols to make it all work seamlessly.

U.S. FORCES

Relationships between commanders are often as important, or more important, than *command relationships*. Sometimes junior officers get so transfixed on the doctrine of who reports to whom that they miss the bigger picture of what makes sense. This is in no way meant to dismiss the importance of clear lines of authority and responsibility, and a command relationship agreement before and during operations. However, in today's dynamic environment, there is a heightened appreciation of a command relationship called *support/supported*. This is where one force is the *supported* effort—and everyone else provides forces *in support* of that main effort. The supported force commander needs to ask for capabilities, and the supporting forces will provide assets that satisfy the requirement. Any disagreement will be settled by the common superior.

MARINE CORPS

I lay out the discussion above as a preface to my discussion of Navy-Marine Corps support. When the ground forces advanced north into

Iraq, they would become the supported force, and the aircraft flying off the Navy carriers would support overhead. Lieutenant General Hailston was the Marine lead in theater. He operated out of Bahrain in proximity to Vice Admiral Keating. He would coordinate Marine Corps efforts throughout the war.

The Marine Expeditionary Force (MEF) was the lead combat team for the Marine Corps. They numbered more than 60,000 Marines. The elements of this force included a ground combat element (GCE), an air combat element (ACE), and a combat service support element (CSSE). They formed up as a Marine Air-Ground Task Force (MAGTF). They were conducting detailed planning ashore as the kinetic (extensive weapons involved) phase of OIF was about to commence. Lieutenant General James Conway was commander I MEF. He had formerly commanded the First Marine Division and was highly respected for his direct, forceful manner. He would work with U.S. Army Lieutenant General McKiernan, the land component commander.

Major General James Mattis commanded the First Marine Division. He was known as the "warrior monk" due to his extensive reading of history and his spartan lifestyle. His assistant division commander was Colonel John Kelly. Under his command was the 5th Marine Regiment led by Colonel Joseph Dunford.

Major General James Amos commanded the Marine 3rd Air Wing (ACE), with Brigadier General Terry Robling as assistant wing commander. He reported directly to Lieutenant General Conway and worked closely with the air component commander. Because *relationships matter*, both Lieutenant General Conway and Major General Amos made their way out to *Constellation* to meet with me on 27 December 2002.

We had an opportunity to discuss their concept of operations. It was clear that air support would be critical to ensure success on the ground. The MAGTF would move swiftly north at the designated time— sometimes outrunning their organic (which was a part of the base organization) support, including air cover. I assured them that I would discuss this with Rear Admiral Kelly, who would be the direct liaison with the air component commander and ensure that there were fighter/attack aircraft overhead 24-hours-a-day from the Navy-Marine

Corps three carrier air wing team at sea. Without overstepping my authority, I made it clear that they had my promise that *Constellation* CVW-2 aircraft would always be looking out for them in the night hours, by tuning in to radio frequencies used by Marine forward air controllers (FACs).

The *face-to-face* *discussions ensure a lasting relationship and form a bond of trust. In our leadership courses, we use the phrase that "trust cannot be surged" when you need it most. It must be developed early and refreshed regularly.*

Part of the CVW-2 air wing on *Constellation* was the Marine Corps F/A-18 squadron VMFA-323 "Death Rattlers" with Lieutenant Colonel Gary Thomas in command. In a recent discussion, he said that the visit of these two senior Marine Corps leaders was a huge boost for the morale of the Marines on *Constellation*. Great leaders that they were, they spent the bulk of their time aboard listening to "their" Marines and providing encouragement and inspiration that was soaked up by the team.

Additionally, air wing staff flew ashore and conducted face-to-face meetings with the Marine Corps FACs. These were fellow Marine aviators who understood the capabilities and limitations of the F/A-18 aircraft. This would prove to be critical, as the pilots would know the faces and voices of the people they would be supporting on the ground.

AIR FORCE

Similar to the Navy-Marine Corps relationship, the connectivity to the Air Force was critical to success. In this case, it was up to the Navy to go to the CAOC in Saudi Arabia to meet with the leadership. I discuss this relationship further later in a section on CAOC operations.

COAST GUARD

The Coast Guard contributed greatly to the effort. The Northern Arabian Gulf waters were too shallow for U.S. Navy destroyers, but not for Navy patrol craft (PCs) and U.S. Coast Guard assets. The Navy requested assistance from the Coast Guard to help patrol these waters. The Coast Guard deployed the 110-foot cutter/patrol boats called WPBs to respond to this request. This would be the first combat deployment of Coast Guard patrol boats since the Vietnam War (other assets served in Desert

Shield/Storm) according to William H. Thiesen, Atlantic Area Historian ("Tip of the Spear").

WPBs *Adak, Aquidneck, Baranof,* and *Wrangell* were transported from the U.S. east coast by the larger motor vessel *Industrial Challenger.* They were craned off on 5 March after a 35-day transit and moved north to the NAG by 9 March.

The Coast Guard team was immediately employed to perform a variety of important missions. They initially supported the MIO near the mouth of the KAA waterway. They worked in support of Captain Jones' team of Sailors in RHIBs to prevent breakouts of vessels from Umm Qasr.

The WPBs played an integral role, and combined with the Navy PCs, became a force that controlled this critical waterspace. They made significant positive contributions in support of MIO, oil terminal protection, mine clearance operations, and waterway escort duties. As the commander of Task Force 55, I can say without reservation that I depended on these four great patrol boats and their diligent crews to work in the shallow waters of the NAG.

The Coast Guard also provided the USCGC *Boutwell* who performed as a shallow water blocker near the Shatt-al-Arab (SAA) waterway, and USCGC *Walnut* who serviced the buoys along the KAA waterway. Additionally, Coastguardsmen provided port security resources in Bahrain, Kuwait, and Umm Qasr.

ORDER OF BATTLE

The coalition was one of the largest gatherings of warships since the Korean War, representing many countries that wanted to contribute to this effort. Who were the 147 ships in the theater? Following is a snapshot of this force from 29 March 2003.

Key

HMS: Her Majesty's Ship (U.K.)
HMAS: Her Majesty's Australian Ship
HMCS: Her Majesty's Canadian Ship
HMNZS: Her Majesty's New Zealand Ship

HMLMS: Her Majesty's Royal Netherlands Ship
HMDS: Her Majesty's Royal Danish Ship
HSV-X1: High-speed Vessel/Ferry
RFA: Royal Fleet Auxiliary
FS: French Ship
ITS: Italian Ship
ORP: Polish Ship
FGS: German Ship
JDS: Japanese Defense Ship
HS: Hellenic (Greek) Ship

Of note:

- Additionally, there were ships in Task Force 155 supporting the defense of Kuwait: from Bahrain (PC—*Al Muharaq*), the United Arab Emirates (FFG *Al Emarat*), and Kuwait (*Al Sanbouk* leading six fast-attack craft).
- See glossary for ship type and location descriptions.

NAVAL ORDER OF BATTLE
29 MARCH 2003

SHIPS: 147 (89 U.S./58 NON-U.S.) NON-U.S. SHIPS
ARE REPRESENTED IN ITALICS

INPORT BAHRAIN
RFA GREY ROVER (AOR)
FS CASSIOPEE (MHC)
HS KOUNTOURIOTIS (FFG)

INPORT DJIBOUTI
FGS ELBE (ARL)

INPORT KUWAIT
RFA SIR GALAHAD (LSL)

INPORT UAE
NIAGRA FALLS (TAFS)

INPORT OMAN
ITS CIGALA FULGOSI (OPV)
ITS CHIOGGIA (MHC)
ITS VIAREGGIO (MHC)

EN ROUTE HOA
GUADALUPE (TAO)
ITS F-MIMBELLI (DDG)
FS ACONIT (FFG)

OPS GOO
HMS SCOTT (AGS)
RFA BAYLEAF (AO)
JDS KIRISHIMA (DDG)
JDS HARUSAME (DD)
JDS TOKIWA (AOE)

OPS HOA
MOUNT WHITNEY (LCC)
AUSTIN (LPD)
PATUXENT (TAO)
FGS M-VORPOMMERN (FFG)
SPS CANARIAS (FFG)
ITS STROMBOLI (AOR)

OEF MIO - GOO/JASK
VANDEGRIFT (FFG)
FS PRIMAUGUET (DDG)
HMCS MONTREAL (FFG)
HMCS REGINA (FFH)
HMCS WINNIPEG (FFH)
HMNZS TE MANA (FFG)
HMNZS VAN NES (FFG)

OPS ARABIAN GULF
WALNUT (WLB)
ADAK(WPB)
AQUIDNECK (WPB)
BARANOF (WPB)
WRANGELL (WPB)
SIRIUS (TAFS)
CURTISS (TAVB)
WRIGHT (TAVB)
CATAWBA (TATF)
GUS W DARNELL (TAOT)
GRAPPLE (ARS)
CAMDEN (AOE)
RAINIER (AOE)
KISKA (TAE)
SHASTA (TAE)
COMFORT (TAH)
JOHN ERICSSON (TAO)
PECOS (TAO)
FLINT (TAE)
OBSERVATION ISLAND (TAGM)
JOINT VENTURE (HSV-X1)
HMS ARK ROYAL (CVS)
HMS EDINBURGH (DDG)
HMS LIVERPOOL (DDG)
HMS YORK (DDG)
HMS MARLBOROUGH (FFG)
HMS RICHMOND (FFG)
HMS OEAN (LPH)
HMS BANGOR (MHC)
HMS BLYTH (MHC)
HMS SANDOWN (MHC)
HMS GRIMSBY (MHC)

OPS ARABIAN GULF
HMS LEDBURY (MSC)
RFA SIR BEDIVERE (LSL)
HMS BROCKLESBY (MCM)
RFA SIR PERCIVAL (LSL)
RFA SIR TRISTRAM (LSL)
RFA ARGUS (ATS)
RFA FORT ROSALIE (AFS)
RFA FORT VICTORIA (AOR)
RFA BRAMBLELEAF (AOT)
RFA ORANGELEAF (AOT)
RFA FORT AUSTIN (AFS)
RFA DILIGENCE (AR)
HMS ROEBUCK (AGS)
FS CDT L'HERMINIER (FFG)
FS BOUGAINVILLE (AGI)
ABRAHAM LINCOLN (CVN)
CONSTELLATION (CV)
KITTY HAWK (CV)
COWPENS (CG)
BUNKER HILL (CG)
MOBILE BAY (CG)
SHILOH (CG)
VALLEY FORGE (CG)
JOHN S MCCAIN (DDG)
HIGGINS (DDG)
MILIUS (DDG)
OSCAR AUSTIN (DDG)
PAUL HAMILTON 9DDG)
CARR (FFG)
GARY (FFG)
REUBEN JAMES (FFG)
THACH (FFG)
TARAWA (LHA)
NASSAU (LHA)
BATAAN (LHD)
KEARSARGE (LHD)
BONHOMME RICHARD (LHD)
BOXER (LHD)
ANCHORAGE (LSD)
ASHLAND (LSD)
COMSTOCK (LSD)
GUNSTON HALL (LSD)
PEARL HARBOR (LSD)
RUSHMORE (LSD)
TORTUGA (LSD)
DUBUQUE (LPD)
DULUTH (LPD)
PONCE (LPD)
SAIPAN (LHA)
DEXTROUS (MCM)
CARDINAL (MHC)
ARDENT (MCM)
RAVEN (MHC)

OPS RED SEA
SAN JACINTO (CG)
ARLEIGH BURKE (DDG)
DONALD COOK (DDG)
O'KANE (DDG)
PORTER (DDG)
BRISCOE (DD)
DEYO (DD)
FLETCHER (DD)
KANAWHA (TAO)

MIO NAG
BOUTWELL (WHEC)
CHINOOK (PC)
FIREBOLT (PC)
HMS CHATHAM (FFG)
HMAS ANZAC (FFG)
HMAS DARWIN (FFG)
HMAS KANIMBLA (LST)
OPR K X CZERNICKI (ASP)

OPS CENTCOM AOR
AUGUSTA (SSN)
BOISE (SSN)
CHEYENNE (SSN)
COLUMBIA (SSN)
KEY WEST (SSN)
LOUISVILLE (SSN)
MONTPELIER (SSN)
NEWPORT NEWS (SSN)
PITTSBURGH (SSN)
PROVIDENCE (SSN)
SAN JUAN (SSN)
TOLEDO (SSN)
HMS TURBULENT (SSN)
HMS SPLENDID (SSN)
HDMS SAELEN (SSK)

CHAPTER 7 | OPERATIONS PART I: SETTING THE FORCE

"For decades, Saddam Hussein has tortured, imprisoned, raped and murdered the Iraqi people; invaded neighboring countries without provocation; and threatened the world... The time has come to end his reign of terror. On your young shoulders rest the hopes of mankind."

—J.N. Mattis, Major General, U.S. Marine Corps,
Commander 1st Marine Division, Commanding General's Message March 2003

ROTATING THE CLOCK FOR 24-HOUR AIR COVERAGE

The ground forces had arrived by air and sea. More than 200,000 U.S. Marines and Soldiers were now positioned along the northern Kuwaiti border with Iraq. U.K. forces were embarked in the Royal Navy ships off the coast. As we approached potential combat operations, it became clear that one carrier air wing should be designated the *night operations* team to ensure 24-hour coverage was provided to the ground forces headed north from the Kuwaiti border to Baghdad.

I met with Captains Miller and Fox to review options before entering discussions with Rear Admirals Kelly and Moffit. I wanted to ensure that I represented their views on this issue as it might turn out to be one of the most significant decisions of the war for *Constellation* and CVW-2 teams.

As we had so often done in our months together, the three of us fell into a healthy discussion of the pros and cons of taking on such a duty. It would have a huge impact on the daily battle rhythm throughout the ship, and everyone would be affected, from the cooks to the engineers, to the maintenance personnel, to the pilots and flight deck crews. Everyone would have to adjust for night responsibility success.

Ultimately, we agreed to volunteer to have the *Constellation* air wing take on the night mission. No one from *Lincoln* or *Kitty Hawk* argued. They were happy to conduct the day support.

Constellation rotated the clocks, beginning on 21 February. Normally reveille occurred at 0600. Consistent with medical guidance from our staff, we adjusted the wake-up time over a six-day period. On day one the wake-up call was at 0800, day two 1000 until reveille was at 1800. Once this was achieved, the team settled into a rhythm. Breakfast was from 1800–2000; lunch ran from 2330–0100; and dinner was served from 0500–0700. What an amazing transition; the ship's routine had been rotated by 12 hours to support the war effort. The crew adjusted magnificently.

FIREPOWER SHIFT FROM THE MEDITERRANEAN TO THE RED SEA

The Turkey overflight rights assumption proved to be erroneous. The Turkish government would not grant this right of access despite the efforts of several high-ranking envoys from the United States. The impact was as follows.

No Turkish *basing*:
- Loss of U.S. Army's 4th Infantry Division access to the Northern Front
- Loss of Incirlik, Turkey-based U.S Air Force fighters and tankers

No Turkish *overflight*:
- Loss of Mediterranean carrier support for special forces in the North.
- Loss of Mediterranean carrier, destroyer, and submarine support for strategic targets.

Ships and submarines that had planned to fire Tomahawk missiles from the Mediterranean into Iraq would now need to transit the Suez Canal and prepare to attack from the Red Sea. Thus, Commander Destroyer Squadron 22, Commodore Stewart O'Bryan led a force from the Mediterranean through the canal 13–14 March to reposition for their tasking.

The transit groups consisted of the following ships:

OPERATIONS PART I: SETTING THE FORCE

Group 1:
USS *Arleigh Burke* (DDG 51)
USS *Deyo* (DD 989)
USS *San Juan* (SSN 751)
USS *Boise* (SSN 764)
USS *Toledo* (SSN 769)

Group 2:
USS *San Jacinto* (CG 56)
USS *Donald Cook* (DDG 75)
USS *Porter* (DDG 78)
USS *Augusta* (SSN 710)
USS *Providence* (SSN 719)
USS *Newport News* (SSN 750)
USNS *Kanawha* (AO 1)

These groups represented the firepower of a sizable number of Tomahawk missiles.

Commodore O'Bryan was designated commander of Task Group 55.6 and reported to me. He understood his role in command of Red Sea ships. My guidance to him was:

"You are Commander TG 55.6, command this group. Figure out what you need to accomplish and then execute it. You will *not* get the 1000-mile screwdriver from the Gulf telling you how to be a commodore. As you work issues, keep me posted regarding challenges, solutions, and areas where you could use an assist.

Subs will be under CTF 54 tactical control, but you will all be operating in the relatively close quarters of the northern Red Sea, so keep an eye out for them, literally and figuratively.

I look for you to work together to keep your ships ready to execute the Tomahawk mission shortly. I am Launch

Area Coordinator for the Red Sea shooters (eight surface ships and 10 submarines), and Lieutenant Commander Pietrantoni is my point of contact. We have been doing this since 14 December and have learned something new and better nearly every day.

Keep me posted, and welcome to the team. Barry."

Rear Admiral Boomer Stufflebeem, the commander in the Mediterranean who was Commodore O'Bryan's normal reporting senior, was superb in his direction. He said:

"Know Rear Admiral Costello is well served to have you there to help out. Let me make this easy for you and your staff—Rear Admiral Costello is your boss for now, so an occasional update from you would be terrific but certainly do not try to juggle working for two bosses simultaneously... it doesn't work that way. Let me know where, when and if I can help with logistics or other support stuff from here. Call if you get work and have fun!"

–Boomer

———————

Even while preparing for war, one must keep a sense of humor. Vice Admiral Scott Fry was the commander 6th Fleet during this timeframe. I had the pleasure of working under his tutelage while serving on the Joint Staff in a prior tour of duty. At the time, he was the director, and I was a newly minted rear admiral in the J-5, Strategic Planning and Policy Directorate. He was a 1971 Naval Academy graduate, one of the Navy's top achievers, who had aspired to the director position—the best job for any three-star in the military—orchestrating all activities of the Joint Staff on behalf of the chairman. His intelligence was matched by his sharp wit.

In 2002, I was scheduled to brief him on an issue, and the occasion called for Navy whites uniform. I was in my khakis as a normal work uniform in the Pentagon, and as I checked my whites in my office closet, I noted the lack of required shoulder boards. I requested my executive assistant, an Air Force major, to head to the Pentagon uniform shop to procure a set for me. He returned with the boards, affixed them to my shirt, and I quickly changed and headed for the front office for the one-on-one brief.

After a few minutes with Vice Admiral Fry, it became clear to me that I had lost my audience. He was staring at my uniform. I inquired as to what was amiss. He stated, "Well Admiral Costello, I was unaware that you had transitioned to the Chaplain Corps!" Unbeknownst to me (my fault) the boards had a cross on them, which is the designation for the Chaplain Corps. Hence from that day forward, Vice Admiral Fry referred to me as Father Costello, including during holiday celebrations in the Pentagon, where he would call on me to provide a grace before the masses enjoyed the delights of the festive foods.

Now, in 2003, it should have come as no surprise to me that when I sent him a message indicating that the transfer of forces under his command, from the Mediterranean to the Red Sea was proceeding smoothly, he replied with a note that began: "Padre Costello! What a delight to hear from you! You just go right ahead and get all the Irishmen* lined up the way you want them." Of course, he copied Vice Admiral Keating, and that elicited a note from him with question marks. I told him I'd have to explain it later over a cold beverage. *Referring to Commodore O'Bryan and RADM Costello's heritage.

COMMANDER'S GUIDANCE

At the higher levels of any government, there is a certain comfort and desire for ambiguity. It allows flexibility in dealing with a changing landscape and does not pin one down to specifics that may later prove inaccurate. This ambiguity causes a natural tension as the concepts get passed down to the forces that are going to execute the plans. At the tactical level, the opposite occurs. There is a desire for specificity that deals with any ambiguity, such that commanders are well versed in the intent of their superiors—right down to the most junior serviceman. If ambiguity remains, additional information is sought (Commander's Critical Information Requirements (CCIRs)), and planning and execution options (branch plans) are created to deal with the assumptions.

Now it was time to evolve the extensive planning to tangible actions across the force. *Strategic* guidance was coming from President Bush, being refined at the *operational* level by Secretary Rumsfeld and General Franks, and more detail provided at the *tactical* level by Vice Admiral Keating.

At the strategic level, President Bush was meeting with his National Security Advisors to work through the ramifications of a wide set of actions to be pursued in the Iraqi situation. These discussions dealt with building coalitions, working with the United Nations, and coordinating with allies to shape various courses of action. Additionally, discussions typically addressed ramifications of actions. What would be the *current* cost in lives and treasure, and what would be the *long-term* consequences?

At the operational level, Secretary Rumsfeld and his Department of Defense (DoD) team were drilling down into the details of executing the *military aspects* of the plan, while the State, Treasury, CIA, and other government departments were doing their individual planning—attempting to coordinate across boundaries of responsibility. This was a step down in scope from the presidential discussions, but more detailed in the specifics.

General Franks played a critical part in these DoD meetings. He would return to his staff and field commanders with guidance emanating from both the White House and DoD leadership.

Vice Admiral Keating was in the follow-on component commander meetings with General Franks. He and the other commanders provided their insight as to the pros and cons of various courses of action. They would advocate for the optimal use of their forces on behalf of the overall fight. The synergy of these complementing forces would exceed the whole of the individual pieces.

Vice Admiral Keating then hosted his Commanders Conferences to take the higher-level guidance and distill it down to how the naval component would operate, either being *supported* or *in support* of other forces at the tactical level.

I hosted three Warfare Commanders Conferences on *Constellation* in February and March to discuss details of upcoming operations. All commanding officers were present. The discussions covered every aspect of the upcoming conflict including:

- Responsibility for various warfare areas.
- Achieving harmony with coalition partners.
- Working with the air, land and special operations components.
- Achieving stability in the Northern Arabian Gulf waters.
- Addressing the mine threat.
- Securing the oil terminals to the north.

These conferences presented opportunities for me *to listen, learn, and lead—in that order.* I believe in this order of action for commanders, or anyone leading an organization.

There is much to be learned by first *listening* to subordinates. In listening, you provide an amount of empowerment to the speaker. The act of asking for input itself is sometimes startling to people who have not had that experience. In every case, the organization is stronger for having the discussion.

Learn from their perspectives and have an open mind as to the best way forward in dealing with a situation. It is only through this appreciation of other perspectives that a commander learns critical information that will make the ultimate plan stronger. I have found, time and again, that *excellent ideas emerge from more junior people. You just need to ask for their opinions, thoughts, and recommendations.*

I had the benefit of an all-star team of commanders, officers who had vast experience, education, and common sense. Talented officers, including Commodore Robert Harward, Commander Michael Gilday, Commander Jeffrey Harley, and Commander Kevin Campbell, figured out how to best maximize the potential of the force. Listening to their inputs provided an immense amount of insight from their unique experience that was not resident within my immediate staff.

Once the first two steps are completed, then—and only then—can the commander *lead*, fully equipped with input from those who will be held responsible for executing the plan. That is what I believe, and that is what occurred in Task Force 55. This process made me cognizant of many issues that needed to be addressed in my commander's guidance.

On March 10, during the last conference, I provided my thoughts on *perspective*.

> "Perspective is important here, and you as group leaders need to provide that to your crews. On the one hand, we will be here as long as required. On the other hand, this group has been and remains in the thick of the action— and many of their contemporaries would be very happy to be here in their place. Your leadership will make a dramatic difference in the outlook of your crews. Seize this as an opportunity. You have been chosen to lead because of the great potential you have demonstrated in the past... this is the time to put that potential to full use."

At the end of the conference, I reminded the commanders that:

> "We are part of the greatest armada seen in decades, with 147 ships, including six carriers and three expeditionary strike groups. Our discussions this morning regarding escort operations, oil terminal takedown, Al Faw assault, KAA waterway clearance, Umm Qasr pier operations, and Tomahawk strikes were well thought-out and have us well positioned for tasking by higher authority. This will be the last time we meet as a group before hostilities commence."

It became more apparent daily that conflict was on the horizon. The media was polling citizens about the potential of war. Polls showed that 35% of Americans thought it necessary to get U.N. authorization for military action via another resolution, while 56% said it would be desirable but not necessary. As international tensions increased, in my daily meeting with the press on 12 March 2003, I said:

> "There is well-founded confidence that if we are ordered to go forward (in combat), it will be lightning quick, it will be persistent, it will be precise, and it will be lethal."

The U.S. and its coalition partners were ready. It was now time to provide my commander's guidance to Task Force 55 and, unlike the previous lesson *identified* (when I learned back in November that my guidance was not getting through to the entire force), the message must permeate all the way to the deck plate, to the most junior personnel. On 13 March I wrote:

> "I want to ensure that every commander, commanding officer, and tactician in Task Force 55 is aware of my expectations for the coming conflict. We will not be risk-averse, but we will use good judgment to ensure we preserve our national treasure. We will take advantage of our technological superiority to control the battlespace. As you read the rest of this guidance, keep in mind that I want to be on the offense once this operation begins. We will go forward to take the KAA waterway and prepare the Port of Umm Qasr to receive humanitarian assistance shipping while providing surface protection to the force throughout the area of responsibility. Keep the ROE simple. "Self-defense" will cover most situations; use your best judgment to ensure that you do not take the first round but ensure that you develop the situational awareness to make sound decisions which avoid indiscriminate kills.
>
> My foremost concern is avoiding blue-on-blue engagements... Our operating areas will have U.S., coalition, enemy and noncombatant forces, as well as civilian craft and merchant vessels all in proximity.

Limited maneuver space makes target discrimination and avoidance of blue-on-blue challenging.

The objective is to defeat Iraqi military forces while leaving their society and civilian infrastructure intact to the maximum degree, consistent with operational objectives.

Enemy prisoners of war and civilian detainees will be taken during operations in the Northern Arabian Gulf. Treat them humanely and tend to their immediate needs for medical treatment and food.

Awareness of the tactical picture, current intel, and positive identification of all contacts approaching the force are vital. While I am concerned about fratricide and minimizing collateral damage, I cannot stress this final point enough: *If you feel threatened, act accordingly. There is no—repeat no—provision in the ROE nor any guidance from me which limits your right and obligation to take any and all measures to defend yourselves and other U.S. and coalition forces."*

I informed the press, "We are finished planning, and ready to support any action the president directs."

FOG OF WAR

As the time for hostilities approached, the force was in a heightened readiness state, both in the sense of the people and equipment. Everything was tuned to the highest possible degree. This is when the "fog of war" begins to roll in. Carl von Clausewitz, a famous Prussian general and military theorist in the 19th century, wrote of this concept. His book, *On War,* was published in English in 1873. The *fog* to which he referred was meant to capture uncertainty on the battlefield regarding one's own capabilities, the adversary's capabilities, and the adversary's intent. Intelligence collection is meant to reduce this fog.

However, while intelligence might mitigate some confusion, the reality is that the fog exists in one degree or another in every situation.

With that as a backdrop, coalition intelligence assets were at a fever pitch. At sea, some ships had specially configured systems to collect communications from the enemy. The Sailors assigned to these responsibilities were very bright and very secretive regarding their mission. Operators were trained that the fewer people who know what they were doing, the better. Their information went back to the intelligence community via separate communications channels, only being shared with the ship leadership in the case of a direct threat.

One day I received a call from an unusually unhappy Vice Admiral Keating. He wanted to know about the report emanating from one of my ships about a chemical weapons attack ashore in Kuwait. This was a surprise to me (not good), and I queried the captain of the ship reporting this information. I asked him about the report, how he had verified the information, and how he had communicated this to the highest levels of the government—without a call to his boss?

The silence on the other end of the line was deafening. This was a superb captain who had a key role in multiple ongoing mission assignments. His response, after a moment of shock and thought, was that he would get back to me shortly. He asked his ship's crew what they knew of this report—nothing. Then he ventured into the area where the intelligence specialists worked and asked the question there. He found the answer. One of the junior specialists had heard something about a *possible* chemical attack ashore in Kuwait (did not happen) and had immediately forwarded this information back to the intelligence chain of command... including the White House. Let's just say that this uncorroborated report, based on hearsay at best, caused quite a stir. A very embarrassed captain called me back, relayed the situation, and assured me that he would get a tighter handle on the reports emanating from his ship. He would review any report before launching it to the rest of the world.

That is only one example of the fog of war. Others included the report of a possible mine sighting in United Arab Emirates water (determined invalid), and possible activity at the Al Faw Seersucker missile site (proved to be of no consequence). There were many more.

However, commanders at all levels were trained to anticipate this reality.

INFORMATION WARFARE

Information Warfare (IW) is defined as "actions taken to affect adversary information and information systems while defending one's own information and information systems." IW is comprised of Electronic Warfare (EW), Operational Security (OPSEC), Military Deception (MILDEC), Psychological Operations (PSYOP), and Computer Network Operations (CNO). Each of these subsections of IW deserves its own exhaustive description. For brevity sake, I simply point out that they are extraordinarily complex, and actions in any of these areas have the potential to win or lose a battle. They are brought together under one commander to ensure consistency of effort. Successfully deployed, these disciplines have the potential to provide a great advantage over an adversary.

Captain Miller, in addition to being the *Constellation* commanding officer, served as the Information Warfare Commander (IWC) for the strike group. It was a first for the U.S. Navy—having the commanding officer of any carrier take on this role. It was initiated by Vice Admiral Bucchi. He called me to his headquarters shortly after I took command of the strike group and asked that Captain Miller join us. He "suggested" we consider having Captain Miller take on the role of the IWC, elevating it above the typical lead of a more junior specialist. This would place IW on the same level as surface, air, and submarine warfare—with a big stick to ensure priority in both planning and execution. Since the 3rd Fleet commander was "interested" in this initiative—we were "fascinated" and ran with the ball. We intended to make this experiment a great precedent-setting success for the Navy.

There were many pieces of special equipment installed on strike group ships before deployment. Several of these supported IW operations. Due to classification, I cannot go into specifics of these systems. Suffice to say, they made a significant difference in protecting our electronic systems. The threat was real. That was 14 years ago. These systems have since been replaced by more sophisticated technology, but the threat has continued to mature and, in some cases, outpaced the defensive systems. IW is now one of the most challenging realms for the warfighter. Initiatives during this conflict made it clear that it would be a major naval warfare area in the future, and that critical gaps remained in the ability to affect the adversary command and control systems.

One of the many successful aspects of IW operations was HMS *Chatham's* conduct of radio broadcasts. They logged over 250 hours of broadcasts with 25 different radio programs. These proved very effective as the Iraqi people could tune to these outlets and received accurate news regarding the conduct of the war, and the intentions of the coalition forces. USS *Valley Forge* provided similar broadcasts.

Leaflets were another tool used to deliver messages to various audiences. Aircrews practiced dropping leaflets versus bombs on the transit to the Gulf. *Constellation* crew printed millions of leaflets and stuffed them into weapons canisters. This was *not* a mission that excited the pilots; they referred to it as "Operation Litter Bug." It was more, "Really, you want me to fly into harm's way and drop leaflets?" But they practiced this skill set, one that *would later prove to be critical to the success of the operational and strategic mission. The more mundane tasks often have significant reach and impact on the overall conduct of the campaign—tactical actions with strategic effects.*

Captain Miller's IW team executed the operation. Millions of dollar-sized leaflets were printed on both sides. The leaflets included a variety of messages with the Iraqi soldiers as the target audience. Two of the messages were: "Soldiers go home to be with your families, and do not oppose the ground forces of the coalition," and "Do not blow up your oil well structure, as this will provide the money to support your country in the future."

There were drops every day after 1 March. Each drop involved 100,000+ leaflets on a wide variety of "targets" throughout Iraq.

On 11 March, 27 CVW-2 aircraft launched from *Constellation* to deliver 120,000 leaflets. These had the message to tune to a certain radio frequency to hear a U.S. message about the possibility of war, and the actions Iraqis should take to protect themselves.

On 16 March there was a similar leaflet mission, dropping on six military and industrial targets south of Baghdad. The message was, "Do not fight for Saddam, return to your homes."

ENGLISH (FRONT)

ARABIC (FRONT)

ENGLISH (BACK)

ARABIC (BACK)

INFORMATION WARFARE: IRAQ LEAFLETS

MEDIA EMBARKATION

From February to April, 32 journalists from a variety of news outlets embarked aboard the carrier. Similar contingents embarked on *Lincoln* and *Kitty Hawk*. Guidance from the secretary of defense to CENTCOM was passed to the groups. Specifically, "Media will be given access to operational combat missions, including mission preparation and debriefing whenever possible." It was clear that the chain of command wanted to allow the media to experience and report on every aspect of operations at sea.

They arrived in groups. Each group met collectively with me, Commodore Balmert, Captains Miller, Fox, Hepfer, and our Public Affairs Officer (PAO) Lieutenant Commander Wendy Snyder. After a "welcome aboard" we would explain our vision for their stay: where they would sleep and work; the ship routine; their access to the Internet to transmit their stories, except a brief window during the anticipated first-night strikes; and their access to the crew for their stories.

In addition to those aboard, reporters would call in for live interviews as the action occurred. These included Seamus McConville from Ireland (*The Kerryman News*) and Bruce Edwards from my hometown of Rutland, Vermont (*The Rutland Herald*). All were provided with stories for their audiences, usually with the roar of aircraft taking off in the background.

The embedded press corps represented an interesting mix of backgrounds and cultures. Language and cultural differences brought challenges to the PAO on how to firmly but diplomatically enforce rules, like no smoking except in specific areas of the ship. Some reporters were experienced in military matters. Some had previously embarked on a carrier (Otto Kreisher, *Copley News San Diego Union*; William McMichael, *Navy Times*; Cesar Soriano, *USA Today;* and Frank Buckley, *CNN*). There were others who had never been to sea and had never reported on the military. When one young reporter was asked why she was there, she answered that she happened to be standing by the water cooler when the leadership came around looking for "volunteers" to go underway for six weeks to the Arabian Gulf.

I met with the reporters daily from 0930 to 1000 and provided them with a summary of events that occurred over the past 24 hours. (See

Appendix D for daily highlights that show the overall flow of operations). Our daily briefing topics ranged from the serious to the lighter side of life on a carrier.

Reporters were advised of operational security and told of the potential for disaster for the troops if they tried to report events in advance via knowledge gained by their access to ships and Sailors. Universally the press understood their responsibility, and I never had an issue with a "leak" from our contingent.

They were informed they could go nearly anywhere on the ship and talk to any Sailor, *with no PAO "supervisor" to monitor their interviews.* The reporters were both amazed and skeptical that we would follow through on this transparency. I felt that there were nearly 5,400 individual stories on the ship and I wanted them told to the audience in every corner of the U.S. and overseas. I wanted the moms and dads to read of the exploits of these great Sailors and Marines, and the only way that was going to happen was to set the press corps free. *I accepted that there would be a negative story or two but determined that the benefit far outweighed the risk.*

An additional benefit I saw of the transparency policy was that it provided a meaningful lifelong impact on the reporters. They learned of the challenges of shipboard life and received a much better understanding of the environment, and the intensity of work performed 24-hours-a-day. How was it trying to sleep under the flight deck as aircraft launched and recovered throughout the night? How was that hot/cold shower? Equally important, they learned about warfighting concepts, flight operations, weapons, and maritime interception operations.

From having free rein of the ship, the reporters quickly learned about general quarters drills and how the ship quickly locked itself up in practice to preclude progressive flooding if the ship took a hit. They learned to be in awe of the young people running the day-to-day operations from the flight deck to the operations centers to the engine rooms. Each time reporters would interact with these proud professionals they would return with, *"I had no idea how much responsibility is vested in these young Sailors."* The reporters would *never be the same because of the experience of living alongside the young volunteer Sailors and Marines.*

It reminds me of stories of when U.S. military leadership would take their counterparts from Russia or China aboard ships to show the competence of the U.S. Navy. The counterparts, on more than one occasion, would not believe that they were talking to enlisted Sailors as they were so very confident, composed, competent in their rating skills, and held the same sophistication and professionalism as officers. They are that good!

Sometimes inexperience was an advantage. Joellen Perry, *U.S. News*, Technology and International Economics reporter, published her report on flight deck operations. It was the most descriptive article I have read because she had fresh eyes, ears, tongue, and nose... and assumed nothing. It was all new to her, and she used her gift of writing to tell a story such that all readers could feel like they were there on the deck with her:

> "In the middle of the night, in the middle of the Persian Gulf, the flight deck of an aircraft carrier offers an unlikely feast for the senses. The sharp scent of jet fuel mixes with hot, sweaty steam from the *Constellation's* catapults to form a lush brew that hangs heavy in the otherwise crisp Middle Eastern air. Deckhands don headsets that barely diminish the soul-shaking din of aircraft roaring and slamming onto and off the carrier's 300-foot airstrip. Wind whistles around the deck so wildly it's been known to blow unwitting sailors into the sea. And in the inky blackness of a nighttime ocean, tiny white landing lights burn steadily, while the dragon-breath burners of an F-18 Hornet blur orange and blue as the sleek aircraft, heavily pregnant with huge bombs attached to its underbelly, hurtles down the deck into the night sky...
>
> Each night, between sunset and sunrise, the *Constellation's* gravelly, greasy flight deck bears the

thundering weight of nearly 100 takeoffs and landings, as pilots of the ship's 72 aircraft carry out operations... the *Connie's* aircraft keep flying, as the ship maneuvers its flight deck in a terrible, beautiful ballet that has an aircraft landing or taking off every few minutes throughout the night. The immense Prowler, a four-seater that jams enemy radars... rolls to its spot on the strip. In 20 seconds, its low rumble ratchets up to a belly-of-the-Earth roar. For the prolonged second that the Prowler runs at full throttle, waiting to be catapulted off the deck, its monstrous moan completely immerses you, fills your lungs, becomes the air you breathe. The brief climax, two seconds in which the aircraft hurtles from 0 to 150 miles per hour, almost disappoints. The catapult releases, the aircraft shoots off the deck, and a thick curtain of steam is all that remains. Deckhands swarm into the smoke, preparing the tarmac for another takeoff. Within seconds, another Prowler makes its dramatic entrance onto the runway, nudging its nose into its sister's steam.

On this clear March night, with so many aircrafts circling overhead it looks like the stars themselves are moving, one sight stands out. From the deck of the *Constellation*, a deep orange glow dominates part of the horizon, spreading out like an anachronous sunset over the midnight sea. It's the tip of an oil refinery in Saudi Arabia, a flame that shoots some 200 feet into the air as it purifies its precious, controversial brew."

Most stories were positive, describing the human-interest aspects of working on a carrier at sea. An example of the many personal stories is an interview with Petty Officer Scott Smart from *Constellation* by Britta Arendt of the *Hibbins Daily Tribune* (Nashwauk, Minnesota):

"One important lesson I was taught, from growing up... is talking about it doesn't get it done. Someone has to do it, whatever the task, whatever the sacrifice, whatever the danger. That is what has made our country great and free. The morale of the crew is high. They miss their families, but know they have a purpose and mission to accomplish... every Sailor and Marine here does a vital job... everyone has to pull their weight and more. We don't get paid much compared to our civilian counterparts. We do it for Pride of Country... I am very proud of my wife. She takes care of the homefront while I am gone and is my support network. For every one medal I will earn, she deserves 10."

The Sailors understood that I would accept a less than flattering story. *But* that did not mean that *they* had to accept it. The note below was published in a Long Island, New York paper in response to an article published by one of its reporters. The fact that the paper gladly printed the "response" was appreciated by the crew.

"Greetings, my name is Chad Runge. I'm a Petty Officer Third Class in the United States Navy. I write from the deck of the USS *Constellation*, 'America's Flagship,' on 13 Mar 03 (4 months and 11 days into our current deployment) in response to a story that was recently run by your publication regarding my ship.

Though your journalist reported the truth, with minor errors, in fact, I know, being a journalist myself that she took a negative angle on everything she wrote. Not once was anything positive mentioned about my ship or my shipmates. She reported that life on board "*Connie*" is mundane and boring. I would like her to tell that to the gentlemen that spend countless hours risking their lives working in one of the most dangerous environments in the world, the flight deck.

Life on board *Constellation* is anything but boring. Although daily life may be routine for many, this is not the case for most. I know that I am proud of the job I do, regardless of how "mundane" it is. I'm proud to be sitting here today, fighting the global war on terror in whatever way the U.S. military needs me... My shipmates, Sailors and Marines, make up the *Constellation*. Without my shipmates, this aircraft carrier is just a boat. We ARE the *Constellation*... Each of my shipmates takes pride in this ship... Each Sailor on board does his time on the mess decks (cleaning dishes). This person's normal job may be as an air traffic controller that guides pilots back on to a runway that is ¼ of the size of your closest commercial airport's runways. He may be a 19-year-old 'kid' that navigates this 1,069-foot ship through the hostile waters of the Arabian Gulf.

The reporter also mentioned that she saw dingy and wrinkled uniforms. There is no doubt in my mind that she did. I'm also quite sure they were drenched in sweat from spending 12 to 18 hours in a hot, steamy machinery room. I'm sure they may have been covered in grease or smelling like fuel from the jet blast of an F-14 Tomcat. I ask this reporter to change the tires on her car without soiling her hands or clothes. These are the perks of mundane jobs. The jobs we all take pride in.

We take pride in the fact that we can be called Sailors or Marines, Soldiers, or Airmen. We take pride in the uniforms we wear. Believe it or not, we even take pride in this misguided journalist's story. It is because of my shipmates and fellow servicemen and women that she is able to write this story.

I fight so that she can write whatever her heart desires. My uncles, they fought so that people could stand outside the White House to protest. My grandfather, he fought so people could burn 'Old Glory' without consequences. It is because of myself, my family, and millions of other active duty and retired military personnel that you may voice your opinion freely. We are PROUD TO SERVE.

When we all return to Coronado Island, you will all see how proud we really are. With thousands of people sure to be awaiting our return to the San Diego Bay, you will see. 'Manning the rails,' lined up shoulder to shoulder along the sides of the ship, in our dress white uniforms, you will see how proud we are. Not one person will slouch. We'll all stand tall, chests in the air and heads held high as we transit through the bay to the pier. Slowly we'll leave the ship, see our husbands and wives for the first time in six months, some seeing their newborn child for the very first time (more than 50 of us so far will have this privilege). Watch as tears roll down our faces. Our heads will remain high. You'll see how proud we are.

We'll wear our uniforms for a bit longer that day, nobody will be quick to change. We will strut around all day long in these uniforms, heads held high. PROUD of ourselves. PROUD of our country. PROUD of our ship. PROUD of our shipmates, and PROUD of the 'mundane' jobs we do."

Petty Officer Runge's letter conveys the genuine passion of this fantastic crew.

———

Occasionally there would be a question in the daily brief that would not warrant an answer either because of security or another reason.

However, I never wanted to embarrass any of the reporters so I would utilize an acronym I created a decade earlier to respond. That acronym is *COPE*, which stands for *challenge, opportunity, professionals, and education*. If I used those four words in a series of sentences, it was an acceptable answer to any question. For example, if asked about potential issues with a future operation, rather than admonish the reporter that we do not discuss future operations—the answer would go something like this:

> That is an interesting question. There will be great *challenges* in the days ahead. But here on the *Constellation* team, we see that as an *opportunity* to move the ball forward and help achieve our mission; and with the proud *professionals* on our team, and the *education* they have received via training before we left San Diego, we are confident we will succeed.

That might sound a little sophomoric, but I found it very effective to give the reporter a sound bite that did not violate any trust, but at the same time it conveyed a positive message.

The other part of preps for any gathering of reporters was to *have three points prepared ahead of time*, and regardless of the questions, I would ensure I got those points out on the record. You will see that tactic every Sunday morning when senators and congressmen are on the television talk shows.

Finally, there is a natural tendency to feel like one must answer a question if asked. This is *not* the case. *The art is to turn a bad question into one that you feel is appropriate to answer, and then go for it.*

In my opinion, *there is no such thing as off the record.* Everything you say is on the record. If you approach the press with that mindset, there is less opportunity to be lulled into a false sense of security and camaraderie. I've seen too many leaders fall into that trap with twisted words, out of context quotes, or simply by providing personal feelings that are inappropriate to share.

The embedded press would be hungry for details of the good and the bad and were anxious for the story when the *Constellation* air wing suffered its only aircraft loss during the entire deployment. An S-3 experienced a loss of hydraulic control while flying a night mission. The aircraft had no brakes and limited ability to control the movement of the rudders. Captain Miller tells the story:

"The aircraft was the recovery tanker and had a cockpit indication that the hydraulic system that powered their nose wheel steering and brakes (among other things) was low. Per standard procedures, the crew radioed into the Carrier Air Tactical Control Center (CATCC) to talk to a squadron representative, who happened to be the squadron commanding officer.

They talked over the issue, and the crew indicated a desire to get towed out of the wire once they recovered on deck. But the squadron commanding officer thought they would be fine to taxi out under their own power. No one else in CATCC was informed, so no one in the tower or on the bridge was aware that the aircraft had a hydraulic system problem."

The aircraft successfully landed at 0510. It caught the wire and cruised to the end of the flight deck with the wire extended. Then the situation deteriorated. The aircraft released the arresting gear and shut down its engine, awaiting either chocks and chains or a tow to a parking area. There it was sitting on the deck at the mercy of any movement. The flight deck crew did not get the chocks and chains out immediately (unaware of the loss of brakes on the aircraft), *but* the bridge team did what it does at the end of every recovery cycle—turn the ship to starboard and run back downwind. The aircraft, with no brakes, turned to port on the flight deck and it began an uncontrollable roll to the edge of the deck, hit the deck edge lip, rolled over it, clipped the Challenge Athena communications antenna, and plunged into the waters of the Arabian Gulf. The two-man crew held on until the last possible second and then ejected as the aircraft headed over the carrier side. A rescue helicopter plucked the pilots from the water, and a rescue boat was on the scene as a backup.

A few hours later it was time for our daily press meeting. The reporters had seen the videotape of the incident and were eager to get my take. When I addressed them that day, I said that the pilots were in sickbay, that the press could go down and talk to them momentarily, and that we would have the appropriate investigation to determine what led to this mishap (*not knowing all the details at that point that are provided here*). I then related what I saw immediately *after* the incident:

> "The experienced flight deck crew swung into action. Aircraft were repositioned. The deck was prepared. Crews took their positions for the launch of the next wave of aircraft north into the skies. In fact, 11 minutes after the S-3 went into the water, the next wave of fighters was launched."

That is what I saw, and that became the headline in the press clips the next day, versus a negative story. *In every negative situation, there are people who do amazing things that are often overlooked, and those heroes should be the headline news. Figure it out, be prepared, and go on the offense.*

———————————

In summary, these daily briefings on *Constellation* were the source of 300 printed articles. There were also 30 live television feeds, and numerous taped segments. There were over 24 live radio feeds. I believe this coverage is exactly what the Department of Defense had in mind when they established the embedded reporter program.

Following are some of the outlets who came aboard for periods of time while we were in the Gulf, some for a month. This list gives you an idea of the challenge faced by Lieutenant Commander Snyder, as she worked tirelessly to ensure everyone had an opportunity to get their story. She handled the myriad tasks masterfully.

ABC	Daily Express	ITN	RTE Ireland
Afton Bladet	Dallas Morning News	Jordan News Agency	Rutland Herald
AP	DAPP	Knight-Ridder	Sky TV
APTN	DELO (Czech News)	KTRK	Time Magazine
ARD Radio	der Spiegel	L.A. Times	Toronto Star
ARD TV	der Tagesspiegel	London Daily Telegraph	Turkish TV
Arizona Republic	Die Welt	London Times	U.S. News & World Report
Asahi TV	Dutch TV	Mittle Deutsche	USA Today
Australian Neuss	ESPN	MSNBC	Virginia-Pilot
Austrian Broadcasting	Fox News	National Journal	Voice of America
Bahrain Tribune	German Press Agency	Navy Times	Washington Post
BBC Radio	Getty Images	Newsday	WNBC
Canadian Broadcasting	Glasgow Herald	Newsweek	World Journal
CBS	GovExec.com	People Magazine	Wrposzt
Chicago Tribune	Greek TV	Polaris Images	Yomiuri Shimbun
CNN	Gulf News	Pro Sieben	
Copley News	Hong Kong Daily	Reuters	

The reporters were professional and described their experiences to a worldwide audience. I believed in the embed program and did everything I could do to make it a success.

The media was welcomed aboard as a *teammate*. Evidence of this was reflected in the fact that they were featured in several air wing cartoons, a daily feature of the air-plan.

Air wing personnel find creative genius in crafting the daily air-plan cartoon. These cartoons typically choose an event of the past day and lampoon it, to the great entertainment of the masses. They are crafted in good humor and extend a long tradition in the air wing ranks. No discussion of strike group operations is complete without reference to these classics. A few are attached throughout the book to capture the incredible imagination of the authors.

Media "Credibility"

"Stay tuned to our continuing coverage. Next, well be speaking to a retired General, a retired Army Captain, and a guy who's thinking about enlisting, to get their expert opinion on the Coalition's military strategy - after this."

CNN AMERICA, INC.
6430 Sunset Boulevard, Suite 300, Los Angeles, CA 90028

323.993.5000

April 18, 2003

Rear Admiral Barry M. Costello
Commander, Cruiser Destroyer Group ONE
Unit 25064
FPO AP 96601-4700

Dear Admiral Costello:

I hope this letter finds you in good spirits and calm seas. I just wanted to thank you for your gracious hospitality and assistance while we were embedded aboard the USS Constellation.

Your good humored manner and your leadership in the area of media relations truly helped us to tell the Navy story during Operation Iraqi Freedom. It has been my experience that the personality of a ship's crew reflects the view of its senior leadership and I have to say that virtually everyone we dealt with–from the seaman on his first deployment to the salty veterans of the Constellation–treated us with respect. And more importantly to me perhaps, they did their best to answer our questions.

My fellow journalists on other ships were not so lucky and I sincerely believe that our superb experience aboard Constellation is directly attributable to you. So, thank you.

On a more personal note, I wanted to thank you for the kind words in your note that I will always keep in a special place. As the son of a retired Master Chief, it was humbling to receive your card and you should know that my parents later read the words with great pride.

I look forward to seeing you again in a couple of weeks as you get closer to San Diego. We are hoping to come aboard one more time to do some on-air reunions between the Constellation sailors and their families as you steam from Hawaii to California.

Thanks again and if I can ever be of assistance to you, please don't hesitate.

Respectfully,

Frank Buckley
National Corresondent
CNN

MINE STORAGE AREAS AND RULES OF ENGAGEMENT

One of the initial planning assumptions for the combined force, based on intelligence reports, was that Iraq planned to mine the Northern Arabian Gulf and its territorial waters. This would impact coalition combatants operating in those waters. Carrier operating areas were well to sea, but not impossible to reach. There was also a concern about mining efforts in the southern part of the Gulf, near the U.S. base in Bahrain and port facilities in the United Arab Emirates. If successfully deployed, the mines would have a significant impact on all naval operations, commercial shipping, and relief supplies.

The coalition intelligence on the Iraqi mine warfare capability was extensive, based on years of study and analysis of reports. Iraq had a known significant quantity of sea mines, both moored contact—those that would explode when bumped by the hull of a ship (LUGM 145 or AL-TAHADDI) and bottom influence—those that would explode due to a mix of pressure, magnetic, acoustic and seismic influences in the water when a large ship passed over (MANTA or SOMAR-250s) types. The Iraqis had the potential to deploy these mines via a variety of watercraft. These ranged from tugs, modified oil barges, dhows, pilot boats and small combatants (TYPE-15s).

They deployed at least 60 MANTA mines in the NAG in 1990 to defend against amphibious landings in Kuwait. USS *Princeton* passed over one of these mines during Operation Desert Storm on 17 February 1991, incurring considerable damage. The USS *Tripoli* struck a LUGM mine the same day, with equally profound consequences.

Having the intelligence was the good news. The bad news was that to most effectively disrupt this capability, it must be dealt with *ashore*—before the mines are deployed. The reality is that national leadership will not typically authorize ROE for preemptive strikes on these facilities. It is one of the commander's responsibilities to fully appreciate these constraints *and ask for clarifying guidance*. I continually pushed to get the mine storage areas and mine-laying vehicles on the target list for the first day of strikes, or earlier if conditions allowed.

As combat operations neared, there were reports of possible Iraqi mine deployment, for what and to where were questions yet to be determined. This was another example of the fog of war, and it certainly heightened my sensitivity to the need to deal with both the mines and the minelayers—soon. On 17 March *Chatham* changed the readiness posture of the ship in response to the mine threat warning of *yellow*, requiring all personnel to sleep above the waterline.

One of the options I pursued to address the mines on the land and at the piers involved close communication with Commodore Robert Harward (CTF 561—Naval Special Warfare), Captain Mike Tillotson (CTF 56—EOD), Captain Allen Painter (CTG 51.9—Naval Coastal Warfare), Captain Michael O'Moore (CTG 55.4—Mine Warfare), and U.S. Marine teammates. These leaders and their forces would be ashore in the first hours of the conflict, and I wanted them to focus on dealing with mine-laying vessels that had not yet gotten underway, as well as the mine storage areas—ensuring there was no movement of mines.

MINE CLEARANCE OPERATIONS

The mission of the coalition mine clearance team was refined over several weeks. Ultimately, it was to open the KAA waterway and Port of Umm Qasr 72 hours after Umm Qasr and the Al Faw Peninsula were secure. Planners estimated that it would take 96 hours for the coalition forces to secure these areas, thus the total of seven days for the entire effort.

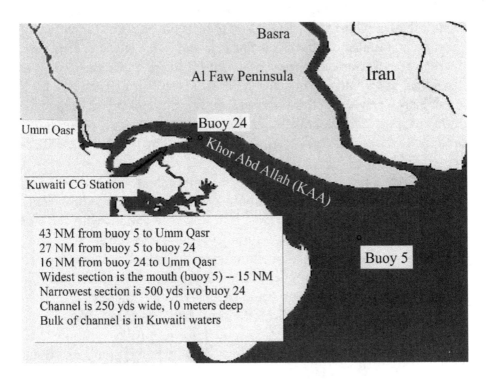

Basra

Al Faw Peninsula

Iran

Umm Qasr

Buoy 24

Khor Abd Allah (KAA)

Kuwaiti CG Station

43 NM from buoy 5 to Umm Qasr
27 NM from buoy 5 to buoy 24
16 NM from buoy 24 to Umm Qasr
Widest section is the mouth (buoy 5) -- 15 NM
Narrowest section is 500 yds ivo buoy 24
Channel is 250 yds wide, 10 meters deep
Bulk of channel is in Kuwaiti waters

Buoy 5

To provide a sense of geography for this mission, the following statistics are provided:

- Buoy 5 marked the southeast end of the KAA waterway
- Buoy 24 marked the narrowest section of the waterway (northwest of Buoy 5)
- From Umm Qasr to Basra—32 miles northeast
- From Umm Qasr to Al Faw Peninsula—33 miles east

Lieutenant Tracey Green, executive officer of USS *Dextrous,* advised, "The waterway had not been surveyed since 1992, so there were no accurate charts. There were also a lot of damaged and sunken vessels in the waterway."

Captain O'Moore, CTG 55.4 (Mine Countermeasures Squadron 3) would direct this operation from his flagship, USS *Ponce* (LPD 15). The forces supporting these efforts were from the U.S. Navy, Royal Navy, and Royal Australian Navy.

My initial meeting with Captain O'Moore in February was memorable. He came to *Constellation* to brief me on plans for clearance operations. I indicated that I was familiar with mine warfare. However, my surface warfare experience to-date had not emphasized that discipline, so I would rely heavily on his expertise: listen, learn, and lead. He painstakingly walked me through the traditional methodology for mine hunting and clearance. At the end of this very professional briefing, I was left with several questions, including risk factors and the expected timeline.

Captain O'Moore explained that it would take 14 days to cut a 43 mile 200-yard swath from the mouth of the KAA so that ships could safely reach the Port of Umm Qasr. He was very patient with me as I continued with my questions. I anticipated that Vice Admiral Keating would be pressed by higher command and the political element to expeditiously get relief support to the people of southern Iraq via this waterway; the 14-day number would be hard to sell. That said, I was also not interested in putting our brave Sailors at unacceptable risk.

I asked what planning factors went into the 14-day estimate, and Captain O'Moore replied that the force would be in Situation Alpha (minimize risk to mine warfare assets). This situation allowed for a slower pace and no opposition. I queried, "What happens in Situation Bravo (balance risk to mine warfare assets and time available to complete the task) or Charlie (timely completion of the task is primary concern... risk to mine warfare assets is secondary)?" Taking other factors into play, the timeline could be reduced by a few days. I emphasized that we would be entering a wartime situation, and a combination of self-defense measures by the mine warfare forces and the security to be provided by the patrol craft would be appropriate to allow them to proceed up the KAA in Situation Bravo.

The next questions were a series of *what ifs*. What if the mine force started at opposite ends of the waterway and met in the middle? What if the helicopters and ships worked in tandem in real-time communications cutting out the time loop of tape analysis back at the mothership? None of these ideas reflected existing doctrine for mine warfare.

Captain O'Moore patiently worked through the alternatives. I suggested he go back with his staff to see what might be done to reduce the 14-day estimate. We were already clearly out of his comfort zone, yet he was open to suggestions. We were in a position where mine warfare was going to have a front seat in the action. It had to be done correctly, professionally, with an appreciation of risk, and finally, and as expeditiously as possible for operational and strategic reasons associated with the overall campaign.

In a recent conversation with Jay Cavilieri, one of my watchstanders in 2003, he recalled the discussion about refining options for this important mission. Jay smiled and noted that Captain O'Moore returned with a 12-day plan, and I had an unhappy reaction, asking "What is it that I do not understand?" Clearly, the answer was "a lot," but my rhetorical question was indicative of my attempt to remain calm while getting across the message that 12 was not the answer I had hoped for and would not lead to mission success.

By 25 January the estimates had been groomed. The transit to Umm Qasr timing estimate was nine days for the best-case and 31+ days for the worst. The best-case scenario assumed that no mines would be found. It consisted of two to three days for mine hunting; four to six days for harbor clearance; four days (simultaneously with the harbor clearance) to establish waterside port security; and possible requirements to deal with sunken ships and wrecks in the harbor. The worst-case scenario reflected *challenges* in each of the aforenoted areas. Planning factors included up to 4+ knot currents that limit dive windows, lack of waterway bottom data, and hazards to divers such as pollution, hazardous marine life, and unexploded ordnance.

During this time in the planning effort, Vice Admiral Keating received a note from the admiral in charge of the Mine Warfare Command in Corpus Christi, Texas, suggesting that he come forward into the theater as the mine warfare effort should be led by a Flag officer (admiral). I then received a note from Vice Admiral Keating inquiring "Aren't you a Flag officer?" I replied in the affirmative... and the boss suggested that the admiral remain in Texas and provide support from there.

Ultimately Captain O'Moore returned with a plan to cut the swath through the 43-mile transit in seven days. The priority was to open the KAA waterway and Port of Umm Qasr. The secondary mission was to open the Khor Al-Zubair (KAZ) waterway to the Port of Az Zubayr. The challenges included dhows loitering in the waterway, possible mines in the water, and Iraqi naval threats.

The planning effort included a wide variety of players and precise timing to coordinate our actions.

- The *Information Warfare (IW)* campaign would distribute millions of leaflets to inform the Iraqi ship crews not to mine, and how/when to depart the KAA waterway.
- Next would be the daylight only *Air* Mine Countermeasures (AMCM) exploration and sweeping operations. The AMCM force consisted of MH-53E helicopters of Helicopter Mine Countermeasures Squadron 14 embarked on *Ponce*. They would conduct precursor mine hunting with the AQS-24 Side Scan Sonar which they towed. They would also conduct precursor mine sweeping with the MK 106 countermine sled that emanated electromagnetic waves to set off "influence mines" such as the MANTA. The helicopter could also conduct a mechanical sweep,

trailing wires that could cut the moorings of contact mines such as the LUGM. This activity would occur in front of the Surface MCM force.

- The *Surface* MCM (SMCM) ships would work in groups of two, marking and neutralizing mines. They would use mine-hunting procedures, without mechanical or influence sweeping.
- The *Underwater* MCM (UMCM) forces would work the port area utilizing U.S. and coalition divers, unmanned underwater vehicles (UUVs), and marine mammals.
- *Task Force 561* (special operations forces) would be clearing derelict vessels and controlling the flow of all shipping from north of the port.
- *Task Force 56* (explosive ordnance disposal) and *Task Group 51.9* (naval coastal warfare) would clear the port facilities, provide water and land security, inspect vessels north of Umm Qasr, and work closely with the MCM forces in Umm Qasr.

The key to the successful execution of this mission would be the ability to deal with the challenge of deconfliction of efforts with the land component forces that would be operating on the Al Faw Peninsula. This would only be successful by face-to-face coordination before commencing these operations.

We briefed Vice Admiral Keating on the plan. Reflecting Captain O'Moore's concerns, the last slide of the brief was titled "Bottom Line:"

- There were several significant planning assumptions.
- The operation was feasible, but at a higher level of risk, "while executing mission outside of doctrine norms."
- Risk would decrease after 72 hours to more acceptable levels.
- After 72 hours Umm Qasr still had a medium risk of buried mines.
- Many unknowns—the situation would gain clarity once mine clearance forces were in Umm Qasr.

I was able to "sell" this seven-day timeline to Vice Admiral Keating. *That agreement would be significant as events unfolded.*

On 6 March, we assembled all commanding officers on *Kanimbla* for a KAA Concept of Operations Conference. I provided my thoughts on the operation and presented my priorities and concerns. I did not want sailors injured chasing a number, but rather establish a target timeline to frame the problem. Captain Cochrane (*Chatham*) wrote of this meeting that:

> "The key point from the admiral for all commanding officers was that the 72-hour target (beyond the initial 96 hours to secure the Al Faw Peninsula) to clear the KAA of mines and commence humanitarian aid shipping was only a goal and not a fixed target."

The crews of the helicopters and mine hunters were the embodiment of coalition operations as the U.S./U.K./Australian navy sailors successfully worked side by side to neutralize the mine threat along the KAA and KAZ. The Task Group 55.4 team included:

U.S. Support Ships:
USS *Gunston Hall* (LSD 5)
USS *Ponce* (LPD 15)

U.S. Mine Warfare Ships:
USS *Cardinal* (MHC 60)
USS *Ardent* (MCM 12)
USS *Dextrous* (MCM 13)
USS *Raven* (MHC 61)

NSCT1 (Naval Special Clearance Team) with marine mammals
EODMU6 (Explosive Ordnance Disposal Mobile Unit)
HM 14 (6 x MH 53 helicopters)

United Kingdom Support Ships:
RFA *Sir Bedivere* (L3004)
HMS *Roebuck* (H130)

United Kingdom Mine Warfare Ships:
HMS *Ledbury* (M30)
HMS *Brocklesby* (M33)
HMS *Sandown* (M101)
HMS *Grimsby* (M108)
HMS *Bangor* (M109)
HMS *Blyth* (M111)

U.K. Fleet Diving Group

Australia:
AUST CDT3 Diving Team

The scheme of maneuver for the SMCM ships was for *Brocklesby* to lead while controlling the Shallow Water Influence Minesweeping System (SWIMS). This is a remote-controlled precursor sweep to increase the safety of the follow-on force. *Dextrous* would be second in line, followed by *Blyth* with their One-Shot Mine Disposal System (OSMDS), which was superior in high tidal streams. *Raven* would follow, with its SLQ 48 sonar system to hunt, locate/relocate, identify, and neutralize mines. *Cardinal* and *Bangor* would be last of this initial group, to widen the channel search as time permitted.

In the meantime, AMCM operations would be ongoing. Coordination of air and surface asset operations would be key to success.

Lastly, UMCM would be airlifted to Umm Qasr to survey the port and commence a search of the port seawall. Underwater vehicles would conduct exploratory missions along the piers to map the bottom. However, these could not detect buried mines. This is where the well-trained, well-fed and well-cared for marine mammals would go to work, to identify buried mines along the pier. Navy divers would also be involved in this effort to ensure the Port of Umm Qasr was safe so that relief supplies could successfully be delivered by ship to the Iraqi people.

It would take 20 helicopter lifts to get the team of marine mammals, EOD personnel, and other supporting forces to Umm Qasr. This group would work together on the land, in the water, and in the air to ensure the port was secured and ready for shipping.

VIEW FROM THE DECK OF USS *RAVEN*

I had the privilege of interviewing Captain Ken Long in 2017. In 2002, Lieutenant Commander Long was the commanding officer of USS *Raven*, a ship that was 188 feet long, 38-foot wide, had a 900-ton displacement, and sailed with five officers and 46 crew. I was at sea on *Constellation* in the middle of the Gulf several hundred miles from the action, and Captain O'Moore was embarked in *Ponce* (sometimes operating from *Gunston Hall)*, many miles away from the KAA. It was enlightening to get his perspective from the pointy end of the spear.

Captain Long kept a journal that detailed his thinking as events unfolded. He took command of *Raven* on October 3, 2002, in Bahrain. The following summarizes his story:

> On November 24, 2002, during a call with Commander Hall, the possibility of going to war was discussed. On November 27 Vice Chief of Naval Operations Admiral Bill Fallon arrived in Bahrain and spoke of the importance of having mine warfare ships in the area.
>
> In December the mine warfare ships were underway conducting surveys of established Q Routes (pathways for ships to transit in the case of mine dangers). They were making a record of all objects on the Gulf floor so that they could later determine any anomalies. The focus of the survey was in the waters off the coast of Kuwait, very close to the territorial waters of Iraq.
>
> In January 2003, the force continued internal preparations for any future action. This included:
>
> - "Magnetic offloads," removing metal items such as soda machines that could set off an influence mine.
> - Receipt of chemical, biological, and radiological (CBR) protective gear, and conduct of drills to ensure crews were aware of how to don this gear.

- Running the ship through the Forward Area Combined Degaussing and Acoustic Range (FACDAR) to measure the ship acoustic signature.

Vice Admiral Keating visited the ships one final time on February 13 to give them a sendoff. His ability to inspire is well documented, and this proved to be the case that day. "Do your job… take care of your people… spring training is over… people will shoot at you." These ships would operate only a few hundred feet from Iraqi shores. They were armed with twin .50 caliber machine guns, M60 machine guns, and small arms.

The crews practiced their defensive reactions in the case of attempted boardings by Iraqi marines and soldiers. February brought M60 machine gun practice from the bridge wings, and additional underway time to practice their craft. Personnel were armed 24-hours-a-day as there would be minimal time to react in these close quarters with Iraq.

On 17 March *Raven* tied up outboard RFA *Sir Bedivere*. Lieutenant Commander Long met with Commander Hall, and they listened as President Bush addressed the nation. There was every indication that there would be war within 48 hours.

The *Raven* crew witnessed a long series of merchant vessels of various sizes headed southeast out of the KAA on 17 and 18 March. After hostilities had begun on 20 March, the U.K. marine forces moved up the Al Faw Peninsula, and mine-hunting assets moved northwest up the KAA. *Dextrous* discovered a suicide craft on the shore of the KAA. Fortunately, the speed of the U.K. ground forces at the beginning of combat operations prevented this vessel from being launched.

This waterway had uncharted unlit buoys, making it a navigational challenge. The water was described as "like chocolate milk." The ships secured their water making capability for four days for fear of contamination.

I enjoyed hearing this young commanding officer's story. Perspective depends on where you sit. He had minimal connectivity, so his view of the world around him was limited to what he could see. This was supplemented by face-to-face interactions with his chain of command, but these were infrequent as operations gained steam. I filled in some of the operational level details for him during our conversation, and he enjoyed hearing "the rest of the story" for the first time.

ESCORT OPERATIONS

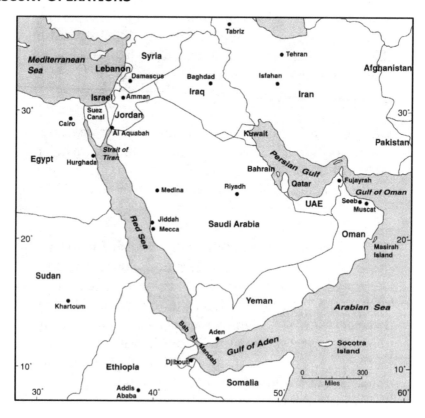

The intelligence community determined that the threat of attack on or seizure of shipping vessels by Al-Qaeda terrorist groups was significant. In addition to threatening the lives of countless merchants, an interception of shipping could seriously interrupt international commerce. Shipping lanes would need to be kept open from the Suez Canal to the Northern Arabian Gulf (NAG). From February through early-April escort support would be required from coalition forces. Several assumptions were identified as the plan was crafted to address this challenge. These included:

- Egypt would support passage through the Suez Canal, and provide force protection.
- Escort through the Red Sea would not be required.
- Iran would remain neutral, though interaction would be frequent.
- Oman and Iran would conduct overt surveillance and query of forces transiting the Strait of Hormuz.

This was a ship-intensive mission requiring a large force to ensure security. There would be one to two coalition ships in the Gulf of Suez to escort vessels in those constrained waters after leaving the canal at Port Suez, and before heading out to the Red Sea. Then two to three ships would be positioned north of the Bab-el-Mandeb Strait, and escort ships through those constrained waters bordered by Yemen and Somalia, areas of known threats to shipping. In the Bab-el-Mandeb Strait, there was a requirement for an armed helicopter aloft, an embarked security team on the escorted vessel, communications with the escorted vessel, and pre-planned responses to deal with any threat.

Once clear of these waters, ships would transit northeast to the Strait of Hormuz, between Iran and Oman. Then eight to 10 escort ships would be required for the transit from the Gulf of Oman to Kuwait (port of debarkation). Hundreds of ships transit these waters on any given day, and at this time of pending conflict, the traffic was even greater than normal because of the shipping support to military operations.

Considerations for the Strait of Hormuz to Kuwait transit included the following:

- Establishing a holding area to the south of the strait
- Making airborne armed helicopters available for the transit
- Conducting covert night transits to deny visual search by terrorists
- Avoiding carrier operating areas
- Avoiding mine danger areas
- Understanding that ships might need to wait in the NAG for a space to unload in Kuwait

There would be a force of five to seven ships in the NAG available to guard the shipping once it arrived.

There were many moving parts to this operation. Rear Admiral Veri was CTF 150, in charge of operations near the Bab-el-Mandeb Strait, from the Red Sea to the Gulf of Aden. Commodore Girouard as CTF 151 was responsible for safe passage through the Strait of Hormuz. The NAG escort ships were organized and supplied by Commodore Peterson and Captain Jones. They all coordinated with Commodore Balmert who was responsible for the overall master plan for these operations. Ultimately, while authority was delegated, I was responsible for these operations, confident in the ability of my team of leaders.

To say that this was complex would be an understatement. The professionals of many navies came together to make it happen successfully. There were hundreds of escorted ships. None were attacked by terrorists because of the outstanding leadership and coordination of the coalition forces.

MARITIME INTERCEPTION OPERATIONS AND FLUSHING THE KAA

Escort operations are focused on getting the good guys to their ports safely. Maritime interception operations (MIO) are focused on finding the bad guys seeking to do harm, and eliminating their threat. Coalition ships had been enforcing U.N. sanctions resolutions 661, 665, and 986 since August 1990. These were authorizations to use MIO to interdict smuggling operations near the KAA and SAA (waterway going north at the top of the Arabian Gulf between Iraq and Iran, forming a portion of the border between these two countries) waterways.

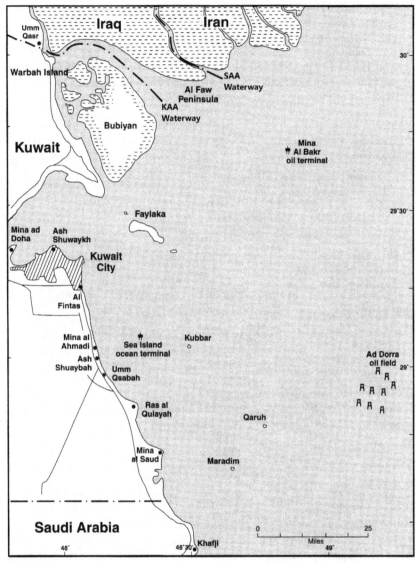

NORTHERN ARABIAN GULF SHOWING SAA AND KAA WATERWAYS, OIL TERMINALS, AND OIL FIELDS. THIS IS A VERY COMPLEX WATER SPACE.

On 30 October 2002, the Australian navy's Captain Peter Jones took command of the MIO force. He was an experienced commander, having served in the Gulf on several occasions. He wrote of his initial impressions as he returned, and stated something all military people could appreciate, "There were more acronyms and procedures than you could poke a stick at."

When we arrived in December 2002, we considered Captain Jones to be a salty dog. He had a firm grasp on Iraqi patrol boat movements, commercial traffic coming out of the Iraqi waterways, the protocol of inspections, and Iranian Revolutionary Guard fast boat activities in his vicinity. There were lots of moving parts in the shallow waters, complicated by a series of oil rigs, oil platforms, and territorial seas claims by Iran. On any given day there could be several interactions by his forces with a wide variety of actors.

Constellation Strike Group brought several new players to join his team. Captain Jones now added the cruiser *Valley Forge*, destroyers *Milius* and *Higgins*, and the frigate *Thach* to his force. These ships allowed him to have a continuous presence in the mouth of the KAA waterway.

He worked to establish a battle rhythm for his staff and to get his hands around the command and control that was being exercised via *chat*. Chat was commercial software on a classified network that enabled participants to join a *meeting room* online, and reports could be sent, and orders could be given. This method of communication had advantages and disadvantages. On the plus side, it was fast, easy to use, and accessible to all. On the minus side, it could be confusing, discerning what were *orders* and what were *discussions*, who was talking in these chat rooms (senior or junior personnel), and the reality that chat can be a distraction for personnel who also have other responsibilities... like watching radar screens.

Commodore Balmert was initially my direct representative to Captain Jones. These two professionals worked together in a support (Balmert)/supported (Jones) relationship. *Milius* became the flagship, hosting Captain Jones and his staff. U.S. Navy boarding teams (Sailors assigned to approach ships in small boats to board and search for contraband) joined the team, working closely alongside their Australian (HMAS *Anzac/Darwin*), U.K. (HMS *Cardiff*), and Polish (*Kontra Admiral Xavier Czernicki*) counterparts.

Once I took command of Task Force 55, MIO became one of my primary focus areas. Sailors would perform this duty by boarding and inspecting ships departing Iraq via either the KAA or SAA. The inspection teams looked for contraband, weapons, or illegal oil that was headed south through the Gulf. Captains/masters of these suspect vessels would attempt to skirt along coastal waters to avoid detection and interception. If illegal transporters were successful in making it to a southern Gulf port to unload their cargo, they would be paid handsomely by those dealing in contraband.

I monitored the situation closely and communicated directly with Captain Jones to learn his personal assessment of the challenges facing his force. He utilized liaison officers to facilitate a smooth communications flow and placed his best people on *Constellation*, *Valley Forge*, and *Czernicki*; and with 5th Fleet headquarters and with Royal Marines. This command structure could have presented challenges; however, the commanders and their staffs worked closely together to ensure the success of the mission.

The coalition force received several new arrivals in February to support MIO operations: Royal Navy ships HMS *Marlborough*, HMS *Chatham*, and HMS *Richmond* reported on station ready for tasking. The Australian ship HMAS *Kanimbla* arrived on scene at the end of February, and assumed duties as the command ship, hosting Captain Jones and his staff (moving from *Milius)*. This ship had a shallow draft that allowed it to go close to the Iraqi coastline, a large communications suite, multiple combat information centers, and a planning space and accommodations for coalition boarding groups. In early March U.S. Navy patrol boats *Chinook* and *Firebolt* brought their speed and firepower to the impending fight; and U.S. Coast Guard cutter *Boutwell* and patrol crafts *Adak*, *Aquidneck*, *Baranof*, and *Wrangell* joined the force.

The maritime interception force (MIF) mission sets began to gain clarity. Coordination of these complex efforts in the confined waters of the NAG would be critical to *avoid* blue-on-blue situations. Missions would include:

- Inspecting merchant ships and dhows exiting the KAA waterway and controlling their movements in the Northern Arabian Gulf.

This would include dealing with a potential mass breakout of these vessels.

- Clearing ships and tracking them as they moved south along the western side of the Gulf.
- Supporting the U.K. Royal Marines assault on the Al Faw Peninsula by securing the maritime approaches and providing naval gunfire support.
- Defeating any element of the Iraqi navy that got underway from either the KAA or SAA waterways, including patrol and other small boats.
- Supporting special forces seizure of the offshore oil platforms.
- Escorting mine countermeasures ships up the KAA.
- Conducting riverine patrols to ensure access to the waterway for humanitarian aid shipping.
- Conducting helicopter operations in support of the force.

In early March, the Iraqis moved their large combatants and government vessels southeast down the KAA and north up the SAA waterway to Basra. As Captain Jones monitored this movement, he continued to gather intelligence.

> "Our intelligence was telling us of Iraqi military on tugs and that explosives were to be laid on the Mina al Bakr (MABOT) and Khor al Amaya (KAAOT) oil terminals and on navigational marks. Rumors of mines abounded among local mariners. We strongly doubted mines had been laid, but we closely shadowed all Iraqi vessels. Equally important was maintaining our overt presence to deter any mine-laying."

On 15 March, USCG cutter *Wrangell* was conducting MIO and observed an Iraqi PB-90 patrol craft closing her position to within one mile. As *Wrangell* maneuvered, the PB-90 matched course and speed. The ship reported the situation to Captain Jones, who ordered *Wrangell* to proceed south, and had the destroyer *Marlborough* steam north and launch its helicopter in support of *Wrangell*. Ultimately, the Iraqi vessel broke off, but this incident was an indication of the Iraqi navy's new interest to interact with the coalition forces at sea and get closer to interfering with ongoing MIO activities. Commodore Peterson emphasized his intent to keep the coalition force posture de-escalatory in any interaction with the Iraqi navy and to avoid any situation that might allow Iraq to dictate the time of confrontation.

To give an overview of this mission, the following figures are provided for the first three months of 2003:

- Vessels queried (asked a series of questions by the coalition force): 1480
- Boardings (coalition sailors going aboard): 893
- Diverts (likely illegal activity, sent vessel into a holding area): 413
- Illegal oil metric tons: over 3,300

Reports were emerging of the Iraqis loading mines on dhows. I wanted to "own" the NAG waters, to eliminate the possibility of the Iraqi navy deploying mines and I pursued many options to achieve that goal.

The first was bottling up all vessels in the KAA waterway, precluding any opportunity to deploy mines in the Gulf. Dhows would transit southeast to the mouth of the KAA only to be met by coalition sailors, who would turn them around and send them back to Umm Qasr. This procedure remained in effect from mid-February to mid-March 2003. Approximately 95 vessels, based on overhead imagery, were being held in Umm Qasr. The international community (likely including some business interests awaiting products from Iraq) petitioned Vice Admiral Keating to allow the vessels to depart Iraq for the safety of the southern Gulf or places outside the Gulf.

Releasing the awaiting vessels in a group as late as possible would provide benefits to the coalition forces. The first was that these ships would act as minesweepers on their transit out of the waterway, effectively letting us know that as of the time of their departure the waterway was clear of danger. Secondly, once the flush was complete, any vessel coming out of the waterway would be considered potentially hostile and would be thoroughly inspected. Finally, it would help simplify the situation on the waterway once hostilities commenced.

I sent a note to Deputy Commanding General I Marine Expeditionary Force (MEF) Major General Keith Stalder letting him know my intentions to flush the KAA. He supported this idea and agreed that deconfliction of the vessels by both time and space would be very helpful. This seam between the land and maritime commander's areas of responsibility would be closely watched during the opening hours of the conflict, with a concern for blue-on-blue due to many missions ongoing in the same battlespace.

Small crews of Sailors operating the RHIBs were critical to security in the KAA. This represented the border between Kuwait and Iraq. It was the path from the southern Iraqi Port of Umm Qasr to the Arabian Gulf. They would speedily roam the waters at the mouth of the waterway, providing a protective seal, ensuring no mine-deploying boats emerged. The decision had been made early on that we would press our forces very close to the Iraqi border and control the water in such a manner that any dhow or other vessel that exited the KAA would be inspected, with a focus on looking for mines.

On 14 March, the decision was made to base the 130 RHIB coalition sailors and their boats on *Kanimbla* to centralize the necessary pool of manpower to deal with the large dhow rush envisioned in the KAA clearance plan. The ship was the perfect choice to be the support vessel for these teams, allowing them to rest and be fed while stationed near the mouth of the KAA. Many of the teams came from U.S. Navy ships that were repositioning to support either Tomahawk missile launches or air defense. These extraordinary Sailors would be the leading edge of the fight up the waterway, working all day and throughout the night.

Captain Cochrane (commanding officer *Chatham*) described the situation clearly in his war diary:

> "The CONOPS for the clearance of the KAA involves
> *Kanimbla* sailing up the river together with the MCM
> (*mine countermeasures*) force protected by U.S. Patrol
> Craft and armed aircraft. By pooling the NAG escorts
> boarding teams on *Kanimbla*, CTU 55.1.1 now could

board, search and clear large numbers of vessels within the river without delaying the MCM effort."

I wrote of the situation to Vice Admiral Keating:

"Thirty dhows came out waving white flags... they have been shot at by Iraqi naval forces and told to leave the KAA. These are pawns in the KAA game. I am concerned that if they are being pushed out (again), it is not a good sign, and may be a foreshadowing of things to come in mine warfare."

Vice Admiral Keating responded an hour later:

"Barry: If you can, inspect the dhows, ensure no mines or contraband onboard, let the dhows proceed... don't have to tell you to tell them this is a one-way pass."

Thus, on 17 March, we flushed the vessels from Umm Qasr and the KAA waterway. Each ship was inspected by boarding teams from the U.S., U.K., or Australian navies. These would prove to be the last meetings between the dhows and other steel hull vessels and the boarding parties.

A total of 58 dhows and 47 merchant ships were processed in three days. Mission focused young Sailors protected the coalition ships, ensuring that nothing got through their net. Before the departing ships were released, Captain Jones had each vessel marked with a painted circle so that they could be accounted for by coalition helicopters. Skippers were provided a chart to follow as they moved south along "Red Route One," complete with instructions to visit check-in points with coalition ships along their transit out of the Gulf.

On the same day, we received information that the Iraqi navy was loading mines aboard four barges at the Umm Qasr Port facility. Masters/captains of the exiting dhows were more than willing to pass along information on Iraqi plans to place mines in the water near certain watermarks. The stage was set for an alerted coalition intercept force to be prepared for the worst.

DISCOVERY OF TUGS AND BARGE WITH MINES

After the KAA was flushed of all shipping, there was a brief period of calm on the waterway. However, that calm was quickly dashed. On the evening of 20 March *Chinook*, *Firebolt*, *Adak*, and *Aquidneck* were patrolling at the mouth of the KAA waterway. While conducting these operations, the force discovered Iraqi tugs *Al Jumhuriyah* and *Al Rayiah* and a barge coming down the KAA. Captain Jones ordered the coalition forces to stop and hold the vessels for inspection. The boats guarded the vessels while an American and Australian boarding team inspected the cargo bay areas for contraband or mines. This was a common event, regularly occurring before hostilities. But the events that followed were not common, as young Sailors approached the tugs and tow.

I had the opportunity to stand jury duty in March 2016. My panel of jurors was selected, and as we exchanged small talk, one of the jurors told me he had served in the Navy. His name was Steven Sharrard, and he had been an Electronics Technician First Class. We started exchanging experiences, and the next thing I knew, he was telling me of his experience in 2003 while part of the boarding party on these Iraqi tugs in the KAA. The following summarizes his story:

> We boarded the tugs, made our way to the bridge, noting that the number of tug crew members was larger than normal. The boarding party asked the captains a series of questions. Why were they heading out? Where were they headed? What was their cargo? The answers indicated a mundane voyage to Dubai to offload the contents of the barge, oil. Suspicious, the boarding party proceeded to conduct their inspection. The deck cargo on *Al Jumhuriyah* appeared to be a series of 40-gallon drums. As the team made their way through the aisle of drums, it became clear that there was more than met the eye. The

drums turned out to be camouflage. Beneath the drum shells were LUGM and MANTA mines.

The team realized that anything the pilots said was likely false. They noted an electrical cable running from a hut into the internals of the barge. They found an access to the inside of the barge. Once the trap door entrance was opened, it became clear that there was no oil inside. Two sets of angle iron were welded into the barge to provide mine rails. The mines would be rolled along these rails and exit the barge via two cutouts in the rear of the hull. The sterns of the tugs had also been modified with doors to allow the deck loaded mines to be deployed. There was a combination of 48 LUGM (contact) and 20 MANTA (influence) mines on the deck of the tug and in the barge. They would have been deployed without detection.

The captain of the vessel knew that his ruse had been uncovered. He had a change of heart and revealed his real intentions to the team. He had been directed to take his load of mines to the Northern Gulf and drop them in the waters where the coalition ships were operating. There would be no tether, and these mines would simply drift and be a threat to any vessel that came in their proximity. The boarding crews noted that there were five empty slots on the mine rails. Thus, there was a real possibility that these had been dropped in the water on the way out of Umm Qasr.

On *Al Rayiah* there were an additional 18 LUGM mines concealed on the deck under drum covers and tarps.

The boarding party called Captain Jones with a report of their findings, and he directed *Chinook*, an Australian landing craft vessel, and an explosive ordnance disposal (EOD) team to the scene. Captain O'Moore provided several mine experts to support the effort.

A third tug was subsequently boarded and seized. This was *Ninaiwa*, with a military crew, small arms and naval communications/encryption gear. It was the mothership that would direct the other two tugs to their drop off points for their deadly cargo.

The actions of the boarding team saved many lives and paved the way for the successful execution of the maritime portion of war plan 1003V. This was one of the most momentous events of the war. The Sailors, whose attention to detail and professionalism ensured this discovery, were true heroes.

CHAPTER 8 | OPERATIONS PART II: OPENING STRIKES

"I think it is a dangerous time in Baghdad and each person in Baghdad whether a news person, inspector or in some other capacity, has to take a look at whether or not it is time to leave."

—*Colin Powell, U.S. Secretary of State*

WAR IS IMMINENT

Vice Admiral Keating wrote to his admirals in the Arabian Gulf on 16 March 2003:

> "Following the component commanders' meeting with General Franks in Qatar Friday morning, I believe we will undertake a military option against the current regime in Iraq within a week.

> Our president is reported to be preparing to deliver an address to our nation and the world Monday, 17 March, after his meeting with the coalition leaders in the Azores tomorrow. General Franks told us the president may provide Saddam with an ultimatum in the speech, and that military operations could follow within 48—96 hours of that address should Saddam fail to comply with our president's terms. Not much reason to believe Saddam will.

> Thoughts:

> ROE are on the streets. We must know them cold, as must a good number of those in our charge.

Deal in as forthright and open a manner as you can with the many media in your midst, but guard carefully against inadvertent disclosure of critical information.

Pace yourselves in the days ahead. Much will be required of you, and all those in your groups will look to you for guidance and example. Start by being rested and fit.

The flow of information out of theater when hostilities commence will be an issue. Thirst at higher headquarters will be voracious. Guard against overuse of the bubba network. *

Know that General Franks is remarkably comfortable with the command structure he has to fight and win this war. You are an integral part of that structure. He trusts you. So do I.

WE WIN. GET READY."

My Best, Tim

(Bubba network: Navy friends who were not in the fight, but interested in how things were progressing)

He then sent a communication indicating that General Franks had told him to be ready for "D-Day" to be 19 March, with the air campaign to follow 48 hours later. We were to move ships as necessary to ensure they were in position to support that timeline. He made it clear that this information was to be kept close hold, to not tip our hand to anyone. Vice Admiral Keating intended to visit the crews of the carriers on 19 March in the hangar bays with press allowed, and then speak to the air wing in the forecastles (forward section of the ship) with no press.

The U.N. (with France and Russia leading the opposition) refused to back President Bush's bid for another resolution sanctioning military force. This diplomatic defeat left the U.S., Britain, and Spain to lead other nations in a "coalition of the willing." (The coalition would grow over time to include 48 partners.) The British House of Commons voted 412–149 to support the use of force in Iraq.

President Bush met with British Prime Minister Tony Blair and Spanish Prime Minister Jose Maria Anzar in the Azores on Sunday 16 March to ensure alignment of messages to the nations. This was characterized as a summit of the Big Three. The diplomatic instrument of power had run its course. The military instrument now moved to the forefront.

On Monday 17 March, President Bush gave Saddam Hussein an ultimatum.

"Saddam Hussein and his sons must leave Iraq in 48 hours. Their refusal to do so will result in military conflict to commence at a time of our choosing."

As the president's deadline loomed, measures were taken to attempt to minimize Iraqi casualties in the pending conflict. Aircraft from the air wing dropped two million leaflets over southern Iraq just before the deadline ended, with a variety of messages including instructions to Iraqi troops on how to surrender.

Vice Admiral Keating sent the attached letter to all Sailors and Marines of U.S. 5th Fleet, which was published in the daily air-plan on the carrier, and throughout all ships:

18 March 2003

Dear Sailors and Marines of COMFIFTHFLT,

You are about to begin a momentous task: the liberation
of Iraq. You have worked very hard preparing for this moment.
You are ready. For some of you, this is a culmination of
years, decades perhaps, of training. For others, this is your
first exposure to the frightening reality of armed conflict.

In any case, you will be called upon for sacrifice, for
strenuous labor, for gut-wrenching, split second decisions.
You will make the right call; you will find a reservoir of
strength and wisdom. I know you will, because you have been
schooled in the traditions of our glorious service, our United
States Navy. When all is said and done, when Iraqis have
rejoined the league of nations and are able to speak freely,
to worship as they choose, to engage in commerce, to travel
and enjoy life and liberty, then you will know the true
satisfaction of an important job done well, done better than
anyone else can do it, done as only Sailors and Marines in the
United States Navy and Marine Corps can do it, because you are
members of the finest Navy in the history of the world.

Now, it is time for us to go to work. Do so
aggressively, intelligently, with audacity and courage. Go
fully confident in the knowledge that you have earned the
support of your countrymen and of millions of freedom-loving
people around the world.

May God continue to bless you and your families, and may
He hold each of you in the palm of His hand now and always.

All the best,

T.J. KEATING
Vice Admiral, U.S. Navy
Commander, U.S. Naval Forces
Central Command
Commander, US FIFTH Fleet

The chief of naval operations sent a note to all members of the U.S.
Navy.

```
P 182210Z MAR 03 ZYB MIN PSN 285172M25
FM CNO WASHINGTON DC//N00//
TO NAVOP
BT
UNCLAS //N05000//
NAVOP 004/03
MSGID/GENADMIN/CNO WASHINGTON DC/-/MAR//

SUBJ/WE ARE READY//

RMKS/1.  SOON, OUR NATION WILL CALL UPON YOU, THE MEN AND WOMEN OF
OUR NAVY, TO MEET THE NEXT CHALLENGE IN THE GLOBAL WAR ON TERRORISM.
WHEN THE PRESIDENT ADDRESSED THE WORLD MONDAY, HE SAID, "THE UNITED
STATES AND OTHER NATIONS DID NOTHING TO DESERVE OR INVITE THIS
THREAT. BUT WE WILL DO EVERYTHING TO DEFEAT IT. INSTEAD OF DRIFTING
ALONG TOWARD TRAGEDY, WE WILL SET A COURSE TOWARD SAFETY." YOUR
EFFORTS IN LEADING THE DEFENSE OF THE NATION AWAY FROM OUR OWN
SHORES AND OUR OWN HOMES IS CRITICALLY IMPORTANT TO THAT SAFETY.
AFTER ALL, WE KNOW ABOUT SETTING A PROPER COURSE - AND WE ARE READY.
2.  THIS IS THE MOST READY NAVY I HAVE EVER SEEN IN MY CAREER.  OVER
HALF OF OUR NAVY, 167 SHIPS, ARE FORWARD DEPLOYED AND ON-STATION
AROUND THE GLOBE, TAKING SOVEREIGN POWER TO THE FAR CORNERS OF THE
EARTH.  SEVEN OF TWELVE AIRCRAFT CARRIERS, NINE OF OUR TWELVE BIG
DECK AMPHIBIOUS SHIPS (LHA/LHD), AND DOZENS OF SURFACE SHIPS,
SUBMARINES, AIRCRAFT, SEALS, SEABEES AND SUPPORT COMMANDS ARE
DEPLOYED.  MORE THAN 130 SEALIFT SHIPS ARE SUPPORTING THE JOINT FORCE
HALF A WORLD AWAY.  NONE OF THIS WOULD BE POSSIBLE WITHOUT YOUR
ENERGY, EXPERTISE AND DEDICATION.  YOU ARE PROVING EVERYDAY THE
UNIQUE AND LASTING VALUE OF DECISIVE, SOVEREIGN, LETHAL FORCES
PROJECTING OFFENSIVE AND DEFENSIVE POWER FROM THE VAST MANEUVER
AREA THAT IS THE SEA.
3.  WHEN YOU RAISED YOUR RIGHT HAND, TOOK THE OATH, AND DONNED THE
SAILOR'S UNIFORM, YOU CHOSE TO MAKE A DIFFERENCE IN THE SERVICE OF
THIS NATION - AND YOU ARE.  REST ASSURED, YOUR SERVICE IS
UNQUESTIONED; YOU HAVE THE SUPPORT OF THE CITIZENS OF THE UNITED
STATES OF AMERICA AND YOUR FAMILIES.  THEY CARE, AND THEY BELIEVE IN
YOU.  MAKE THEM PROUD.  I COULDN'T BE MORE PROUD TO SERVE WITH YOU.
4.  YOU ARE PART OF THE GREATEST JOINT AND COMBINED MILITARY FORCE
EVER ASSEMBLED.  IF OUR COMMANDER-IN-CHIEF GIVES THE SIGNAL, FIGHT
AND WIN.
5.  ADM VERN CLARK SENDS.///
```

When 19 March arrived, Vice Admiral Keating made his way around to all task forces and provided both pep talks and his commander's guidance directly. You could have heard a pin drop as he spoke of the preparations that had occurred over the last year; of the ongoing efforts to resolve the issues peacefully; and of his confidence that if force was required, the Naval Forces Central Command was up to the task. He said, "Thank you for what you've already done. And more importantly, thank you for what you're about to do."

Vice Admiral Keating understood that these young Sailors and Marines would soon be working 24-hours-a-day in very dangerous operations. He appreciated the reality that it was exciting for them to meet a Navy leader and made time to shake many hands as he walked about the ship. Yeoman 3rd Class (SW) James Dillon, a Texas native, said:

> "When he spoke to us, chills went up my spine. He made
> us all feel better about the possibility of going to war. I
> was really inspired."

Next, Vice Admiral Keating spoke directly to the aircrews. His message was from the heart, from one aviator to others. He had seen battle and wanted to look his team in the eye and express his confidence in their ability to carry out the mission while noting their sacred responsibility to minimize loss of life.

During my one-on-one closed-door meeting with Vice Admiral Keating, we talked about his authority and responsibility for coordination across the warfare disciplines. He spoke of his engagement with the other component commanders as well as the various coalition leaders that he interacted with daily. Additionally, he was a part of General Franks' battle rhythm—being on daily VTC conferences with him to provide the Navy input to the overall battle situational awareness. This input would make its way from General Franks through Secretary Rumsfeld to President Bush. The president had regular VTCs where General Franks reported directly from the front.

Vice Admiral Keating looked at me and said, *"Execute the plan... let me know if you need any assistance."* That's it. Perfect. There would be no daily VTC with him. He would *not* be the senior asking for minute detail of all tactical operations. If a deviation was required, his staff would work with my team. Otherwise, move out. He would provide the top-cover with higher headquarters so that we could go about our business without responding to their endless stream of interrogatories. He had confidence in his commanders that they would execute the plan and keep him advised. All task force commanders understood this and worked feverishly to *not let the boss down.*

Rear Admiral Snelson sent an Execute Order to all U.K. forces on 19 March, directing action according to national objectives in Operation Telic, and telling his force to keep him apprised as to any tasking from coalition commanders beyond that guidance. In true leadership style, he made it clear that commanding officers *had the authority to seize the initiative if time was of the essence,* even if it exceeded their authority. Leaders of the other coalition countries issued similar directives to their forces.

Operation Falconer, the Australian name for their engagement, was also set into motion. Their team was ready.

———

The clock ran out. President Bush's deadline passed with silence from the Iraqis. The president authorized the formal execution of CENTCOM Operation Plan 1003V as Operation Iraqi Freedom (OIF).

General Franks said:

"This will be a campaign unlike any other in history. A campaign characterized by shock, by surprise, by flexibility... and by the application of overwhelming force... You have my highest personal confidence and the confidence of your Commander in Chief. You are now in harm's way. Our task will not be easy, but we are fighting for a just cause, and the outcome is not in doubt. I am proud of you—all that you have done and all you will achieve in the days ahead."

The 20 March commander U.S. Naval Forces Central Command *Daily Intentions* message laid out the current situation and activities for each of the subordinate task forces for the next several days. Vice Admiral Keating's depth and breadth of responsibility would include the following tasking for his forces:

- CTF 50: coordinate the 386 naval aircraft with the CAOC
- CTF 51: conduct amphibious operations
- CTF 53: conduct fleet logistics
- CTF 54: coordinate submarine operations

- CTF 55: conduct maritime interception operations, mine warfare operations, and Tomahawk strikes
- CTF 56: support other task forces with maritime security forces
- CTF 561: conduct oil platform seizure
- CTF 57: conduct airborne surveillance in support of other task forces

Captain Harry Harris, the operations/plans officer, would exhort the force to execute the plan, be wary of fatigue, expect surprises, and plan for the worst but be prepared to exploit fleeting opportunities.

A *Wall Street Journal* reporter was allowed access to the 5th Fleet morning briefing on 20 March. His report provided a sense of the atmosphere as the force engaged:

"When VADM Timothy Keating, the senior U.S. naval officer in the Persian Gulf, walked into his war room in Bahrain, his senior staff greeted him in loud, jocular unison: 'Good morning beloved fleet commander.'

Adm Keating took his seat at a large conference table facing two large video screens. For the next hour, slides flashed onto the screen as aide after aide described elements of the naval air and sea campaign that had just begun to unfold.

'Got it,' Adm Keating would respond to most of the slides. After nearly an hour, he motioned to the technicians working the screens. 'Run it,' he said.

A video appeared of knights in armor speaking in perfect verse, footage from the 1989 film of 'Henry V.' The scene was the king's St. Crispin's Day speech, delivered to his men before the battle of Agincourt.

We few, we happy few, we band of brothers;
For he today that sheds his blood with me

Shall be my brother; be he ne'er so vile,
This day shall gentle his condition;
And gentlemen in England, now a-bed
Shall think themselves accursed that they were not
here.

The admiral's audience was rapt.

'We're underway,' he told them. 'It has seemed like a
long time to get here. But we've been baptized. Now we're
in it.'"

(*Wall Street Journal* online 21 March 2003)

MABOT AND KAAOT OIL TERMINALS TAKEDOWN

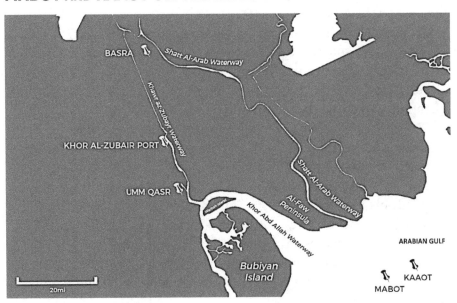

During the 1991 Gulf War, Saddam Hussein ordered his army to destroy
Kuwait's oil fields as they fled from Kuwait with American Soldiers in
hot pursuit. This economic, ecological and medical disaster cost Kuwait
billions of dollars to remedy. Additionally, Iraqi troops dumped the
equivalent of five million barrels of oil into the Arabian Gulf. The
environmental impact of this action was assessed to be 20 times worse

than that of the 1989 Exxon Valdez oil spill off the coast of Alaska. Oil dumped on the ground contaminated groundwater supplies, while oil discharged in the Gulf waters put desalinization plants at risk throughout the region. In arid climates such as Iraq, Kuwait, and Saudi Arabia, repeating this destruction would be a disaster of huge proportions.

Iraq's exported crude oil was sent through the Al Faw manifold facilities on the southeast point of the peninsula. The oil then flowed through underwater pipes to the Mina al Bakr (MABOT) and Khor al Amaya (KAAOT) oil terminals. This infrastructure was a critical asset for the Iraqi economy, capable of pumping 1.6 million barrels of oil a day. The terminals provided oil to huge tankers, serving four supertankers at a time at peak operations. These tankers would take their cargo to the east—China, Japan, and Korea, as well as west to Europe and the Americas.

These oil terminals are located approximately 22 (MABOT), and 16 (KAAOT) miles southeast of the Al Faw Peninsula and are 60 miles to the northeast of Kuwait. This geography is relevant, as it gives an appreciation of the distances required to execute any takedown operation, and of the coordination required.

The mission was to prevent a catastrophic oil discharge in the Northern Arabian Gulf. CTF 561, commanded by Commodore Harward, supported by Task Force 55, had the task of planning and executing the mission to secure these Iraqi oil facilities. He was a SEAL warrior, attended high school in Iran (father served in U.S. government overseas), fluent in Farsi, with experience on the front lines of Afghanistan, as well as other conflicts. He continues to hold several records for physical stamina at the Naval Special Warfare Center in Coronado, California and challenges any student who has the temerity to threaten them.

Commodore Harward positioned his special operations forces, ready for action, close to the fight. He conducted several rehearsals with RHIBs, Mark V fast boats, and helicopter assets to identify specific challenges that would need to be addressed in capturing these platforms. This included covert swims under the terminals, taking pictures, and surveilling Iraqi activity.

He worked closely with Commodore Peterson and placed a maritime deconfliction team of SEALs aboard *Valley Forge* (CTG 55.1 flagship) to ensure the continued smooth flow of communication. Captain Phillip Beierl, commanding officer of HSV *Joint Venture* (high-speed vessel—ferry), would provide the staging base for Commodore Harward's forces.

Commodore Harward provided his concept of operations to me, Lieutenant General Conway (I MEF), Rear Admiral Kelly, Rear Admiral Marsh (amphibious forces in the area), and Brigadier General Dutton (Royal Marines). The coordination required for the success of the mission to secure the oil terminals was extensive.

These face-to-face synchronization efforts were critical, as I MEF would be moving into the Rumaila oil field (the third largest oil field in the world, producing in excess of one million barrels of oil a day, making up 40% of Iraq's oil production), and the U.K. 3 Commando Brigade would be assaulting the Al Faw Peninsula nearly simultaneously as the special forces would be taking the oil terminals at sea and the pumping stations ashore. Timing would be critical to success. Lieutenant General Conway wanted to ensure the operations were not too early, providing Iraqi soldiers incentive to torch Rumaila before the arrival of the Marines. (Of note, U.S. Army forces would be initially positioned farther to the west, and therefore not impacted by this operation.)

Beyond the deconfliction discussions with the ground forces, there were three component commanders involved in the actual takedown operation:

- Combined Force Air Component Commander (CFACC)—air support
- Combined Force Maritime Component Commander (CFMCC)—maritime support
- Combined Force Special Operations Component Commander (CFSOCC)—special operations

The air team was eager to establish the timing of the assault on the oil terminals so they could fence off supporting air assets. Naval forces were arrayed in the Northern Arabian Gulf, with a wide variety of other missions. Therefore, clarity of timing would be very beneficial from the maritime perspective. The special operations forces were eager to get moving. Rehearsals were complete, and there was consensus, let's do the mission!

The stage was set. Time marched on. Boarding of vessels coming from the KAA and SAA waterways continued to occur daily. On 16 March, *Darwin* intercepted a vessel and interviewed the master. The master brought the Australians out to the bridge wing, and in guarded tones indicated that the Iraqi military and weapons were being embarked at Basra for transfer to KAAOT and MABOT. This information was consistent with that gained by boarding parties from *Marlborough*, as they interviewed Iraqi crews from other vessels, and was determined to be highly credible.

The day of the initial assault on Iraq approached. There continued to be many discussions among the components as to the timing of A-Day (air) and G-Day (ground). How many days of unfettered air bombing should occur before the ground forces should head north? The ground commanders were eager to move out, but the air component wanted to eliminate the possibility of blue-on-blue by holding the ground forces back while the air forces continue to pound Iraqi targets.

According to the campaign plan, once D-Day (decision to launch the operation) was established (19 March), A-Day (wartime air attacks) would follow 48 hours later. Then two of the three pieces would be in place. *As the timing of the third and last element—G-Day (the ground advance into Iraq)—was being considered, fortune intervened.*

I received a 0300 call from Vice Admiral Keating on 19 March. This was unusual; he normally worked through his staff. He indicated that five Saybolt Company (Netherlands) employees, working under contract as U.N. Oil for Food representatives (from Estonia, Denmark, Philippines, Russia, and Portugal), were on the oil terminals monitoring production. This group phoned their local contact in the Kuwait Maritime Liaison Office in the early evening, informing them that Iraqi commandos carrying boxes of explosives had landed on the oil terminals. Iraqi soldiers told the representatives that they would be transported to the Port of Basra the following morning. The U.N.

Kuwaiti office immediately alerted the 5th Fleet staff to this situation and requested help in rescuing their people.

Vice Admiral Keating laid out this information and directed me to intercept the boat carrying these U.N. representatives and ensure they were *not* transported to Basra. This is any warfighter's dream! Receive a call late at night from the boss, for a very time-sensitive mission, with no PowerPoint slides, staff interpretations of Commander's Intent, or exhaustive concept of operations briefings. The coalition had trained for months to execute this type of mission.

I immediately gathered a small team to consider options. It was clear that Commodore Peterson was in the best position to carry out this tasking. I communicated with him, provided the appropriate guidance, and told him to let me know if he needed anything else and keep me advised. Commodore Peterson rallied his team and created a force of helicopters, U.S. Navy patrol craft, and U.S. Coast Guard assets. This team would scour the waters between the oil terminals at sea and the SAA waterway that led to Basra. They worked throughout the night to identify possible boats that might be used to transport the U.N. representatives. With .50-caliber machine guns at the ready and boat crews determined to succeed, cooperation from all vessels was ensured.

The Sailors found the transport vessel on its transit north and rescued five very relieved U.N. workers. The U.S. Coast Guard Law Enforcement Detachment embarked in *Chinook* conducted the transfer, with *Valley Forge, Boutwell*, and an overhead helicopter in support. The U.N. workers were quickly transported to the *Valley Forge*. Mission complete; the Iraqi vessel was sent on its way to Basra.

Ironically, a U.N. spokeswoman said the evacuation of the five was done with the "full cooperation of Iraq." I do not think the five workers on a boat in the Northern Arabian Gulf headed to Basra would have seen it the same way as the spokeswoman in New York City.

Once the rescue was completed, information raced through the appropriate channels. The representatives retold their story firsthand to the U.N. leadership. The details of this story were passed quickly to Vice Admiral Keating, who passed them to General Franks. The information was then sent to Secretary Rumsfeld and finally to President Bush.

The message was that the Iraqis were preparing to blow up the main oil terminals that would provide the lifeblood for any future reconstruction of the country. The fact that this complex was in imminent danger of being destroyed from explosives planted by the Iraqi army set off alarms throughout the chain of command. The coalition leadership determined that these facilities must remain operational to export oil through southern Iraq for the future economic well-being of the country, as 90% of Iraq's income came from oil.

Discussion of the timing of A-Day and G-day accelerated. The enemy indeed does get a vote. In this case, the Iraqi army voted by preparing to blow up the oil terminal platforms, and their actions would change the course of the war.

I had discussed the need and requested permission over several months for the mission to secure the oil platforms. Planning and rehearsals by the naval special warfare and coalition surface warfare teams would now pay huge dividends. This would be a *non-compliant* boarding of the terminals, and support facilities on shore would also be defended by the Iraqis. The coalition team needed to be prepared for armed opposition.

It was time. On 20 March the war commenced. Vice Admiral Keating sent a message to the force announcing that President Bush had authorized the execution of Operation Plan 1003V, as Operation Iraqi Freedom (OIF). The order to execute the takedown of the oil platforms and the support facilities ashore followed immediately. I believe this mission (and the concern for the security of the Rumaila oil field) was the trigger that initiated the ground war. To succeed, there had to be simultaneous assaults on the two platforms at sea *and* on the Al Faw manifold facilities. These facilities on shore included a MABOT support facility, a KAAOT support facility, and the actual manifold and metering station.

The Navy SEALs of Task Force 561—supported by coalition special forces, *Valley Forge*, *Anzac* and helicopters from five squadrons from four locations—executed the well-rehearsed plan flawlessly. Commencing at 2200, two speedboats pulled alongside each terminal facility, and two SEAL platoons quickly boarded the platforms. They were backed up by four Mark V patrol boats, each armed with .50 caliber machine guns, along with snipers placed inside helicopters overhead.

The oil terminals were now secured, and the Iraqi soldiers were captured. Task Force 561 packed up and sped away to support the Royal Marines as they fought their way north toward Basra. A detachment of U.S. Marines with Navy EOD personnel arrived at the terminal to guard the prisoners and search for booby traps. Confirming our intelligence reports, a cache of rocket-powered grenades and explosives were found on the terminals.

WPBs provided perimeter security, which thwarted Iraqi reinforcements and prevented escape by any of their forces already on the terminals. Once Iraqi personnel and their explosives were cleared, Coast Guard personnel secured the facilities, as the Marines left to execute other missions.

The facilities on shore were also secured by Navy SEALs and coalition special forces, quickly overcoming Iraqi resistance. The U.K. ground forces followed to take the entire Al Faw Peninsula. U.S. Marines rushed into the giant Rumaila oil field (20 miles north of the Kuwait/Iraq border) to secure those assets. Iraq had laid a ten-mile-long defensive minefield, with 100,000 mines, that the Marines breached. No blue-on-blue incidents occurred due to superb coordination.

What is the measure of the effectiveness of leaflets in the information warfare mission? In this case, it was very easy to determine. Three examples highlight the success.

One: The Iraqi army put up resistance, but many of their soldiers evaporated as the coalition headed to Baghdad.

Two: Very few explosives were activated in the oil fields. In the case of the oil wells, coalition forces approached an oil field that was occupied by Iraqi soldiers. The soldiers surrendered after a brief time. The coalition forces noted that there were explosives rigged to destroy the oil wells, but they had not been activated. *When they asked the Iraqi soldiers why they had not blown up the infrastructure—they pulled leaflets from their back pockets and smiled "we got your message."*

Three: Oil was not dumped into the waterways. A senior non-commissioned Iraqi officer captured on the tug Al Rayiah told the coalition forces that the leaflet addressing the release of oil into the waterways had a significant impact on him. He was referring to the leaflet that stated: "Dumping oil poisons Iraqi waterways, as well as your family's future... it will kill or taint the sea life that feeds your family. Saddam has poisoned your waterways before. You must not aid him in doing so again."

I was interviewed by Kathy Day of the *North County Times* the next day.

> "It's been an unbelievable 24 hours... 24 hours ago we—with the SEALs and coalition partners—took control of the oil platforms in the Gulf. It's huge to fully appreciate the complexity of this mission and its implications. Now Iraqis can't flood the Gulf with oil because we control these platforms."

This mission provided an early win for the coalition forces, and it would be a foreshadowing of future successes. The Iraq economy continues to thrive today because of the professionalism of the teams that prevented the destruction of these critical platforms.

As the U.S. and Royal Marines moved north into Iraq, the special operations force provided support by controlling the Shatt al-Arab waterway from the Iraqi shore. This waterway formed the borderline with Iran in several areas. TF 561 set up an observation post on the Al Faw Peninsula to execute this mission.

U.S. forces received fire from the Iranian side of this waterway. U.S. policy precluded any response to the Iranian aggression. U.S. leadership was not interested in engaging the Iranians in any way. That said, the incoming fire presented a problem for the safety of the force. Security classification precludes me from telling how this challenge was resolved. Let's just say that the previously mentioned coalition ROE matrix was helpful, and the firing from Iran ceased.

TOMAHAWK STRIKES

It is difficult to describe the sense of excitement on a ship or submarine knowing that you are about to embark on the *largest launch of Tomahawks in history*. The crews had trained for months, some for years, to refine their skills, and learn to appreciate the capabilities and limitations of the system. Time after time they would go through the procedures to ensure a successful (simulated) launch.

The strike group had been exercising procedures for launches as we made our transit west. Once in the Arabian Gulf, there were 13 additional exercises to prepare all ships and planning agencies. The exercises built up to several hundred launches. The teams were set for any eventuality and all taskings. We referred to recent history to get some perspective on the possible number of Tomahawks that could be deployed:

- 282—Operation Desert Storm in 1991
- 235—Operation Desert Fox (targets in Iraq) in 1998
- 220—Operation Allied Force (targets in Kosovo) in 1999

Central Command advised the press that it had more than 1,000 TLAMs in the theater at the start of the war.

On 18 March Tomahawk-shooting ships were discretely pulled from their escort mission assignments and repositioned to their launch points. This required delicate coordination between General Franks (concerned with tipping our hand to the enemy regarding timing), Vice Admiral Keating (wanting to remain in step with strategic guidance from higher headquarters), and myself (wanting to move the ships as soon as possible to their launch baskets to ensure they were ready when called upon to properly execute their missions). It worked because of solid communications and some initiative... *do not ask for permission, beg for forgiveness* thinking on my part.

Anticipate is one of my favorite action words. I believe it is the key to successful execution of any mission. It also helps to preclude crisis mentality that leads to failure. In this 2003 case, moving the ships to their Tomahawk launch positions in the Red Sea and Arabian Sea early ensured they were ready when called upon to fire weapons in the opening hours of OIF.

I reached back to my 1996 experience, while embarked as the commodore aboard the *Nimitz*. We were on notice of a possible transit of strike group ships (except the carrier) from the Arabian Gulf back to

Taiwan in response to China's aggressive stance trying to influence the Taiwanese elections. It is a significant distance, so my team calculated when we would have to leave the Gulf to arrive near Taiwan prior to the elections. We then discretely moved all ships except the carrier to the Strait of Hormuz to get a running start. When approval came from President Clinton for the mission, and the admiral in charge asked how long it would take to move out, the answer was, "We are on our way now."

President Bush had spoken on 17 March, laying out his deadline for Saddam to depart Iraq. There was no indication of movement, so the president directed a mission where Tomahawk strikes, simultaneous with two U.S. Air Force F-117s, would attack as a last-ditch effort to avoid war by taking out Saddam. The targets were homes on the outskirts of Baghdad based on intelligence tips that the Saddam and four of his military commanders had been seen at the buildings.

The decapitation strikes commenced early in the morning on 20 March in the Gulf when the first Tomahawks were fired from the Red Sea (*Donald Cook* and *Cheyenne*) and the Arabian Gulf (*Bunker Hill*, *Cowpens*, *Milius*, and *Montpelier*)—two cruisers, two destroyers, and two submarines (along with USAF F-117s—discussed later). Once the first missiles successfully left their canisters, there was a sense of relief mixed with satisfaction that the training had paid dividends. These strikes consisted of three groupings totaling 39 missiles. Captain Faris Farwell, commanding officer of *Bunker Hill*, told the embedded press that the missile launches went, "Just as they were planned." George Cahlink from the *National Journal* was an embedded reporter in *Bunker Hill*, and he would describe the scene from the deck of the cruiser as 13 missiles were sent on their way:

> "Finally, at 5:15 a.m., amid an explosion of flames and smoke, two missiles emerged from the ship's rear, shaking the 9,500—ton vessel and lighting up the ocean with the bright blue color of a welder's torch. The missiles paused overhead for three seconds, almost appearing to have petered out before their navigation systems kicked in with a loud pop. The upright rockets then flattened out

as they shot across the sea trailing flaming debris. Within 10 seconds, the Tomahawks were out of sight. In short order, two more missiles streaked away into the early-morning sky."

The attack did not achieve the objective (leaders were not at the targeted buildings), so the next day there was a major push to clear the way for coalition ground forces as they moved north into Iraq. More than 380 missiles were fired at a variety of air defense sites, runways, and fixed targets. This would be the largest salvo of Tomahawks of the war (by far) and the largest in the history of this weapon system.

Tomahawk missiles played a vital role in eliminating the Iraqi's ability to see and respond to incoming coalition attacks. The strikes eliminated radars and communications centers, effectively blinding the Iraqis to the incoming ground and air assaults.

I have seen cockpit video from a fighter aircraft where the pilot looked below and saw eight Tomahawks flying as if in formation as they made their way to their respective targets. It was quite a sight, and the pilot was appreciative of the altitude deconfliction regime in place.

From the initial launch to the last on 6 April, there were 802 TLAMs fired. Cruisers, destroyers, and submarines combined to launch these missiles from the Arabian Gulf (417), Red Sea (349), and eastern Mediterranean (36).

Most Sailors deploy for their entire careers without launching a missile in wartime. Yet here there would be 15 submarines, 9 cruisers, 12 DDGs, and 3 DDs whose crews would all contribute to this massive effort putting their endless hours of training to the test in combat.

Preliminary reporting post-strike by a team from the Center for Naval Analysis indicated:

- No big surprises.
- Launch, arrival and hit rates were consistent with Block III performance in previous operations.
- Missile accuracy was as good or better than previous experience for GPS-guided TLAM.
- Preliminary results were similar for high and low fliers.

- Results were similar across different launch platforms, launch areas, and mission planning agencies involved.

COMBINED AIR OPERATIONS CENTER

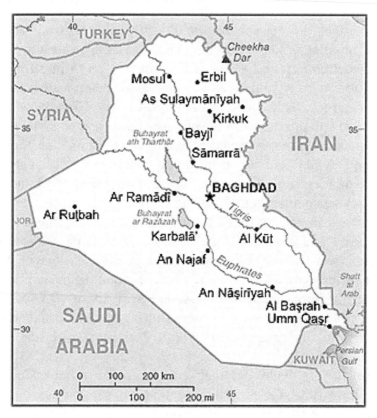

The Navy presence in the Combined Air Operations Center (CAOC) in Saudi Arabia proved critical, as the team assisted in creating the Air Tasking Order (ATO). This daily document assigned missions to everything that flew in the airspace and ensured deconfliction, as well as assured targets, were serviced in priority order.

The magnitude of the mission of this Navy group became evident as the Tomahawks flew to targets in Iraq, and naval air was predominant from the three carrier air wings in the Gulf. Turkey's refusal of overflight rights caused a shift in the primary burden of air operations to the Gulf carriers. These aircraft worked in tandem with U.S. Air Force and U.K.

aircraft under the coordination and tactical control of the air component commander in the CAOC.

Navy air capabilities were underutilized during the 1990 Gulf War. This was due to a combination of factors, including the Navy's lack of investment in placing a robust cadre of personnel with the Air Force in the Air Operations Center where decisions were being made as to assets and target allocation. Also, Navy was retaining an excess amount of air sorties for the defense of the ships at sea. Finally, the combination of tanking requirements and lack of battle damage assessment capabilities caused the Navy air to be supplemental to Air Force assets.

The irony in 2003 was that the situation was nearly reversed. Navy investment in people, in relationships, in precision-guided weapons, along with Saudi restrictions on Air Force flights originating from the Kingdom and Navy leadership mindset of minimizing defensive air sorties in favor of the highly capable cruiser assets in the Northern Gulf, caused the naval air to shoulder a high percentage of the sorties. A review of the record revealed that during the intense period of attacking the Republican Guard forces in early April, carrier air peaked at 326 sorties (flights into the fight) a day. That contribution was greatly appreciated by the ground forces.

Rear Admiral David Nichols was assigned duties as the Deputy Combined Force Air Component Commander (DCFACC) under Lieutenant General Moseley. They agreed to ensure robust joint service representation in the CAOC. Rear Admiral Nichols was an experienced aviator who helped orchestrate the optimal mix of air assets to accomplish the mission, regardless of service. His calm demeanor was a steadying influence in this dynamic environment, and he earned the respect of the entire organization.

The Naval and Amphibious Liaison Element (NALE) in the CAOC played a key role. This team would conduct the face-to-face coordination in the operations center, working 24-hours-a-day to ensure proper assignment of aircraft. Captains William Gortney and Garry Mace led this team, ably supported by liaison officers from the three air wings at sea in the Arabian Gulf and two in the Mediterranean. Additionally, the reserve Joint Force Air Component Command (JFACC) unit from 3rd Fleet forward deployed to Saudi Arabia. Captains Russell Penniman and

Stuart Hendrich led this group, working in the combat plans branch and filling the roles of deputies to the directors of the CAOC. In all, there were 158 Navy personnel (95 USN/63 Reserves) assigned to the CAOC.

There were serious issues that needed to be worked. These included:

- Target prioritization.
- Scheduling of tanker assets.
- Revising target lists based on the V Corps and I MEF ground force advance.
- Command and control in the air using Air Force Airborne Warning and Control System (AWACS) and Navy E-2 aircraft.
- Ensuring NO blue-on-blue mistakes.
- Weather impacts—a significant concern with the sandstorms.
- Time-sensitive targets.

Books could be written on each of these challenges, and how they were addressed. All were significant, but the tanker issue (providing gas for the fighters) and dealing with the speed of the ground force (to remain in their advance and not be shooting behind) caused intense coordination. It worked... confirming the wisdom of placing our best officers in the CAOC.

Captain Gortney filled the roles of leader, coordinator, counselor, and cheerleader. He would write nightly summaries from his position in Saudi Arabia. These would be the communication vehicles between the leadership of the five carrier air wings and the CAOC. This link was critical, as the environment was ever-changing. I include some of his comments here to give a sense of the interaction:

> "The CAOC is going through a time of change as 9th Air Force is moving in alongside their teammates who have been fighting this fight for 13 years. Two heavy groups are merging, and from the ensuing fireball, the new team will emerge. We will be placing our augmentees into this organization with a single mission, to support you.

Our Navy has never fielded a better team, and I am proud to be a part of it.

To think there will be no fog of war, no confusion... is a mistake. Confusion will be there. Our job is to prevent confusion by clearly laying out a plan, and then executing that plan until the enemy decides to change the plan for us. We, the CAOC and you, must understand each other's limiting factors and rapidly counter the enemy's decisions. We will sometimes fail, but we will succeed far more often.

Another bottom line, support to any coalition Soldier or Marine forward of the line of departure and engaged with the enemy—or threatened in an assembly area—is top priority... support to Soldiers and Marines on the ground is number one. We don't rest until they rest.

The environment will continue to be cluttered, there won't be enough time to plan everything to the letter, demands will be placed on everyone, tempers will get short, and the ATO will have numerous changes... all of them coming to you late. It is going to be great.

Last night you were confronted with a less than perfect ATO, flying in varsity conditions, with late changes, surrounded by the most complex air strikes any of us have seen. Well done. Keep up the great work."

Captain Gortney's nightly updates, constant encouragement, and mentorship were the glue that made the system stick together and succeed. He led a team that worked hard to ensure success in the campaign air operations.

In my discussions with Commander Stammer (commanding officer of VFA-137 aboard *Constellation*), he singled out Lieutenant Eddie Paysee, who was his liaison officer to the CAOC, as a key player.

Lieutenant Paysee would be on the watch floor in Saudi Arabia throughout the night while CVW-2 was flying off *Constellation*. He was attuned to quick strike missions that required immediate responses. These could be calls for close air support from the ground forces, or targets that had been identified by the intelligence community. Lieutenant Paysee would quickly get the information to pilots in the air and direct them to the targets. This is the best example of effective use of the liaison officer concept for an immediate impact.

FLIGHT OPERATIONS: *AIR WING OF DESTINY*

Five aircraft carriers had been strategically positioned in the Arabian Gulf and the Mediterranean Sea: *Truman* and *Roosevelt* in the Mediterranean, and *Constellation*, *Lincoln*, and *Kitty Hawk* in the Gulf. They were all within striking distance of Iraq, giving coalition commanders 350 fighter, electronic radar jamming, and surveillance aircraft. The U.S. had deployed this number of carriers before, but *never* with this much striking power. Improvement in weapon capability significantly changed the equation.

In previous conflicts (Operation Desert Storm for example), a Navy/Marine aircraft would launch with a full load of six iron bombs to drop on a single target, and the battle damage assessment would be determined later by overhead satellite photography. Now—in OIF—13 years later, a single aircraft would launch with 6 GPS-guided weapons destined for six *different* targets, fully confident of positive results and able to return with video to prove the success of the strike. *Sorties per target* was changed to *targets per sortie*. The improvement was dramatic, and the effects immediate.

Accuracy and aircrew safety increased with the introduction of GPS-guided weapons. For example, the Joint Direct Attack Munition (JDAM) could be dropped at any altitude and airspeed once the pilot flew the aircraft into a pie-shaped envelope calculated by the onboard computer. Once released, the bomb's tailfins adjusted to guide the weapon to its pre-programmed target some distance away and the crew could exit contested airspace. However, this was the case only with the GPS-guided weapons fired at pre-programmed targets. Once these targets were destroyed, crews flew in close-air support of ground forces urgently requesting assistance, directly into the heart of threat envelopes of enemy surface-to-air missiles.

Carrier aviation requires reliable, precision equipment. Steam-powered pistons catapult jets off a 250-foot runway, slinging them from 0 to 150 mph in under two seconds. An equivalent land-based takeoff would require nearly 6,000 feet of runway. Constellation's four catapults could launch an aircraft every 30 to 45 seconds. The fighters could reach speeds of Mach 1.7, nearly twice the speed of sound. On recovery, the arresting gear brings the aircraft from 150 mph to a halt in just 300 feet. Dedicated, highly trained Sailors make it happen seamlessly.

A *Los Angeles Times* article described the Sailors on the flight deck:

> "On the wind-whipped flight deck, where the roar of jets taking off and landing rattles teeth and sucks the breath from the body, the workers wear bright vests and shirts color-coded to tasks. Blue moves the aircraft. Brown maintains them. Green handles the catapults that thrust the aircraft into the sky. Purple fuels the jets. Red loads the weapons. Yellow keeps everyone moving, and white brings the aircraft in safely. When the jets take off or land, the whole vessel shudders and clanks. The men and women work until their heads hurt and their muscles scream for a break."

The *Constellation* air wing, led by Captain Fox, seemed born to take on the challenges that CVW-2 would face on this historic deployment. Captain Fox referred to his team as the *Air Wing of Destiny*, as he correctly predicted that they would play a leading role in the upcoming conflict. What would follow would be referred to as the Super Bowl of deployments by many in the air wing.

DECAPITATION STRIKE SUPPORT

Electronic Attack Squadron 131, led by Commander John Geragotelis, was always ready for a mission and relished the opportunity to demonstrate their skills. I recently talked with Commander Geragotelis, and he related that the *Constellation* air wing was flying the night of 19 March when a call came to the carrier from the CAOC requesting short notice support for the F-117 decapitation mission (discussed earlier in the Tomahawk section). There was an EA-6B Prowler aircraft on deck ready to launch. That aircraft's main mission—electronic jamming—prevents the enemy's air defense radars from tracking incoming aircraft, preventing radar-guided missiles and guns from targeting aircraft, and disrupting communications by directing powerful beams of electrons in the frequency range of the enemy radars. This is known as a *soft kill*. The aircraft also has the capability of a *hard kill* by launching a High-Speed Anti-Radiation Missile (HARM). The crew was re-tasked from their original briefed mission and launched into the night to support the F-117s who would be headed into the Iraqi Missile Engagement Zone (MEZ) (a high-value area protected by a large concentration of surface-to-air missile systems placing any aircraft at risk) near Baghdad. The Prowler crew never envisioned heading over Iraq that night, but training kicked in, and they provided the required jamming to ensure the F-117s went into and out of the threat area unnoticed. The F-117s' weapons hit the designated targets.

The feedback from the liaison officer in the CAOC reflected the appreciation of the entire force for the mission.

> "...I thought you would like to know how *Constellation*, CVW-2, and Bonanza 05 jumped through their ass and executed an unplanned sortie on last night's event to "downtown." At 1145Z I asked if there were any extra EA-6Bs to support a strike into Baghdad. A few hours later the F-117s struck the target without the Iraqi IADs* having a clue what was going on.
>
> To sum it up the crew and aircraft were scheduled, prepped and launched, tanked, went downtown, on time, for an unbriefed strike, wiped the IADs scopes clean and thus not a single surface-to-air missile (SAM) was launched!"

IADS: Integrated Air Defense System of radars and missiles

IN HARM'S WAY

The decapitation strike was unsuccessful. It was time to execute Plan 1003V. The briefing on the evening of 20 March 2003, the first night of major flight operations, focused the crews. I opened the briefing by providing encouragement:

> "When we first met at the AirPac auditorium in San Diego back in June 2002, I told you we would go into harm's way. *We are here now.* I am very proud of how you have excelled in getting to this peak of readiness. I have every confidence in your ability to succeed. So, go on up, do your job, kick some ass, come on back and I'll see you when you return from your successful strike. God bless."

Captain Fox followed with a review of upcoming mission details. Besides the normal discussion of weather and the air-plan, he reminded the team to bring their *survivor cards*, which give the enemy instructions on how to treat a downed pilot.

Crews talked about getting into their *bubble*—a quiet, emotionless, focused state thinking of the mission—and the return landing on the ship. Sleep was at a minimum, as nerves come into play. In a later interview, Commander Geragotelis said, "I wasn't actually afraid of dying from the anti-aircraft fire, but I'm always scared of landing on the carrier at night." This was an honest admission by one of our best.

Just after 1900, aircraft launched into the night. Aircrews consisted of a pilot, and some aircraft had a radar intercept officer (RIO) running the airborne weapons and sensor systems. It would be an 800-mile round trip flight, and the mission would take seven hours from launch to recovery back on the *Constellation* flight deck. Tanking en route (refueling from airborne big wing Air Force tankers and Navy S-3s) would require precise corrections and steady nerves by each of the pilots.

I welcomed the crews on their return. They were exhausted but had a clear sense of accomplishment.

Frank Buckley, a *CNN* correspondent, embedded in *Constellation* tells the story of the first night of air strikes in a press release:

"Friday night was extremely busy for us. It was the first night of the "A-Day" air-plan. We were given incredible access to the air-plan on the USS *Constellation*. We knew—several hours before the air-plan was launched— what was going to happen. As part of our embed rules, we were not permitted to say what was going to be happening until it happened, and until those aviators returned safely to the aircraft carrier. But we got a great insight into the sense of mission the pilots were feeling before their first flights over Baghdad. I sat in on the briefing of the first strike package that was flying into the vicinity of Baghdad.

The carrier's air wing commander led the briefing. He told the men gathered in the squadron ready room that this day was a day they would never forget. As he put it, the package was 'going downtown.' The atmosphere was quite solemn in the squadron room. It was a group of focused pilots who were ready to go out and conduct their mission. Immediately after the first strike package landed, I happened to be in a passageway when the air wing commander walked by me in his flight suit.

He had just gotten out of his jet, but he came down to the hangar bay and gave us his impressions of the flight. He talked about how he flew in Desert Storm, and they didn't use night vision goggles then. But this time they are using them, and he said he wasn't sure if it was such a good thing, having the ability to look down and see all the fire directed at them. He was a bit facetious, but his point was that a pilot could see everything. Some of the younger guys were talking about how much fire they saw down below, how many explosions they saw simultaneously.

They were just amazed. They told us that no amount of training could prepare them for what they saw. Even though all of them have flown combat sorties over Iraq as a part of Operation Southern Watch, and most of them have been shot at, they all said that last night was unique."

Captain Fox would describe the experience:

"It was like being in a stadium with a million camera flashes going off."

Commander Walt Stammer said:

"Obviously if you're going to kick the beehive, you expect the bees to be flying, and they were... There was lots going on; lots of shooting, lots of talking, lots of aircraft. It was sensory overload."

Otto Kreisher interviewed me on day three of flight operations. I told him that the first-night strikes by Tomahawks and aircraft were to degrade the air defense capability, to knock out radars and anti-aircraft batteries, and to hit leadership or military buildings that are fixed sites around Baghdad. I informed him that the focus was now shifting to targets around Basra, in support of ground forces moving north. Otto wrote:

"Judging from the bombs positioned on the hangar deck for loading on strike aircraft, the second night's and this morning's work for *Constellation*'s aircraft apparently focused more on supporting the ground forces in the south.

In addition to the satellite-guided Joint Direct Attack Munitions used the first night, the bomb load included many laser-guided bombs and laser-homing Maverick missiles. These weapons are more effective against mobile targets, such as tanks or artillery than the satellite-guided weapons.

But at least some of the 61 aircraft launched by *Constellation* early today went into the vicinity of Baghdad. A "strike package" of F/A-18 Hornets, whose pre-flight briefing was observed by journalists, was to hit targets just south of the Iraqi capital.

The Hornets from Fighter Attack Squadron 151 and Marine Fighter Attack Squadron 323 were to coordinate their strikes with Air Force B-52s and F-16s, and Navy EA-6B radar jamming aircraft..."

I have been asked how so many coalition aircraft flew directly into the teeth of the Iraqi air defense network, and none were shot down by Iraqi defenses (unfortunately there was one U.S. F/A-18 and one U.K. Tornado accidentally brought down by U.S. Patriot missiles). Why weren't aircraft shot down? One answer is that although the Iraqis fired nearly 500 missiles, it was estimated that only 12 (2%) were radar-guided because if the operators turned on their radars, they could be detected and expect an incoming missile. Apparently, the Iraqi operators were more concerned with survival from a hit by a coalition HARM missile than achieving success. Another answer is that the jamming aircraft from the coalition force blinded the Iraqi radars, which rendered them ineffective. The definitive answer is the coalition was made up of the finest pilots in the world, able to avoid the barrage of missiles headed their way every day and night.

AVIATION LEADERSHIP PERSONAL PERSPECTIVES

The Navy investment since the 1990s was paying significant dividends. Employment of "smart" weapons totally changed the dynamic from past conflicts. Availability of parts ensured fully ready aircraft to fly more than 1,000 missions in the opening days of the fight.

I interviewed four leaders of the air wing team in 2017 and had access to war diaries of three others. Captain Denneny flew in the F-14, while Commander Stammer piloted the F/A-18. They both flew in the first-night strike on Baghdad. Colonel Thomas was the lead planner for the first strike. Captain Burt was the glue that connected all three air wings on behalf of Rear Admiral Kelly. Commander Hubbard's war diary of VFA-151's exploits is the source of his comments. Commander Andersen's war diary provided insight as to VAW-116's operations. Finally, Captain Fox's writing provided a fitting summary of the action.

CAPTAIN DOUG DENNENY

Captain Denneny was a RIO in the F-14 squadron aboard *Constellation* and the senior executive officer in the air wing. He would be an element lead (in charge of four of the strike aircraft and their support jamming aircraft) as a part of the first-night strike led by Captain Fox. There would be U.S. Air Force B-52 and F-117 aircraft coming in from the north of Baghdad, and a variety of coalition aircraft involved throughout. The following notes summarize my discussion with Captain Denneny.

> The F/A-18s could drop JDAM GPS-guided weapons. The F-14s did not have that capability before the deployment, but there was a software fix in testing. The aviation community came together to push the system to get the software completed. Then they took the risk of inserting this new tape into the aircraft mission computer. It could have potentially downed the entire F-14 fleet if the software had not performed correctly. This would have had a significant negative impact on our ability to carry out the mission, as we would have been without the service of CVW-2s 10 F-14 fighters, who would carry air-to-ground weapons into the fight.

> The software update was successful, and the upgrade in capability was immediate and significant. F-14s dropped

their first weapons with the system in support of Operation Southern Watch in January 2003.

During the pre-brief of the flights for 20/21 March, Lieutenant Colonel Thomas established certain "minimums," criteria that must be met before the strike aircraft could go forward into harm's way.

The weather was one of the criteria as visibility would be important to see surface-to-air missiles (SAMs) coming up to meet the coalition aircraft as they entered the Super Missile Engagement Zone (MEZ) around Baghdad. This zone was protected by Iraqi SA-2/3/6 missiles. Many of these missiles would be unguided, but the Iraqis could get lucky if you were in the wrong place or were not aware of their presence. Radar can provide an indication of an incoming missile but having a visual on its path is important to the pilot as he decides how to maneuver the aircraft to avoid being hit.

Another criterion was to have the required *suppression* package. This meant having EA-6B jamming aircraft with HARM flying alongside. HARM missiles would lock on to any enemy fire control radar that would be used to guide their SAMs, and speedily fly to impact and destroy these radars—leaving the threatening missiles to fly without guidance and making them easier to avoid.

However, the plan often requires adjustment during execution. The timing was imperative, as all striking assets were being coordinated by the CAOC, and on-time arrival over the target area was critical. Thus, when Navy EA-6Bs were unexpectedly delayed, Captain Denneny needed to decide whether to deviate from the original plan. He chose to push forward. As his team moved north, the CAOC assigned two available U.S. Air Force F-

16CJs jamming aircraft to the package. This was Jointness in action (services working together), as these Air Force aircraft seamlessly filled the role of jamming enemy radars and carried HARM missiles to deal with any radar sites that chose to go active, substituting perfectly for the delayed Navy EA-6Bs.

Hundreds of Tomahawk missiles from ships and submarines in both the Red Sea and the Arabian Gulf converged on military targets around Baghdad as the aircraft approached the city. The city lights were bright, and the Iraqi military fired a tremendous amount of anti-aircraft artillery (AAA) into the air thinking the missiles were from the approaching aircraft. Additionally, Iraq launched more than 50 SAMs, including SA-6s, SA-8s, and Rolands. The coalition aircrew, using night vision goggles, could see the fireworks from 15 miles away.

The crews of Captain Denneny's four aircraft element launched their weapons 10 miles from their targets—an Iraqi military radio relay facility and a military complex. Launching of the two 2000-pound JDAMs made a significant jolt to the aircraft. The missiles would fly independently to the target. Once the GPS-guided weapons were away, Captain Denneny accelerated, climbed, and turned south to rendezvous with the Air Force tanker that was waiting over the Kuwait/Iraq border, 180 miles to the south.

Upon returning to the carrier, Captain Denneny exited his aircraft, debriefed the flight, talked to the media, and headed back to his stateroom with shaky legs after the intensity of an 800-mile seven-hour flight. Later he met the Air Force F-16CJ pilots and thanked them for joining the flight with their capabilities. The Joint team was a reality.

COMMANDER WALT STAMMER

Commander Stammer took command of VFA-137 on 15 January. He was part of the same first-night package of aircraft with Captain Denneny. His comments are summarized below:

> There were 10 EA-6B Prowler jamming aircraft assigned for 360-degree coverage in his vicinity. Tomahawk cruise missiles began impacting, and the bombardment lasted 10 minutes. The air wing attacks began immediately after that. He was in the Super MEZ for nine minutes, which seemed like hours due to the threat from the ground. He successfully launched his weapons, and the results were confirmed once he was back on the carrier.

> His second strike was on 23 March. The target was the Baghdad International Airport, headquarters of the Special Republican Guard. He was the overall coalition package commander for this mission. This strike was a part of a bigger overall group of aircraft that included U.S. Air Force F-117s and B-2s (flying from the U.S.). The strike was successful at achieving all goals.

> His third strike on 26 March was to render the Al-Taqaddum Air Base useless. The team used 15 weapons to create 40-foot craters throughout the runway, putting it out of action for the foreseeable future. The Iraqis then began to bury their aircraft since they could no longer use the runway, making them easy targets for coalition aircraft.

Commander Stammer continued flying every other night on a wide variety of missions. As the coalition ground forces moved north, the missions switched to close air support, working with ground forward air controllers (FAC). He and his team were there in support of the ground forces until mid-April, for 22 straight nights.

He would summarize his thoughts as follows:

"We got to do everything we trained for. All the strike planning and other preps during workups paid dividends. The air wing demonstrated sound execution of the basics. There was buy-in to the system up and down the chain of command. There were no 'weak links' in the *Constellation* Strike Group. Within the air wing, all the squadron commanding officers respected each other and got along, very well. And everyone came home."

LIEUTENANT COLONEL GARY THOMAS

Lieutenant Colonel Thomas provided details regarding his memories of 2003 while in command of the Marine F/A-18 Fighter Attack Squadron aboard *Constellation* (VMFA-323 "Death Rattlers"). His recollection was—in a word—thrilling. The following are highlights.

He took command of the Death Rattlers in October 2001. He noted that Marine Corps headquarters had made a deliberate decision to place experienced Marine pilots and crews together for this *Constellation* deployment. There was an appreciation that there would be a high probability of Marine sea-based pilots in support of Marine infantry ashore during this timeframe. When they shifted from assigned targets to close air support of the ground force, the Marines in the cockpit personally knew the Marine FACs on the ground. These FACs were Marine pilots and crew who fully understood the capabilities and limitations of the F/A-18s flying in support. The combination was extremely effective.

Lieutenant Colonel Thomas told me the story of the call from the Air Force U.S. based B-2 aircraft looking for final details of the strike. It was well before the actual strike overhead time. When asked about the urgency, they said: "We are working our own mission planning prior to pre-flight and an 18-hour flight to the target area." It brought into the reality that these aircraft were launching from Whiteman AFB in Missouri and it would be 32-hours before they arrived in the target area.

As he tells the story:

"CVW-2 led planning would include Navy, Marine, Air Force, and coalition aircraft in the first wave of attacks. The timing was critical. The Tomahawks and air-launched cruise missiles had a window of 2100—2110 for impact. The first wave of aircraft-delivered weapons would roll in right behind this window—from 2110—2120. The strike package consisted of 68 coalition aircraft: 20 F/A-18s, 8 F-14s, 10 EA-6Bs, 8 F-15s, 7 F-117s, 3 B-2s, 8 F-16CJs, and four United Kingdom GR-4s. This strike was set against 91 targets in and around Baghdad, including leadership, command and control, air defense, and offensive strike assets. Our mission planning software allowed us to enter in all the planned routes of the aircraft in the strike package and then play back a "rehearsal" that showed where all the aircraft would be at any given time. By doing this, we could deconflict altitudes and ensure that HARM shooters and Prowlers, for example, were in the proper place to provide cover for the strikers.

I was 80 miles from Baghdad on night vision goggles and could see the impact of missiles as they hit their targets around Baghdad. The Air Force F-15 Strike Eagles' weapons were the first to reach their target... but the VMFA-323 aircraft were the first to launch, firing Standoff Land Attack Missile-Extended Range (SLAM-ER) at a distance. In my group, there were four F/A-18s who launched 12 Joint Standoff Weapons (JSOW) at a rocket factory near Baghdad. There was a lot of AAA fired from the ground at the fighters."

Lieutenant Colonel Thomas described the environment in the Gulf as "the harshest operating environment he had ever experienced." Sandstorms and high winds were prevalent in March/April 2003, along with hail and torrential rains. From 25—27 March 65% of sorties were canceled due to weather. The training and discipline experienced in the workups off San Diego prepared the team for most situations; however, some circumstances could not be anticipated, and the crews adapted.

> "On one flight we were flying at 37,000 feet, and the weather turned bad. I made the call to divert but was then contacted by F-14s in the target area. They said the weather was clear. So, we went forward, but the window of good weather closed, and we diverted to Kuwait. It was a good thing, as two other aircraft that returned to *Constellation* were seriously damaged by hail: one EA-6B nose was busted off, and an F-14 had a weapon detach from the aircraft."

Flying intense missions night after night of six-plus-hours was beginning to take a toll on the pilots and their support team members. Fatigue is always a factor and was particularly relevant in the high operations tempo experienced during the opening days of the war. The CVW-2 air wing flew for 22 days straight before finally having a "no-fly" day on 10 April. Fatigue began having an impact on their decision making. Lieutenant Colonel Thomas noted the leading edge of this when the communications in the air upon check-in to various points became delayed. The crispness of the opening day exchanges was replaced by slowness reflecting tired crews.

This phenomenon became apparent in a lessening of the flying discipline that had been the hallmark of the CVW-2 air wing. Lieutenant Colonel Thomas relates what happened:

> "Returning flights were to go to the eastern edge of Kuwait to hit the tanker before returning to the ship. In one instance, a flight of two were late returning and were "feet wet" (over the Gulf waters) with "bingo" fuel (*an amount of fuel that would just barely allow a safe return to the ship*). The pre-brief order was that if you were at that fuel state, you would go to Kuwait and land the aircraft. However, this crew noted an S-3 tanker in the

area and decided to go there for fuel, and then return to the carrier.

The lead aircraft "killed the basket." No fuel would be forthcoming from this tanker. In the meantime, the aircraft had traveled further south, now 80 miles from the divert field in Kuwait. To make matters worse, they would now be flying into a headwind.

The two fighters made it back to Ahmed al Jaber Kuwaiti Air Force base. The flight lead landed, and as he taxied off the main runway, his engine flamed out, having burned all its fuel. The second aircraft flamed out when it touched down. They avoided disaster by seconds. They could have simply fallen out of the air."

In true professional fashion, the pilots reported their mistake and were held accountable. It was a good reminder for the air wing: get rest whenever possible, and do not let either overconfidence or complacency creep into your flying decision-making or disaster will occur.

Lieutenant Colonel Thomas described the strike group leadership team as emphasizing "disciplined flying, accountability, and encouragement." The leadership needed to prepare the unit, wing, and group as a team. Discipline was required in the air, on the flight deck, and in all aspects of planning. Mistakes would be made. Accountability was paramount. The desired end state was to *"execute the mission and return safely."*

As we wrapped up, we discussed the transit home after departing the Gulf. He vividly remembered being on the carrier flight deck elevator looking out to sea as the carrier sliced through the water. There was finally "time to reflect on a job well done for the nation. How lucky I was to be able to participate."

CAPTAIN LARRY BURT

Captain Larry Burt had orders to become the air wing deputy commander. However, Vice Admiral Malone and Vice Admiral Keating decided that a leadership rotation just before the conflict was not appropriate. Thus, we were fortunate to have Captain Burt, an experienced aviator, at the ready as a liaison officer and coach. I sent him as an advisor to Rear Admiral Kelly when *Lincoln* returned to the Arabian Gulf at the end of January, and he assumed the role of CTF 50, directing all Navy air operations from the three Gulf located carriers. I could have retained Captain Burt as a valuable asset on *Constellation* but sending him to *Lincoln* was the right thing to do for the team—where he could influence employment of all naval air assets.

Rear Admiral Kelly knew he could benefit from the experience of a senior aviator at his right hand. Captain Burt filled that role to perfection. He communicated daily with each of the air wings on the three carriers, identifying challenges and opportunities, and coordinated with the CAOC. As we spoke of his experiences, he provided the following information:

> To best fill his advisory role, he flew with the air wing on *Lincoln*. Thus, he was better able to appreciate weather issues, tanking challenges, and weapons deployment considerations. He flew during the first-night major strike. His experience was like others I interviewed. However, his *sweat factor* was a bit higher than the rest, as he found himself amid several SAMs fired by the Iraqis. Training kicked in, and despite guidance not to break below certain altitudes, he found himself diving toward the deck to avoid the incoming missile barrage. This maneuver was successful. Then he pulled up and climbed rapidly on afterburners to move out of the threat area.

I could feel the intensity of the moments as he retold his story. It was clearly a night he will never forget, and one where he fully appreciated the importance of his years of experience and training.

COMMANDER MARK HUBBARD

As I read Commander Hubbard's war diary, several passages exemplified his inspirational leadership as commanding officer of VFA-151 "Vigilantes."

> "Our turn around training cycle had prepared us well. The mood of the squadron is that of not if, but when. What's different for me on this trip is our new suite of munitions. JDAM and JSOW are now the bread and butter of the Strike-Fighter Pilot... Our future lies in GPS aided weapons with pinpoint accuracy... Earlier this past February CAG Fox sent me into Prince Sultan Air Base in Saudi Arabia for the Warfighters Conference... General Moseley passed General Frank's guidance to 'Make it fast and make it final.'

Our tasking was clear:

- First, we would neutralize the enemy's ability to command its forces and govern its state.
- We will maintain our air superiority and deny the enemy the right to fly. We were reminded that not a single Soldier has been lost to enemy air threats since April 1951 and we would not allow that date to be renewed.
- The TBM (Tactical Ballistic Missile) and SRBM's (Short-Range Ballistic Missile) threat must be met head-on, and we would seek and destroy all resources.
- All measures to protect from the ecological disaster of blowing up oil wells and flooding waterways would be afforded.
- We must also neutralize the mine threat as keeping the waterways clean and clear would pave the way for quicker recovery and humanitarian efforts once Saddam was removed, not to mention required resupply routes to keep the battle going as long as required.

Just a few days before the war kicked off, I was making my rounds, and one of my airmen in the Line division had a question for me. He said, 'Sir, are you ever afraid?' I quickly responded, 'Sure, I get afraid.' I explained to him that I divided fear into two categories. Controlled and Uncontrolled. Controlled fear is your friend as it brings all of your senses to attention. Then, all that great Navy training kicks in and allows us to manage it. Uncontrolled fear is your enemy. It distracts you and pulls you away from what you know is right, and if unmanaged it can kill you. I closed by telling him that only fools are unafraid and to respect what threatens you.

First night of the Air War. This is a plan that has changed 10 times already and was sure to change again. Finished up final adjustments to the brief and was able to snag about 3 hours of sleep. Who am I kidding? Couldn't sleep a wink. Kept rehearsing the brief in my mind and thinking about defensive reactions. If hell were ever to be released on us, it would be tonight. Visions of Baghdad in 1991 kept popping into my head. Barrage fire, surface-to-air shots, Speicher's* shoot down—I have been wearing his POW bracelet since we left—and all the many stories of air action remind me of the reality that we face."

*Lieutenant Commander Michael Scott Speicher was flying an F/A-18 Hornet fighter when he was shot down 100 miles west of Baghdad on the night of January 17, 1991, the first night of Operation Desert Storm.

Captain Fox named Commander Hubbard as strike warfare action board chairman, reflecting his confidence in this commanding officer. This faith was well warranted, as Commander Hubbard performed spectacularly in coordinating the efforts of the entire air wing.

Commander Hubbard had "In Memory of Sandra Teague" painted on his F/A-18 and carried her picture on his kneeboard on every flight. She was the fiancé of one of his intelligence officers, and she died tragically on Flight 77 as it impacted the Pentagon on 9/11. He adopted her as his "silent Co-Pilot and Guardian Angel" for the deployment. His recognition of Sandra was a reminder of why he was fighting for freedom, and he inspired his squadron teammates by his dedication and love of country.

-----Original Message-----
From: Hubbard, Mark CDR
Sent: Thursday, January 09, 2003 20:52
To: Fox, Mark CAPT
Cc: Geron, Craig CAPT
Subject: Inspiration

Vigi's, If you are wondering about the name "Sandra Teague" on 301 here's the story....
    I have recently become friends with one of our Intelligence Officers on the staff out here. His name is LTjg Frank Huffman and he volunteered to join our CVW-2 team just before work-ups started this past summer. He was formerly the Public Affairs Officer at the Pentagon and was assigned there during 911. On the morning of September 11th he put his lovely fiancée Sandra Teague on American Flight 77 as she was off to Australia and then back to her hometown preparing to be married that next month in October. He dropped her off and rushed back to work and remembers enjoying the last I love you and kiss, the hug, and I'm sure imagined wonderful thoughts of seeing her dressed in white as he would patiently wait in the front of the Church that they were to be married in just a few weeks. Unfortunately, her flight would crash in to the Pentagon killing all on board and many that worked within the reinforced concrete walls. At the beginning of cruise Frank asked me if I would take a photo of Sandra with me during one of my flights. Since our arrival here in the Gulf I have flown with her picture just inside my pilot kneeboard on every flight so that she will have a first hand look at the great work we are doing here. I know she actually has an even better seat than that as she is looking over each of our shoulders with all of the victims of 911. I have adopted her as my silent Co-Pilot and Guardian Angle for our deployment and this is why I painted her name along side mine on my aircraft 301. This is just one of the many reasons I enjoy working 20 hour days, seven days a week for 6 or more months at a time or longer if it required... Though I hate being away from my wife and children as you do, and its sometimes hard to get out of bed after a long day, and the weather is sometimes poor and not what I would choose to fly in, I still have the luxury to be among us.... Sandra and many with her that day were robbed of that right to live long lives, in a free county, and enjoy everything that comes with being a Proud American. Terrorist hate this and they want to take it away from us.... Yes, I'm talking about freedom.
    You all are a part of this War on Terrorism.... Each and every one of you! Some of you may think that your job isn't important but I assure you that it is. If you are in question about that come see me and I will personally rally with you to reinsure that you are.. I couldn't do what I do without you. We're an awesome team and we have just arrived at the "Super Bowl Game for Warriors", and when called upon we will win! I greatly appreciated the efforts and sacrifices that each of you are making... I'm proud to serve with you as your skipper. Its truly an Honor!

                                 Cdr. M.A. Hubbard
                                    Switch One

<< File: Frank Mutha1.jpg >>   << File: 301 memory.jpg >>   << File: frank mutha2.jpg >>

CDR Mark A. "Mutha" Hubbard
Commanding Officer VFA-151
CVW-2, USS Constellation CV-64
E-mail; hubbardm2@constellation.navy.mil
address: VFA-151, FPO/AP 96601-6122

                                    ' MUTHA '
                                SWITCH ONE

COMMANDER KEVIN ANDERSEN

As a part of my research, I happened upon the VAW-116 commanding officer's unclassified OIF war diary. The E-2C aircraft is a smaller version of the U.S. Air Force Air Warning and Control (AWAC), the big bird in the sky that helps command and control air assets. There were occasions where these E-2C controlled over 75 tactical aircraft. The Commander's Assessment within the war diary provides a vivid summary of the action from the perspective of Commander Andersen, and an excerpt is provided:

> "We flew in the dark of night until the dawn of morning, stationed more than 300 miles away from the carrier and more than 100 miles inside hostile territory to provide Airborne Early Warning (AEW), Threat Warning, Command and Control of Southern Iraq Airspace, and Airborne Battlefield Command and Control (ABC2). Also, Hawkeyes from VAW-116 established a command and control link between coalition ground and air forces located in Iraq and the CFACC located in Saudi Arabia.
>
> After launching and climbing to transit altitude more than 25,000 feet, the E-2Cs crossed over the country of Kuwait. When close to the Iraqi border, they secured the exterior lights and other specific equipment to reduce the risk of detection. Then, unarmed and without threat warning systems or countermeasures normally carried by coalition aircraft entering hostile territory, the crews proceeded to their stations inside Iraq. Each mission was close to five hours in duration, and without in-flight refueling capability, the crews had to fly the aircraft on the edge of its fuel endurance envelope to ensure maximum on station time.
>
> The crews were aware of the risks of flying in hostile territory, marked by occasional instances of enemy surface-to-air fire from AAA and SAMs. Another threat to the E-2Cs operating within hostile Iraqi airspace was the risk of colliding with another coalition aircraft, as the skies above Iraq had become quite crowded. Despite the

risks, E-2C crews did what was required to ensure the utmost support of coalition ground forces... As engagements continued and moved closer to Baghdad, some of the crews stationed further north into Iraq to maintain radio contact with forward-moving ground units while still retaining communications with Kuwait based command centers.

Our major contribution to OIF's success was serving as a communications node to connect the Army's V Corps Air Support Operations Center (ASOC), and the Marine's I MEF Tactical Air Operations Center (TAOC) with coalition aircraft.

We also provided real-time information on battlefield engagements to all coalition aircraft in our area of responsibility (AOR) and assisted in directing them to vital target areas containing hostile troop concentrations, artillery batteries, and enemy armor units. Additionally, Hawkeye crews from VAW-116 provided real-time airspace deconfliction for Tomahawk Land Attack Missile (TLAM), and Army Tactical Missile Systems (ATACMS) launches...With the battlefield changing much faster than the Air Tasking Order (ATO) could support, the E-2C crews were rerolling assets assigned to one agency to get them to another agency more in need of direct support with the air-to-ground munitions being carried by that aircraft."

The VAW-116 team performed magnificently and received appropriate acclaim from the CAOC leadership, especially U.S. Air Force personnel who came to truly understand the capability that the E-2Cs brought to the fight. Additionally, feedback from those directly impacted is always appreciated. On 24 March, the U.S. Army forward liaison officer wrote:

"Having the E-2s up today on Cobalt 10/11 and 13 (radio frequencies) was one of the best things to happen in this war so far. It was great to hear the E-2s relaying comms and clearing people hot onto targets based on information passed from Warhawk. Having E-2s help out in this way is critical. I don't have exact numbers, but a shit-ton of bombs were dropped on bad guys today because and only because the Hawkeyes were airborne acting as a comms relay."

On 21 March, the E-2C crew had a special addition to their team. Lieutenant Commander John "Dice" Gormley was trained as an F-14 Tomcat RIO. Commander Gormley joined the Reserves after eight years on active duty and was reactivated to augment CVW-2 for OIF. While in the Reserves he wore the badge of New York's bravest, serving as a lieutenant in New York City's Fire Department Ladder Company 34 on West 161st Street. Even though he was off-duty at the time of the attacks on the World Trade Center, he rushed to the scene to fight fires at the Twin Towers on 9/11/2001.

He painted "Engine 84/Ladder 34, FDNY, Washington Heights" on the side of the F-14 he navigated, and the FDNY flag was flown from the mast of the carrier. When asked about his experience aboard *Constellation*, Dice said:

"Being here is a tremendous dividend, and it is not in the form of a paycheck. It's the fact that you're able to make a difference, maybe help somebody. I think I'm pretty lucky to be in that position as a firefighter and most certainly out here on the tip of the spear."

Dice presented T-shirts from FDNY firehouses to members of the carrier's flight deck crash crew firefighters "to show they support you." That gesture certainly made a positive difference.

During combat operations in the Gulf, Dice's wife Kathleen gave birth to their third child at White Plains Hospital on 28 March. The *New York Post* reported the story and interviewed Kathleen. A proud Dice phoned to be part of the moment. The separation during important family events is part of the reality for servicemen and women overseas, and they accept it with courage and grace. It is a sacrifice worthy of appreciation by all Americans.

QUICK REACTION STRIKE IN SUPPORT OF U.S. MARINE CORPS

Captain Fox tells this story best, in his article *Air Wing of Destiny*, published in the Fall 2004 edition of the Naval Aviation Museum *Foundation* magazine.

"On March 25th, after trapping aboard in the midst of a terrible sandstorm (at sea!) that produced near zero-zero ceiling and visibility, I (with *Constellation* CO Capt. John 'Fozzie' Miller's consultation and concurrence) recommended to RADM Costello that we knock off flight operations until conditions improved. Minutes later, the CAOC's Navy 'night O-6', Captain Garry Mace, called with an urgent and compelling request: '*We think the Marines are going to get 'slimed' (i.e., a chemical or biological attack) tonight. We really need you to launch a quick reaction strike in support of the Marines.* We have the target coordinates for your GPS weapons; all the ground bases are socked in, and no other carriers are flying, *you're the only ones who can launch right now.*'

My pre-war desire of having the CAOC choose CVW-2 for a really hard job had been fulfilled in a way I could never have predicted. Only minutes after deciding to stop flying because of the sandstorm, I not only reversed my previous recommendation but urged that we increase the size of the next launch to support the CAOC's request.

The soul-searching moment for Captain Miller, me and ultimately RADM Costello, defined the concept of 'operational necessity.' We accepted the risk that we might lose aviators and aircraft based on the need to support the Marines ashore and launched the strike. We continued to fly through the night and into the next day in the most difficult conditions imaginable, ultimately recovering all aircraft without mishaps."

A four-plane contingent of F/A-18s would fly and launch 12 missiles—JSOWs—that night at the Iraqi forces, ending that threat to the Marines on the ground. Some of the aircraft landed ashore because of reduced visibility due to sandstorms and high winds. The weather was as bad or worse than predicted, but the pilots and crews of this strike were prepared to put their lives on the line for their brother Marines on the ground. This was a high-risk operation. I vividly recall the tension as we decided to proceed with the launch, knowing full well that we were putting our team in harm's way, and our people could die.

My air operations officer, Commander Brick Conners, was a part of these talks. In a June 2018 conversation, he could still recall the intensity of the discussion as we reviewed objectives, options, and potential scenarios. He was on watch as reports came over the net of a 1000 vehicle convoy of Iraqi Republican Guard troops was headed south from Baghdad. There might be no place to land on shore, and if the pilots ejected, there would be no one to come and pick them up.

This is where the combination of well-maintained aircraft, advanced weapons, and experienced pilots would enter into the risk-benefit calculus. The risk was significant, yet there was a sense of confidence based on months of training in the most challenging environments. *I am convinced that no other group on the planet could have successfully pulled off this mission in the weather conditions that night.*

INTERVIEWING RETURNING AIR CREWS

Day-to-day life on a carrier does not lend itself to awareness of the external operational environment. One can fall prey to a false sense of security, unaware of what is going on outside the skin of the ship.

My experience years earlier as a junior officer living on a carrier helped me appreciate this reality. In 1985, I served as the operations officer for a destroyer squadron embarked on a carrier. I had the responsibility of determining the group's speed of advance, which consisted of six ships. At one point I slowed the force, much to the displeasure of a captain from the more senior group staff who worked in the admiral's office inside the skin of the ship. He came to the bridge to rage at me and question the wisdom of this move. I worked on the Flag bridge, which had windows to view operations on the flight deck. From my vantage point, I could see the sea state and weather conditions for miles around the carrier. Calmly, I led this unhappy officer to the window to view the outside. Weighing in at 88,000 tons, the carrier was barely affected by the wind and waves. However, in the distance, we could clearly see a destroyer... and then *not* see it as it disappeared into the waves. This was a case where a picture was worth a thousand words. The captain suddenly understood, turned, and walked away without another word.

In light of that early experience, in 2003 operations, I directed that several aviators report to my office after returning from their flights to enhance my situational awareness of events occurring outside the skin of the ship. This was one of my favorite times. Before we rotated the clock 12 hours, they would report just before midnight. After the rotation, they would arrive mid-morning. Day or night, it was an invigorating exchange. The junior officers would come in, complete with greasy boots and helmet marks on their faces. I had a chart of the Gulf and Iraq on my wall. We would go to the chart and discuss their mission. How was the weather—by the carrier, on the route north, over the target areas in Iraq? Tell me about the Air Force tankers—where were they? Were the communications good, any problem connecting? How was communication with ground controllers? Were they able to execute the mission as planned, or any diverts? As a result, my situational awareness of the environment faced by the pilots was enhanced. Also, I was armed with the most current information for the daily senior level briefing sessions in our war room.

I sensed that the crews enjoyed the exchange. This perspective was confirmed by Captain Denneny, Lieutenant Colonel Thomas, and Commander Stammer when I spoke with them after the conflict. It was an opportunity for the junior officers to provide their feedback firsthand, one-on-one with the admiral. In these sessions, our conversations would venture across a wide variety of subjects after we covered the details of their flights. It was as good as it gets.

IRANIAN AIR INTRUSION

The air wing had fully settled into the rhythm of night flying and the challenges associated with the environment. One evening, I received a call from my battle watch captain. He told me that one of our cruisers had issued a *hot dog red* to a CVW-2 S-3 aircraft. There are various levels of warnings given to a pilot if their flight path is getting close to intruding on unauthorized airspace (another country). A *hot dog yellow* warning indicates you are approaching a no-fly area. A *hot dog red* indicates you are already in it.

I called in Captain Fox to find out what was happening. His initial instinct was that the cruiser was likely mistaken. I asked him to go down to *Constellation* battle watch, investigate, and report back to me, sensing there was more to the story. He returned about an hour later. He was more than a bit unhappy, as, in fact, the cruiser was correct. One of our aircraft had unintentionally wandered into Iranian airspace. To add insult to injury, the crew of this aircraft included one of Captain Fox's staff and one of mine. The crew had failed to align their navigation system with the ship position before launch and therefore were 30 miles north of their perceived position from the beginning of the flight.

Fortunately, the intrusion was only momentary, as the cruiser redirected the aircraft back to authorized airspace. However, the event was ripe for the next day's daily air-plan cartoon, and the crew was reminded of their mistake every day for weeks.

"Kitty" Defies the Odds

"Not to worry, Admiral. The chances of
me navigating an S-3 over Iran are about
as great as being hit by a meteor."

HELICOPTER OPERATIONS

Helicopters played critical roles in many missions. They executed important tasking, although they do not receive the same visibility as the fighter teams who conducted their missions over Iraq. Some highlights include:

- Helicopters provided a protective screen around the force, using their sophisticated detection and communications equipment.
- Helicopters supported the maritime interception operations in the Northern Arabian Gulf for months before the conflict.
- A helicopter from *Bunker Hill* supported the rescue of the five U.N. Oil for Food workers as they were being transported toward Basra.

- Crews from five squadrons from four locations came together to support the SEAL takedown of the MABOT and KAAOT oil terminals in the opening days of the war. They supported the operation by hovering above the platforms and having SEALs land via sliding down ropes. They used their infrared viewing system and data link to provide real-time information to the command post onboard *Valley Forge*. They were also staged to provide gunfire support and evacuation of casualties as required.

Bottom line for me as the group commander: they were there when we needed them every time, bringing a wide variety of capabilities that supported the mission.

SADDAM'S YACHT—*AL MANSUR*

The pace of surface and air operations was fast and furious. Over the first 10 days of wartime operations the following remarkable events had occurred:

- The fleet of dhows had been flushed out of the KAA waterway.
- MABOT and KAAOT oil platforms had been seized, thwarting the Iraqi army's preparation to blow them up.
- Australian and U.K. ships had fired NGFS rounds into the Al Faw Peninsula in advance of the ground surge and had responded to calls for fire during the march north.
- Tomahawk missiles were launched against various Iraqi weapons and command and control facilities.
- Mine clearance operations were continuing along the KAA waterway.
- Coalition aircraft had destroyed a variety of targets, including several strategic Iraqi surface craft pierside along the SAA waterway between Iraq and Iran, including the Iraqi OSA missile boat (developed for the Soviets and sold to the Iraqi navy) that was conclusively determined to be armed with SS-N-2 Styx anti-ship missiles, a definite threat to the coalition forces at sea.

- Coalition aircraft sped overhead 24-hours-a-day in support of land forces headed north.

Pockets of resistance remained near Umm Qasr and Basra, despite the superb work of the U.K. forces along the Al Faw Peninsula. I would receive midnight calls from Commodore Harward (sometimes aboard the *Joint Venture* just south of Umm Qasr, and sometimes from points unknown) reporting on activities of his Navy SEAL force, and from Captain Tillotson providing his situation report from Umm Qasr as he conducted the initial clearance surveys of the port. In both cases, I could hear small arms fire in the background. Resistance was continuing from Iraqis who did not get the memo to clear out.

We were in very high tempo operations. There was a professional appreciation that the unforeseen could happen. What might it be? They've laid some mines and tried to lay more. What could be next?

The high alert was warranted, as four Iraqi suicide boats emerged from the SAA waterway. They were intercepted and chased by Iranian navy forces operating in the NAG; the Iraqi's beached their boats to escape. Iranians discovered 500kg of explosives and detonators. From that point forward, Captain Jones positioned *Chatham* and *Darwin* near the mouth of the SAA to deal with any further threats coming from that direction.

Saddam's Yacht *"al Mansur"* (The Victor) was moored in the Port of Basra on the SAA waterway. It had been moved from the Port of Umm Qasr to Basra a few days before the war began to provide it better protection. The Finnish-built ship was a gift from Saudi Arabia for his fight against Iran during the Iran—Iraq war. It measured 360 feet long, weighed 7,359 tons, and was permanently staffed by 120 Special Republican Guard troops.

Combat operations ashore were in full swing. There was a heightened focus on dealing with Iraq command and control facilities. Every possible facility was scrutinized by coalition intelligence forces. The CAOC had received reports that the yacht's extensive communication systems were being used to direct battlefield operations. Was it a *sure* thing—not sure—but *"certainty" is not something that one has in determining enemy positioning, capability, and intent during wartime.* It is part of the fog of war. Coalition forces did not want to have the yacht become either an enemy sanctuary or headquarters.

On the night of 24 March, several aircraft had completed their assigned missions and were stationed above the southern coast of Iraq before returning to *Constellation.* I received a call from my watchstander who passed along a request from the air wing. One of the S-3 Vikings from the Red Griffins of Sea Control Squadron 38 was surveilling the SAA waterway near Basra. The S-3 is a four-seat, twin-engine turbofan-powered jet aircraft that in 2003 was used primarily as a tanker as well as electronic warfare and surface surveillance asset. It is armed with a laser-guided 300-pound Maverick missile (AGM-65E).

The crew (Lieutenant Commander Richard McGrath, Lieutenant Commander Carlos Sardiello, and Lieutenant Michael Harvey) saw the results of previous F/A-18C AGM-65E Maverick missile attacks on a missile patrol boat and a frigate along the pier. They noticed the presidential yacht remained untouched. At this point, they decided to ask the question as to the status of the yacht. They recognized this was no ordinary target. The CAOC had previously placed the yacht on a "no strike" list. However, it was just approved as an authorized target a few hours earlier. After they had moved their request through the appropriate channels, the crew wanted to let me know what was unfolding as destroying this target could have significant operational and strategic level ramifications.

I thought about the options and decided to give Vice Admiral Keating a call. His aide told me the admiral was sleeping. I asked that he be awakened, appreciating that this was a significant "ask" because sleep was a rare commodity. But this was that important, knowing that this attack would receive international news coverage and potentially have strategic effects.

"Keating here." I got right to the point, telling him the CAOC had authorized the presidential yacht as a target and there was an asset overhead awaiting approval to launch. To lighten the moment, I indicated that I wanted him to know that this could be a strike on his "potential future 5th Fleet Flagship." He appreciated the heads up, chuckled, said to proceed, and signed off.

I passed the word back through the watch to proceed as per the CAOC guidance. The crew then readied their launch. The S-3 had a high-resolution radar, an infrared night vision sensor, and other equipment to find surface targets. It would be a team effort. Two F/A-18 Hornets were in the area. One F/A-18 pilot used his targeting laser to mark the *al Mansur*, and the S-3 launched its missile.

The missile hit topside and destroyed all antennas that would be used to communicate with Iraqi forces. It also caused significant fire damage, and the smoke could be seen for miles. The yacht did not sink, even after several later attacks by F-14 aircraft with MK-82, 500-pound unguided bombs. However, that was never a concern, as the mission was to eliminate it as a command and control node. That mission was successfully accomplished. This summary answers the questions posed by a *Proceedings* article in September 2008 entitled "Taking Out Saddam's Floating Pleasure Palace—Smart Move or Mindless Destruction?" that suggested the "mystery" surrounding this attack might never be answered. It was straightforward—knock out a potential command and control node. The author just needed to ask.

New . . . On the E-Bay Auction Block
(Courtesy of the "Red Griffins")

Presidential Yacht. Hardly used. Needs some work.

This would be the Griffins' last hurrah as the squadron would be retired upon return from deployment as part of a phase-out of Navy S-3s. Launching a Maverick from an S-3 at a surface target was a first—a wonderful way to finish a fantastic career of support to naval aviation. The Hornet pilot said, "These guys are the unsung heroes of the air wing. They provide gas for us, and they do not get a lot of glory." I can attest that they would be sorely missed, and many of the pilots in the air wing would sing their praises for saving them with critical gas availability throughout the war.

CARRIER NIGHT OPERATIONS

Combat operations continued for several weeks. The ship rearmed and refueled during the day. The flight deck opened at 2100 and supported operations throughout the night and morning as jets launched in support of CAOC tasking that crossed the entire spectrum of possibilities. The CAOC had a continuous set of targets that needed to be attacked, ranging from Iraqi airfields to ports, to enemy troops, to emerging targets from ground controllers working in a dynamic environment.

After several weeks of this routine, Rear Admiral Kelly offered to shift the night responsibility to one of the other carriers/air wings. I told him I'd get back to him shortly with an answer to this thoughtful offer. I called Captains Miller and Fox to my office to discuss this initiative. They were exhausted. Since the ship refueled and rearmed during the day, Captain Miller was up 24-hours-a-day on the bridge, catching cat naps when possible. Captain Fox was also on a 24-hour-a-day clock, as he flew at night, and supported planning during the day. I had also been operating on very little sleep while overseeing the operations of Task Force 55. This was not good for a wide variety of obvious reasons. Clear thinking and good decision-making were required, and rest was a crucial element that is often overlooked. The rest period I had factored into my personal battle rhythm was now paying dividends.

I explained the offer on the table from Rear Admiral Kelly—the possibility of returning to *normal* operations. Together they agreed this would be the best course of action, accept the deal and let a different carrier pick up the nighttime responsibility.

Appreciating their exhaustion, I suggested they go take a "walkabout" through the carrier work centers and the air wing ready rooms for an hour to pulse their people before I gave Rear Admiral Kelly my answer. It was a big decision. How are they holding up? Are they ready to rotate the clocks back 12 hours? What are their considerations? I do not know what Captains Miller and Fox were thinking when I made this "suggestion," but they left my cabin to gather additional evidence to support their positions.

The hour came and went. Finally, nearly two hours after they left, the captains returned. The looks on their faces and their body language indicated that they had tales to tell.

They polled the air wing maintenance personnel first. Their response was a quick and resounding "no way!" The readiness of the 72 aircraft was better than at any time since leaving San Diego months ago. The maintenance team could work on the aircraft both in the hangar bay *and* on the flight deck during the day, a luxury that was not available when conducting night maintenance. Due to security considerations, lighting on the flight deck was minimized at night, so it was essentially unavailable for aircraft maintenance during normal operations. Night flying opened a whole new world for the maintainers, hence their quick rejection of the concept of returning to daylight flying.

Next, they went to the crew, including those who worked on the flight deck. Crew members were content with the schedule, having gotten used to the shift. They mentioned several reasons why they preferred to maintain the nighttime rotation for as long as necessary. As true teammates, they also expressed consideration for the other carrier team that would have to go through the biorhythm change that they had to experience.

Cesar Soriano, one of our embedded reporters, wrote:

> "'It's very beneficial to be launching aircraft at night when it's cool,' says Senior Chief Jerome Bamaung, 40, of Niles, Illinois. 'During the day, if its 80 degrees outside, it can get to be more than 110 on the flight deck because of the jet blasts.'"

Finally, Captains Miller and Fox went to the air wing crews... perhaps hoping for support of the concept of shifting the night flying responsibility. Surely this team would be receptive to the idea. They must be exhausted. The conditions of visibility and weather had tested all their skills. Yet they delivered their payloads on target on time, every time.

Captain Fox convened a meeting of the air wing commanding officers. One by one they asserted their preference to maintain their nighttime role in support of the ground forces.

The pilots described the decision to volunteer to be the night carrier as "absolutely fantastic." They had access to Air Force tanker aircraft and direct communications to controllers on the ground who had ample targets/aim points for the pilots. Life was good: fuel in the air, lots of targets, and ROE that allowed them to launch their weapons. The air wing *owned the night.*

The groups in the ready rooms, the hangar bay, and on the flight deck had a universal message for the captains, *"We love flying at night, and we do NOT want to relinquish this opportunity to make a positive difference in the fight."*

It seemed like a long walk back to my office for the captains, but professionals that they were, they delivered the message. It turned out that they were the only two people on the ship who wanted to turn back the clocks! I called Rear Admiral Kelly and gave him the news. He took the information aboard and was pleased and grateful. Team spirit was alive and well throughout the strike groups.

As I watched our aircraft return to the carrier in the dark of the night, I reflected to "The Bridges of Toko Ri" by James Michener. This novel was set in the Korean War, and the action was fierce. Admiral Tarrant was one of the senior leaders at sea. One day his favorite fighter pilot and SAR helicopter crew were shot down. As he watched two F-9 Panther jets prepare to launch on the next combat mission over Korea, Rear Admiral Tarrant stated:

> "Where do we get such men? They leave this ship, and they do their job. Then they must find this speck lost on

the sea. When they find it, they have to land on its pitching deck. Where do we get such men?"

That expression summarized my feelings about the professionals of the CVW-2 air wing.

They would be responsible for many innovations, including pushing the Air Force tankers, the Navy S-3 tankers, and the E-2 command and control aircraft north into Iraqi airspace to support strike aircraft and the land component. They were supported by the dedicated Sailors manning the flight deck around the clock. The flight deck data for March 2003 was:

- Traps (recoveries): 1,923
- Moves (of aircraft around the deck): 5,909
- Crunches: 0

These statistics speak volumes about the professionalism of the air wing flight deck crew team who set the standard for all future deployers. The CVW-2 air wing would continue flying throughout the night until 16 April in support of ground operations. Some pilots went 32 days without a daylight recovery. They would receive many "well dones" as noted below from Lieutenant General Conway.

```
O 190845Z APR 03 PSN 043276T22
FM CG I MEF
TO RHRVNUL/COMCRUDESGRU ONE//N00//
UNCLAS PERSONAL FOR RADM BARRY COSTELLO FROM LTGEN JAMES CONWAY
//N00000//
MSGID/GENADMIN/CG I MEF FWD//

SUBJ/BRAVO ZULU CONNIE//

RMKS/BARRY, AS YOU DEPART THE AO, I WISH TO EXPRESS APPRECIATION ON
BEHALF OF THE ROUGHLY 87,000 AMERICAN AND BRITISH TROOPS WHO
CONSTITUTE I MARINE EXPEDITIONARY FORCE. THE COURAGE AND SKILL THAT
YOUR AVIATORS DISPLAYED WAS NOTHING SHORT OF MAGNIFICENT. AS OUR
MARINES AND SOLDIERS WENT FORWARD INTO BATTLE THEY FREQUENTLY SAW THE
RESULTS OF YOUR WORK IN THE SMASHED REMNANTS OF IRAQI ARMOR   THE
"ANGELS ON OUR SHOULDERS" IN THE FORM OF CARRIER AIR, WERE INVARAIBLY
THERE TO HELP COMPLETE THE TASK. WE SALUTE THE TEAMWORK AND
INDOMITABLE SPIRIT-OF-THE-ATTACK SHOWN BY YOUR AIRCREWS.  FINALLY, AS
YOU RETURN TO HOME PORT AND LOVED ONES, WE WISH FAIR WINDS AND
FOLLOWING SEAS TO ALL THE GREAT MEN AND WOMEN OF CONSTELLATION
CARRIER BATTLE GROUP. SEMPER FIDELIS, BOLD EAGLE SIX.//
```

SUBMARINE OPERATIONS

I had the opportunity to review Rear Admiral Kirk Donald's unclassified "Operation Iraqi Freedom—Submarine Force Perspective: Commander Submarine Group 7, Commander Submarine Group 8, Commander Task Force 54, and Commander Task Force 69." The following specifics about submarine operations are culled from that document:

> Among the assumptions during the initial planning for submarine operations in October 2002 were that there would be 16 days between notification and attack and access/basing/overflight would not be concerns. There would be four U.S. submarines (SSNs) and one U.K. SSN in the Arabian Gulf under 5th Fleet command, and five U.S. SSNs and one U.K. SSN in the Mediterranean under 6th Fleet command (requiring overflight of Turkey).

> In December, the original plan evolved into a submarine Surge Plan. There were six U.S. subs in the Mediterranean, four in the Red Sea, and four (two U.S. and two U.K.) in the Arabian Gulf. By 5 March all 14 TLAM submarine shooters were on station as follows:

> ### Mediterranean
> USS *San Juan*
> USS *Newport News*
> USS *Boise*
> USS *Toledo*
> USS *Augusta*
> USS *Providence*

> ### Red Sea
> USS *Key West*
> USS *Louisville*
> USS *Pittsburgh*
> USS *Cheyenne*

Arabian Gulf
USS *Columbia*
USS *Montpelier*
HMS *Splendid*
HMS *Turbulent*

All subs arrived "strike proficient" in the launch baskets due to realistic training. This preparation and training were the keys to their TLAM success.

However, *Turkey would not allow overflight.* Therefore, the six Mediterranean subs were moved south to the Red Sea on 11 March, joining the four already there. To say the least, it became a bit crowded. In the meantime, there were five additional submarines underway in the Pacific, prepared to sail west as required. *From 11 March to 4 April, Rear Admiral Joe Enright (CTF74/54) maintained, resupplied, and directed the operations of 22 SSNs in the 5th and 7th Fleet area of responsibility.*

In the early hours of the morning of 20 March (Gulf time) USS *Cheyenne* fired the first submarine-launched Tomahawk strike of OIF. Thirty percent of the 802 TLAMs fired during the period 20 March to 6 April would be sub launched.

A few Tomahawk engines or guidance failed, and the missiles crashed in Saudi Arabia causing a loss of overflight rights. The Saudis had been very supportive of these missions but were not interested in popular blowback based on missiles landing in the Kingdom. The last Tomahawk fired from the Red Sea would occur on 25 March—completing 6 days of shooting from this vector. The last U.S. SSN TLAM firing occurred on 29 March; U.K. SSN last firing was 3 April, and the last U.S. surface launch was 6 April.

Communication via the Internet (chat) became the choice for strike tasking. Voice circuits were silent. In prior conflicts, the limitation was equipment aboard SSNs to communicate. In 2003 the limiter became bandwidth.

Initial strike analysis indicated a 90% TLAM successful performance. The submarines were totally integrated with the joint and combined force. They trained for this mission, and they executed it with precision.

NAVAL GUNFIRE SUPPORT OPERATIONS (AL FAW PENINSULA)

Lieutenant General McKiernan, the Combined Force Land Component Commander (CFLCC), requested naval gunfire support (NGFS) for upcoming missions from Vice Admiral Keating in a message on 17 March. The British Royal Marines would be the first force to assault the Al Faw Peninsula. They had conducted preliminary coordination with the U.K. and Australian ships in the Northern Arabian Gulf. Major Peter Boyce was the naval gunfire liaison officer, and he flew to each of the ships to provide a detailed brief on the Royal Marine concept of operations.

As the commander directly responsible for this NGFS operation, I flew to *Kanimbla* and met with captains from the U.K. and Australian ships to review the request. They were interested in supporting the Royal Marines. I felt confident that the Marines would overwhelm any opposition on the peninsula. However, the captains pressed their argument to deliver NGFS as a precursor to the assault, and as a weapon of choice for "on call" fire coordinated with the ground force advance.

I questioned the wisdom of this effort, noting that their proposal had a track for operating the ships in very shallow waters of the NAG. They would be operating in the approaches to the KAA waterway. This was a complex battlespace, with many moving parts on the surface and in the air, all of which needed to be carefully coordinated to preclude the potential for friendly fire casualties. What could possibly go wrong... where shall I begin? But the officers pressed on in the face of my opposition, led by Captain Mark Anderson, commanding officer *Marlborough*. Meeting with the officers face-to-face was critical in determining my support of their plan. As Captain Jones relates the story:

"At the final briefing, we elected to dispense with PowerPoint slides and have charts on a table with small markers representing various units. The plan was walked through in detail and had to survive the admiral's searching questions. The role of the commanding officers was critical. They combined both a broader perspective and a good grasp of the practical. I noted that Admiral Costello would ask the difficult questions of the commanding officers. I concluded the captain of a ship still has credibility all his or her own. Their input, ownership, and support of the plan were vital."

The CFLCC had made the case that while the Royal Marines had sufficient surface-to-surface fire support in most areas of the Al Faw Peninsula, there was a void on the extreme southern tip. There were specific targets planned, and then "on call" fires would be used as required by the advancing force. The allocation of NGFS would reduce risk to the force for the target set in the south. The fact of the matter was that these firing ships were the only ones that could operate close to the shore because of their shallow drafts.

We reworked the track such that it ensured the firing ships would operate in safe water, and I coordinated the proposal with the 5th Fleet staff. This was another example of the value of a diverse force with differing capabilities. No U.S. ships would be involved.

A risk-benefit analysis was conducted. The risks included navigation, mining, shore attack, and deconfliction with mine countermeasure forces. Benefits were focused on support of the rapid buildup of combat power on the peninsula. These benefits outweighed the risks, once mitigation measures were established.

I called Vice Admiral Keating, who appropriately questioned the risk-benefit calculus. I explained that I supported the initiative for three reasons. One was to provide additional coverage to advancing Royal Marines; two was to allow our coalition partners to make a significant impact on the fight ahead, and three was that risk factors had been mitigated.

This was mission command at its finest. Once I was pre-briefed by the commanding officers of the ships and approved their plans, I commanded by negation, allowing the ships to coordinate directly with the Commando Brigade as they moved north. The minute-to-minute decisions were left to the force leadership on the scene, and I would only intervene if problems arose—which they did not.

Thus, in the early morning of 21 March, the NGFS force detached from their MIO stations to take position for their bombardment of the Al Faw Peninsula. At 0604, *Anzac, Chatham, Marlborough, and Richmond* began precise NGFS operations, firing into Iraqi defenses. *Chatham* and *Richmond* were assigned to Fire Support Area *Sword*, while *Anzac* and *Marlborough* were in Fire Support Area *Juno*. Both areas were close to the southern tip of the Al Faw Peninsula in shallow water. In a recent discussion with Commodore Luke Charles-Jones, who was the executive officer of *Anzac* at the time, he said that superb ship handling was required in the 2-knot tidal stream, and these ships did exactly that.

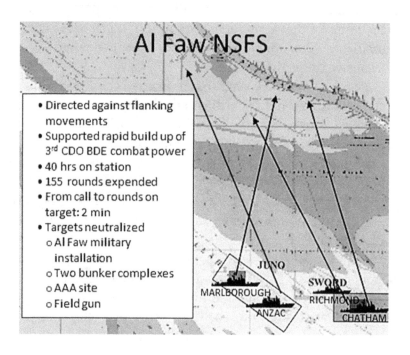

I had the opportunity recently to discuss these operations with Captain Steven Moorhouse (headed to command the second U.K. aircraft carrier HMAS *Prince of Wales*). He was the principal warfare officer on *Chatham* in 2003 as a lieutenant. He provided me a copy of the *Chatham* Operation Telic war diary authored by Captain Michael Cochrane:

> "*Chatham* completed the first operational Royal Navy NGFS mission since the Falklands conflict, firing 18 rounds of High Explosive (HE) into a military installation on the Al Faw Peninsula. (*Chatham* would complete four fire missions... firing a total of 43 rounds of HE.)

> The force would remain on station for 40 hours, executing 17 call for fire missions including 155 rounds. The nearby coalition mine warfare ships and patrol boats felt the impacts as explosions wracked the shore. The rounds neutralized an Al Faw military installation, two bunker complexes, an anti-aircraft artillery site, and field guns. Importantly, they successfully removed the CSSC-3 missile and 130MM gun as threats to the maritime forces.

> Shortly after that, the British Royal Marines commenced the assault on the Al Faw Peninsula. This movement was massive in size and scope, and the largest such effort in decades. Once on the peninsula, the U.K. Marines called for additional fire support from the ships, and another 30 rounds were fired on 22 March in support of the advance. *The time from calls to rounds on target was less than 2 minutes.*

> The arc of fire covered the southern part of the Al Faw Peninsula. There were grid squares established for coordination. The CFLCC liaison officers (LNOs) proved

to be critically helpful in coordinating the fires, used primarily against Iraqi troop movements."

I appreciated that these officers were very capable and did not need meddling from higher headquarters as they executed their mission. They did not let me down; they performed superbly. In the end, supporting this NGFS initiative was the right decision, and the ships provided valuable support to the Al Faw Peninsula assault, saving lives as the coalition forces moved north. It would later be called "Five-Inch Friday" by those involved, as 5.0 inches was the caliber of shells fired from the *Anzac* guns.

Joint Venture (HSV-X1)–The Mothership

The U.S. military wanted to know if a high-speed vessel (HSV) could effectively support missions, including mine warfare, special operations, homeland security, humanitarian assistance, and shipment of troops and cargo (tanks and other heavy equipment). To find out, they leased a former car and passenger ferry, built in 1998 in Australia by Incat. The ferry was an aluminum catamaran the length of a football field (315 feet), and about half the width. Steered with a joystick versus a wheel, it was highly maneuverable, capable of making 90-degree turns at full speed and stopping in three ship lengths. Most importantly, it had a shallow draft (11 to 13 feet) and could operate in waters as shallow as 16.4 feet. *Joint Venture* could cruise for 3,500 miles at 35 knots (with a top speed of 45 knots), powered by four diesels/water jets. It had two .50 caliber machine gun mounts and was armed with Stinger surface-to-air missiles.

It was called *Joint Venture* because of joint testing by the military services. It was modified by adding a helicopter deck and a hydraulically operated vehicle ramp. Once outfitted, it was sent to the Arabian Gulf to contribute to the war effort. The Army-Navy crew consisted of 50 people.

I recall listening to Commodore Balmert's surface combatant team trying to figure out how they were going to escort the high-speed *Joint Venture* through the Strait of Hormuz. How would they provide support if the Iranian Revolutionary Guard navy speedboats decided to harass/attack the ship? Transiting at 40+ knots was optimal for the *Joint Venture*, minimizing the ship's time in the threat area. However, no combatant ship in the coalition force was capable of coming close to matching that speed. It was a wonderful problem to solve. Ultimately, Commodore Balmert assigned a helicopter the task of escorting this high-speed vessel transit.

The commanding officer in 2003 was Commander Phil Beierl, a diving and salvage officer by trade. He was the perfect detail for the missions that would follow. He navigated *Joint Venture* over 5,000 nautical miles from Rota, Spain to Kuwait in seven days, ferrying supplies to the theater of operation. Once on station, it served as the special operations mothership. Commander Beierl said:

> "If you think of what you can do with a high-speed ferry, you can carry a lot of things and carry a lot of people. Right now, we don't have a medium-sized ship that will do that. We don't have any that will do it fast."
> *(tech.tv.com, 28 Jan 2002)*

The *Joint Venture* was used as an Afloat Forward Staging Base (AFSB), deploying Navy SEALs and Marine Fleet Anti-Terrorism Security Teams (FAST) in Mark V craft and RHIBs. This was the most forward ship in the Navy, operating near Umm Qasr for the duration of the support effort. The ship was under the tactical control of CTF 561, Commodore Harward, and it participated in each of the rehearsals for special operations missions.

In the early days of the deployment in the Arabian Gulf, *Joint Venture* operated out of Kuwait Naval Base (KNB). The ship would get underway daily for the training of flight crews, for ship handling, for practice launching and recovering boats, and for testing of communications connectivity between the mothership and the small boats in the water.

On 8 March *Joint Venture* transited to Bahrain to onload cargo and conduct engineering repairs. The next day Vice Admiral Keating came to the pier to tour the ship, listen to the crew, and provide some final guidance before combat operations.

On 18 March, while in port KNB, the *Joint Venture* crew conducted the final loadout to support the special operations forces. This included extra food, water, ammunition, and a fuel pumping and storage system for refueling the small boats that would be patrolling the waterways 24-hours-a-day.

On 19 March, a 50-man U.S. Marine FAST company embarked on *Joint Venture*. They would provide security on the MABOT and KAAOT platforms after the takedown by the SEALs. Over the next 24 hours, *Joint Venture* participated in the successful mission to capture and secure these critical oil terminals. The ship was prepared to act as an Emergency Decontamination Platform. It supported the Mark V and 11m RHIB assault force over 60 miles to the target and transported the assault force back to Kuwait upon completion of the operation.

The SEALs wanted to move close to the southern Iraq Port of Umm Qasr as soon as possible. *Joint Venture* was their base; however, its logical route, through the KAA waterway to Umm Qasr, had not yet been cleared of suspected mines by the mine warfare forces.

Thus, on 21–22 March *Joint Venture* performed the near impossible. Captain Beierl navigated *Joint Venture* through the shallow entrance bar of Khawr As Subiyah (KAS) *west* of Bubiyan Island at high tide and held station until low tide so that it could transit under the Bubiyan Island bridge, with six-feet overhead clearance and 32-feet side clearance. Then the ship hovered on station in the narrow channel fighting a three-knot current and 25-knot winds for 24 hours, awaiting orders to proceed north to establish the AFSB just south of Umm Qasr. Unbelievable. This transit defied all odds. This was essentially like coming in the back door of a building, except it was in the shallow waters of the NAG.

On 23 March *Joint Venture* continued north through the KAS waterway, anchored just south of Umm Qasr, and commenced operations. The ship would be the base for up to 150 people at a time, including coalition special forces. People seeing the ship from the Iraqi shore must have exclaimed: "What is that ship, and how did it get here!"

During the next week, TF 561 personnel would stage from Joint Venture and search over 115 vessels in the KAA and Khor Al-Zubair (KAZ) waterways during round-the-clock operations, using the 14 Naval

Special Warfare (NSW) combat craft based in *Joint Venture*. The derelict vessels were in the way of future relief efforts, and it was imperative that they were searched for contraband, explosives, and people before any coalition force and eventually commercial traffic moved up the KAA to Umm Qasr. This could not have been possible without the proximity of *Joint Venture*. Additionally, the ship remained on station through the 55-knot winds that gusted to 70 knots on the evening of 25 March, with just 300 yards to shoal water. They used their engines throughout the night to prevent dragging anchor.

The experiment with the HSV was a resounding success. It delivered a capability previously unheard of in the U.S. Navy. Its speed and volume were force multipliers and made a significant difference in the conduct of operations in the opening days of OIF.

After OIF, the U.S. Navy expanded its use of the HSV and renamed it Expeditionary Fast Transport Vessel (T-EFP). These vessels continue to deploy to the forward theaters, contributing to a wide variety of missions for the commanders. *It all began with the successful deployment of Joint Venture in OIF.*

Missile Defense Support to U.S. Army

In December 2002, the CFACC requested an Aegis radar-equipped ship to support an early warning mission for short-range ballistic missile (SRBM) launches from Iraq. These SRBMs had very minimal burn times, and therefore might not be detected by other coalition sensor equipment. The primary threats were from the Ababil-100 and Al Samoud II missiles, which had ranges up to 93 miles. This range, launching from Basra, Iraq, could threaten Kuwait, northeastern Saudi Arabia, and ships in the Northern Arabian Gulf.

Higgins was assigned as the Theater Ballistic Missile Defense Commander (TBMDC) for the *Constellation* Strike Group and would support the CFACC request for early warning of Iraqi missile launches. *Higgins* was a destroyer with special capabilities to track missile launches, identifying both the genesis (launch location) as well as the expected crater (impact area). The crew worked with Army and Air Force groups for several months to develop tactics, techniques, and procedures to streamline this critical mission.

On 1 March, *Higgins* was assigned *spotlight* duties for the overall force at sea in the Northern Gulf and retained this responsibility throughout combat operations into April. A direct voice communications link was established with Army units ashore as well as operators at the CAOC. This link would allow two-way flow of information, such that operators aboard *Higgins* at sea were talking to operators of Patriot missile air defense batteries ashore dealing with incoming missiles, *and* to those in the CAOC assigning aircraft to eliminate the launch platform. (Patriot is a surface-to-air missile system whose name is derived from the radar component for the system.)

Brigadier General Bromberg, commander of the U.S. Army 32nd Air and Missile Defense Command, visited *Higgins* on 8 March. He conducted face-to-face talks with Commander Gilday and his team, to ensure that his command and *Higgins* would work seamlessly against the missile threat.

As the Iraqi army prepared to fire their missiles, *Higgins* would scan the entire horizon, identify a launch, and then pass the information to the Patriot batteries so that they could look down a specific bearing, significantly increasing the probability of an intercept. This was especially valuable in the close quarters of the Iraq/Kuwait border, as time of flight was only a few minutes. *Higgins* helped identify which ones presented the most danger to coalition forces. This allowed the Patriot operators to appropriately discriminate incoming missiles, choosing which ones to shoot down and which ones to allow to crash into the water or desert.

On 20 March, Iraqi forces launched five surface-to-surface missiles (SSMs), likely Ababil-100s, from the Al Faw Peninsula toward Kuwait. They were either intercepted or allowed to fall harmlessly to the earth due to *Higgins* support. As of 28 March, they had provided this "heads up" for 11 missiles. Seven of these missiles were successfully engaged by Patriots, three impacted in the desert, and one self-destructed. This was an unprecedented lash-up between the Navy at sea and the Army and Air Force ashore, and the *first* time an Aegis Class destroyer was used in a Tactical Ballistic Missile (TBM) warning role.

The significance of this support was brought home to me years later. I was facilitating a Combined Force Maritime Component Commander

(CFMCC) course on behalf of the Naval War College in Naples, Italy at the 6th Fleet headquarters. I used this story to emphasize the point of the power of joint and combined operations, where the strengths of various units are spliced to enhance the capability of the whole force. One of the students in the class was U.S. Army Major General Bryan Owens. He came up to me on a break, and with an interesting look on his face, said "I never knew of the *Higgins* support. I was there in Kuwait, at the command center in Camp Doha, when there was a missile headed for our position on 27 March. The Patriot battery shot it down. There would have been a considerable number of deaths. I owe my life to the *Higgins* team."

I later had the opportunity to pass this exchange back to then Vice Admiral Mike Gilday. He was appreciative of the feedback and applauded the professionalism of his crew for their success in saving lives.

CHAPTER 9 | OPERATIONS PART III:
CLEARING A PATH FOR RELIEF SUPPLIES

"They paved the way for humanitarian aid to flow."

—Tony Blair, Prime Minister of the United Kingdom

CLEARING THE **KAA**

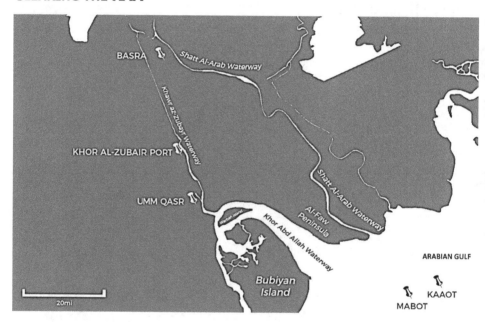

Vice Admiral Keating sent out the order to commence mine countermeasure operations up the KAA to the Port of Umm Qasr. The order directed channel clearing, taking measures to mitigate risk (the Al Faw Peninsula—northern border of the KAA was not yet secure), and communicating directly with the ground forces to prevent blue-on-blue situations.

In the opening hours of the conflict, there was a strong pull from higher headquarters for details on all aspects of operations to feed back to the Pentagon. I worked closely with my leadership team to pass information minute-by-minute to the 5th Fleet staff to feed the beast. On 23 March, I sent the following note to Vice Admiral Keating:

"As we discussed this morning the thirst for information is upon us. Provided a one slide status to your staff at noon for LTG Abizaid. Provided the concept of operations (on taking the KAA) you approved to Mark Milliken to help him answer questions. Watched TV pictures of Umm Qasr, talking of reopening the port soonest for the humanitarian aid, and saw U.K. reference to *Sir Galahad* in Kuwait in a press conference today—ready to go up the KAA.

We play the cards we are dealt. We avoided a catastrophe by getting the mine-laden barge before it dropped the mines in the Northern Arabian Gulf. Hopefully, there are not any behind us... and the Dubai caper (*intelligence indicating that there was a ship in Dubai loaded with sea mines*) turns out to be unreliable. Hopefully, the other barges up the KAA have not dispersed their mines. If the cards fall differently, and we come across the mines in the KAA and harbor, then we will have to dampen expectations—when those who have no appreciation of the pace of MCM operations come calling."

I MEF had moved into Umm Qasr, discovering numerous sea mines at the Iraqi coast guard station. Also, they discovered five vessels modified to carry six mines on deck, and six below deck. Fortunately, these ships did not make it to sea.

On 23 March, Captain O'Moore sent me a report of his forces' activities. He was upbeat, as the helicopters were ahead of schedule, generating 47 contacts to be analyzed. But as he listed his issues, he was prescient when he stated:

"Although there is no hard evidence to suggest mining has taken place, given the background noise regarding

249

mines and mining, in addition to the clandestine minelayers captured, there is every reason to at least suspect parts of the KAA are mined. Areas further north around the narrower parts of the river will require particular attention."

For the next week, WPBs joined *Chinook* and *Firebolt,* as the group escorted minesweeping ships moving up the KAA waterway toward Umm Qasr.

On 25 March, President Bush spoke to the world, providing an update on the progress of the war effort. In the Gulf, it was late at night and I was watching as the president announced that among other upcoming initiatives, "I was told this morning in my briefings that massive amounts of humanitarian aid should begin moving in the next 36 hours." This was alarming as President Bush's timeline would fall short of what we had set forth as the minimum time to clear the 100-yard swath the 43 miles from the mouth of the KAA to Umm Qasr.

I called the 5th Fleet headquarters to talk with Vice Admiral Keating. He had also seen this broadcast and anticipated my call. True to his word, the admiral remained supportive of the seven-day mine clearing effort and assured me that he would inform Central Command leadership that we would proceed along the planning timeline.

This proved to be the right answer. We established 28 March as the date for the *Sir Galahad* transit of the KAA. I told the press that,

"A number of different people clearly are making it a priority to get humanitarian relief up there… our job is to make sure it gets there safely."

The mine clearance team discovered a line of five mine-like objects on the night of the 27 March as they approached the bend in the river across the narrow part of the channel at the entrance to Umm Qasr. This was a spot any ship headed northwest must pass. The coalition sailors deployed their unmanned vehicles. After they attached charges to these objects, the resounding secondary explosions confirmed that these were MANTA mines, the silent killers. These were likely placed in the channel choke point by the Iraqi tug *Al Jumhuriyah* on 20 March as it proceeded out the KAA towards the NAG with its deadly cargo.

NAVAL SPECIAL CLEARANCE TEAM 1

I had the opportunity to interview Commander Tony Rodgers in 2016. He was the commanding officer of Naval Special Clearance Team 1 (NSCT-1) and had a treasure trove of pictures, some that are shared in this book. These pictures showed the magnitude of the Iraqi mine inventory.

NSCT-1 was a new mine warfare team deploying for the first time. This group was composed of 50 Navy SEAL divers, EOD divers and Marine Corps force reconnaissance divers, as well as marine mammals and Remote Environmental Measuring Unit (REMUS) unmanned vehicles. They were joined by a British Fleet Diving Group and the Australian Clearance Dive team, making a total force of 110 people. This group was divided into three divisions: deep and shallow water, very shallow water, and Special Warfare Combat Craft.

Before they swung into action clearing the Port of Umm Qasr, a different challenge arose; how to deconflict fires from the U.S. Marines and British Commandos taking the peninsula with the mine warfare forces making their way up the waterway, along with SEALs and patrol craft. The forces would be operating within a few miles of each other, sometimes sharing the same battlespace, each of which had some priority and real urgency for speed of execution.

Each time we thought there was closure, another issue arose. The last one was particularly thorny. There was a desire to use U.S. Landing Craft Air Cushioned (LCAC) to transport Royal Marines across the waterway. For this plan to succeed, there was a need to clear obstacles in the Surf Zone of the Al Faw Peninsula. In late March, there was a request from Major General Dutton and Rear Admiral Snelson to have U.S. support for this effort. This *had* been discussed, but *not fully planned*. Time was short. The U.K. sense was that it would simply be "chaps with bolt cutters and explosives who can shift things that are in the way, where the LCACs transition from water to land."

My initial response was that it was a "last minute unstaffed idea... contrary to our plans in place... need to spike this unguided missile." Our intelligence was incomplete as to the conditions along the beach on the south side of the peninsula where the LCACs would transit across to the land. What *was* known was that there were at least two fence lines and obstructions along the beach. The question as to who would be responsible for clearing a path was discussed at length. No one seemed to have the answer or capability. I sent a note to Vice Admiral Keating indicating that my team (U.S./U.K./AUS.) had concerns, and I felt that this was not a mission to be thrown together at the last minute. There was significant jeopardy, with no Operational Risk Management (ORM). Rear Admiral Clyde Marsh, owner of the LCACs, weighed in with similar legitimate concerns.

Ultimately, I sent Captain O'Moore to meet with the land component commanders and their leadership. They emerged with a well-defined requirement with acceptable risk for a reconnaissance mission. I asked Vice Admiral Keating for his permission to proceed with this exploratory initiative, and he concurred.

Enter Commander Rodgers and his team. The team explored the actual conditions on the mudflat of a beach at first light on 21 March. The area was *not* secure (still in Iraqi military control) when his team made their way across the KAA waterway. The mission was to clear obstacles before bringing heavy LCACs onto the peninsula. As the team conducted their survey, it became clear that there were landmines scattered across the beach, and the density was *high*. Commander Rodgers passed his findings to Captain Tillotson in Kuwait, who would soon be operating on the ground in Umm Qasr, and the information made it back to Rear Admiral Marsh. At that point, it was game over for this possible crossing by the LCACs. There was no simple way to clear a path through a minefield, and it would be much more effective to go the land route around and through Umm Qasr. There would be enemy resistance, but not to the degree of encountering a beach minefield threat.

Commander Rodgers then returned to Umm Qasr to lead a site survey. He would lay out the plan for clearance of the landside of the Old Port, the grain facility, and the berths. This team also came to help get the port back up and running, since there were no Iraqi workers on-scene. Civil Affairs forces would reach out to the Iraqi people and eventually get some to return to assist in getting the port functioning.

Divers and EOD teams of NSCT-1 worked to clear berths five and six within the port. They had to deal with the 4+ knot current alongside the pier that allowed dive windows to be only one hour. There were high winds and very poor underwater *hand over hand* visibility. Lieutenant Commander Scott Craig, Royal Australian Navy would say, "In the dark hours of the morning after their arrival, a number of CTD3 divers slipped below the coffee-colored surface of the harbour and by touch alone located a sunken minelayer with four live ship-killing mines onboard." (This was a Type 15 patrol boat that would later be raised to the surface.)

The bottom was silty, and U.K. divers could insert their arm up to the shoulder—hence heavier mines could certainly be buried. Commander Rodgers would say: "It's very slow and methodical. It's an unending process of collecting from sensors, then resolving mine-like contacts and determining that they're not mines before you can say, 'clear.'"

Divers were effective, conducting over 482 force protection dives, and marking 97 man-made objects and shapes. The tapes from their dives were reviewed to distinguish 55-gallon drums and tires, eliminating the need for further investigation of those objects. Divers were the major factor in clearing an 800-meter x 400-meter area around the piers, helping assure safe access for *Sir Galahad.*

Divers used the REMUS, an unmanned underwater vehicle similar to a mini-torpedo to search a pre-programmed track looking for mines. After a mine would be detected, divers would pinpoint the location and prep for detonation. This was one of the many innovations in the mine warfare operations in 2003.

In the meantime, Task Force 561 sanitized wrecks and derelict vessels along the main channel of the KAA. This would mitigate the threat to coalition forces and prevent enemy attacks. They would also provide boats north of Umm Qasr to act as a blocking force preventing any movement of southbound shipping that would interfere with military operations particularly the mine clearance effort. This would be accomplished in the face of a storm that created six-foot waves and hurricane force winds that exceeded 65 knots.

SEALs were critical to ensuring the safety of operations on the waterway, working side by side with coalition partners. During their operations in the KAA waterway and waters around Umm Qasr, the SEAL team boarded 113 vessels resulting in the discovery of 55 Iraqis. They also found 12 MANTA mines on two dhows. These SEALs were part of a 700-member task force that represented the largest assemblage of Naval Special Warfare forces on foreign soil in history.

The minesweeping efforts would continue to widen the channel to 400 yards. The channel would receive new markings, and the port would be dredged. These initiatives would allow shipping to return to Umm Qasr without an escort, consistent with guidance from Central Command to "Transition to post-hostility tasks as ground is secured." Electricity to the port was restored in early April.

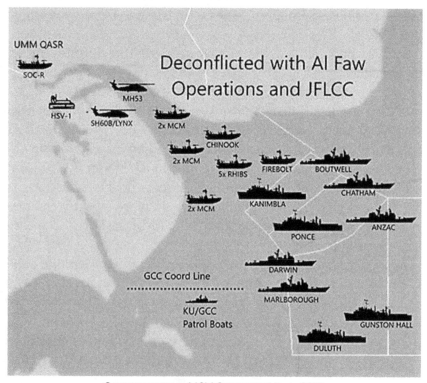

COMMENCEMENT OF MCM OPERATIONS MARCH 2003

SECURING UMM QASR

Umm Qasr needed to be secured while the mine clearing operation was underway. Captain Tillotson took charge of this effort and commanded Task Force 56 ashore in Umm Qasr. This group represented Navy Expeditionary Combat Command (NECC) in the 5th Fleet area of operations and would grow to 800 people over the course of operations in and around Umm Qasr. Task Force 56 was comprised of various groups with a variety of missions, including:

- Explosive ordnance disposal
- Naval construction
- Riverine operations
- Military intelligence operations
- Combat camera (imagery to support operations)
- Diving
- Expeditionary logistics support
- Maritime expeditionary security
- Expeditionary combat readiness

Captain Tillotson provided me regular situation reports on his progress in securing the port and getting the facilities up and running. He had gone forward on the heels of the Marines, moving north from Kuwait to Umm Qasr on 22 March, and assumed on-scene commander of the port on 23 March. We were working the timing of moving the underwater mine countermeasures (marine mammals) to Umm Qasr. I sent him a note looking for his input regarding that timeline.

The captain responded with a note on the evening of 23 March, outlining his five specified tasks and his progress.

- Access port facilities—completed.
- Identify underwater explosive objects that deny use of port facilities—not completed.
- Clear headquarter lay down area of booby traps—not completed.
- Conduct battle damage assessment of Old Port facilities—not completed.

- Evaluate enemy threat to follow-on forces—not completed.

He made it clear that the security environment was *not* as permissive as reported by the press. His personnel remained dressed out in protective clothing in case of a chemical/biological attack. Task Force 56 reconnaissance teams, along with a Marine Security Element, were taking sporadic small arms fire.

The Old Port area was hotly contested, and Marines were in a firefight. He attempted to get access to the main oil pier but was waved off by Marines, too dangerous at that point.

That afternoon he sent another element of his team to the Old Port area. His goal was to clear a landing zone for the next day so that he could receive helicopters, loaded with EOD personnel and marine mammals. This would be the beginning of his efforts to identify and clear underwater explosive objects. He was focused on getting access to warehouses, such that he could assess the progress of clearance efforts, as well as plan for offload and storage of humanitarian relief supplies. However, there were still significant pockets of resistance. The Marines had seized several Iraqi weapons caches, including MANPADs (man-portable air-defense systems)—shoulder-launched SAMs.

A second call later that evening from Captain Tillotson was revealing. I could hear the firefight going on close to his position. He remained cool and collected as the Marines pushed back the Iraqi force. He passed along his intentions for the next day. These included:

- Insert a small boat in the water to clear the waterside of the pier.
- Clear warehouses near berths 1 and 2 where he would set up the marine mammals.
- Continue survey/clearance of 200-meter x 200-meter landing zone for helicopter operations.

One of the issues he faced was the lack of electricity and water to support the force in this hostile environment. He was looking for an assist, and *Gunston Hall* provided support from their position in Kuwait. The next day a convoy of trucks, HUMVs (four with .50 caliber machine guns and four with grenade launchers) and helicopters arrived

OPERATIONS PART III: CLEARING A PATH FOR RELIEF SUPPLIES

on the scene. They brought generators, gas, ammunition, and water. Additionally, they brought four Navy and four Coast Guard small boats to provide harbor security.

Commander Scott Jerabek, CTU 51.9.3, led this group. He reported to Captain Allen Painter, CTG 51.9 (Naval Coastal Warfare Group 1, operating in Kuwait). Commander Jerabek was an experienced hand at port security, having set up the security organization at two Kuwaiti ports. He and his complement of 207 people quickly went to work erecting a secure perimeter around the port area of operations. Additionally, they established a mobile operations center that provided an excellent communications capability.

Sniper fire persisted for several days. However, working side by side with Captain Tillotson and British forces in the area, Commander Jerabek's team created a secure environment and helped bring Umm Qasr back to life. These were Reserves who had known each other for years and worked together seamlessly. Commander Jerabek described their efforts as "routine professionalism," but I can attest that there was nothing routine about the amazing work they accomplished in support of the overall mission. They established a command and control center and communicated effectively with a variety of agencies. They would stay in Umm Qasr until 20 June to provide necessary continuity.

Captain Tillotson was under pressure to get the port safe for receipt of relief supplies. This was a *strategic* goal of the coalition leadership, to be able to show the intent to help the Iraqi people. Basra had been without power for several days, and Red Cross personnel were reporting on a potential humanitarian disaster as fresh water supplies were limited. President Bush indicated that relief supplies were close at hand, while British Defense Minister Geoff Hoon stated that "I'm not going to allow ships into a dangerous port area while there was still fighting going on... Nor are we going to take ships into a waterway that has been heavily mined."

Over the next several days Captain Tillotson's team successfully secured the port and made way for the introduction of MCM operations. By 25 March, 20 airlifts of personnel, supplies, and marine mammals to Umm Qasr were complete. It would take eight to ten hours to get the teams set up on the ground.

Marine mammals (dolphins and sea lions) were a key part of this force. They made their way from their home in San Diego via U.S. Air Force C-5 aircraft. Once in theater, they lived in pools in the well deck of the *Gunston Hall*. The mammals had three years of training at the Space and Naval War Systems Command in San Diego to make them experts so that they could work as a part of NSCT-1 under Commander Rogers. These flippered Sailors traveled with their own staff of veterinarians and got daily medical checkups. They do not touch the mines but leave a small marker near them, and then divers further investigate and dispose of the objects/mines.

The mammals were the only asset that could work *outside* slack tide, overcoming the swift currents. They are extraordinarily intelligent and use their natural biological sonar to find mines. Their sonar system is so sensitive that it can detect a metal disk the size of a quarter 100 feet away. The dolphin locates an object by emitting a pulse of sound from a specialized structure in its head called the melon and waits for the echo to return after it strikes an object. The pulse is called a *click*, and as the dolphin closes on the object, the clicks occur at shorter intervals. Aviation Ordnanceman 1st Class Dee Jennings said it best: "Their search rate is incredibly fast. Detection is 100 percent. They can find anything." They were sent forward to conduct their mission of surveying the pier area of the Port of Umm Qasr and mark any mines they discovered. They performed magnificently, confirming that the area was clear of bottom mines. There were mines on ships there, but they were dealt with by other forces.

They were provided with superb dining, eating some of the best sushi on the planet. This proved to be key, as one of the mammals went AWOL (absent without leave) for a swim into the Gulf. He was gone for several days but returned, a little worse for the wear... with a smile on his face, and hungry for some great sushi!

On 27 March, Captain Tillotson reported that divers were proceeding on or ahead of schedule in clearing the port pier area. In the process, they found six pilot boats rigged with makeshift mine racks alongside the pier or sunk. There were four LUGM and two MANTA mines aboard one of these boats. Additionally, their inspection of the scene revealed scrapings, lines on the decks, and empty spaces indicating the potential recent deployment of several mines from these vessels.

The land clearance effort was completed, and rail movement was ongoing—bringing the port back to life. Captain Tillotson met with Commodore Harward that afternoon to coordinate future efforts.

On 28 March, Iraqis reopened a pipe factory near the port, and schools would be open the next week. The coalition leadership was very confident about their ability to talk to the local Iraqi people and convince them of the coalition intentions to restore order.

On the morning of 28 March, HMS *Sandown* led RFA *Sir Galahad* to Umm Qasr along the 43-mile corridor paved by the mine clearance efforts, delivering over 400 tons of bottled water, as well as tons of chickpeas, sugar, rice, and other food staples contributed by the Kuwaiti government and private aid agencies. These supplies were desperately needed by the ¼ million people in southern Iraq and represented the beginning of the delivery of significant humanitarian relief supplies. The patrol crafts *Chinook*, *Firebolt* and the WPBs trailed the ship providing force protection. *Sir Galahad* was met by Christiane Amanpour from *CNN*, and she conducted several interviews broadcasting this good news. The transit of *Sir Galahad* would later be followed by *Sir Percival* and other U.S Agency for International Development (USAID) ships carrying grain.

The mines discovered directly in *Sir Galahad's* path would have sunk the ship. Loss of life would likely have occurred. Vital relief supplies would not have reached those in need. The ship herself would have become a static display in the waterway, hampering future operations and relief efforts. The strategic and political impact would have been significant, as the well-intended relief would have been sunk. The Iraqi forces could have claimed some degree of victory, despite the reality that a relief ship certainly was not their primary target for these mines. *But none of that happened*, because of the leadership and professionalism of coalition Sailors.

RHIB forces continued supporting the mine countermeasure ships. They worked with the U.S. Navy and the U.S. Coast Guard patrol boats to provide protection on the flank facing the Al Faw Peninsula.

The RHIB trips were getting longer, and the intense Gulf heat presented significant challenges to the health and welfare of the Sailors in the uncovered RHIBs. With the larger patrol craft now in control, on 28 March Captain Jones chose to cease the RHIB support operations.

On 31 March survey work of the KAA waterway was complete, and mapping of the Umm Qasr Port had begun. Four berths had been declared ready to receive shipping by the mine warfare and EOD teams. These teams then worked northward toward the Port of Az Zubayr and discovered 23 LUGM mines hidden ashore under tarps, suggesting this was a staging area before they would be loaded onto dhows. Additionally, U.K. forces discovered and destroyed eight surface-to-air missiles (SAMs).

Captain Jones went to Umm Qasr on 4 April to visit with the force on the ground. He, his staff, and the brave Sailors of the maritime interception force made a critical difference in the conflict. They were dedicated professionals, and the coalition was proud of their superlative performance.

On 11 April the WPBs escorted the motor vessel *Manar* up the KAA. This vessel carried 700 tons of Red Crescent Society aid in food, water, medical supplies, and transport vehicles to Umm Qasr.

On 12 April, I rode *Firebolt* up the KAA to Umm Qasr to gain firsthand situational awareness. This was my first time on Iraqi soil after plying the waters of the NAG for over a decade enforcing U.N. sanctions. It was also an opportunity for me to look the exhausted Sailors in the eye and thank them for their incredible efforts to open the port so that relief supplies could flow. Having completed a mission for which they had long trained, they had a well-deserved air of satisfaction. I sent a trip report to Vice Admiral Keating:

"Provided a good ground level overview of the challenges our forces had while patrolling during the war and received a whole new appreciation of what a superb job the team did in discovering the minelayers before Iraqis executed their mission.

Met with Brigadier General Jim Dutton and resolved all issues.

Met with Peterson, Harward, Tillotson, Painter, U.K. reps, and a variety of other resource providers working on Umm Qasr rehab. It was an impressive gathering of warriors who had been through some amazing experiences over the last month. After listening to their issues, I gave a wrap up of the month's highlights for their situational awareness and laid out the way ahead. It was a very positive environment with an appreciation of the success to-date, and the challenges of tomorrow.

Rode with naval coastal warfare (NCW) Sailors in one of their speed boats patrolling the harbor. Very impressive craft and people. Commodore Painter has 900 people in theater providing security at a variety of locations.

Flew up to Az Zubayr along the waterway. Many steel hull wrecks—a scrap worker's paradise. Environment was calm, and the biggest challenge will be to dispose of these vessels over time. CTF 561 has already been through and cleared them—markings noted on the sides of the vessels.

Flew back down the KAA. Favored the Al Faw side to closely observe the security concerns. It is very flat—so easy to see inland. We were accompanied by a U.K. Lynx, which patrols the shore twice a day at very low altitude.

Overall impression: security environment stable, with the U.K. and NCW tightening their grip on all aspects of the potential threat."

Umm Qasr was declared open for commercial operations. Air and surface mine countermeasure operations would continue, as they moved the effort up the KAZ waterway toward Az Zubayr, 27 miles north of Umm Qasr.

This entire mine clearing operation was a demonstration of close coordination between several forces moving in the proximity of the waterway and peninsula. The naval gunfire support, mine hunting, naval coastal warfare, special operations, and land component movements were coordinated expertly, precluding any blue-on-blue casualties. This coordination, with early planning and constant interaction, ensured success.

During Operation Iraqi Freedom, mine forces investigated a total of 478 contacts in the water, 86 of which were determined to be mine-like objects. Since the visibility in the water was zero, forces conducted "blow and go" operations. Once they found a mine-like object, divers and mine neutralization vehicles were employed in the area to detonate it. Of the 86 charges, 11 of them caused major detonations (six confirmed by visual, and five by high order sympathetic detonation)—indicating they successfully blew up a mine. The 11 identified mines in the water consisted of:

- Five Iraqi Sommer (indigenously produced MANTA mine, discovered at the approach to Umm Qasr).
- Two historic mines from the Desert Shield/Desert Storm era.
- Four unknown type/origin.

Additionally, the coalition forces captured:

- 140 mines at the pier or on shore.
- 86 mines afloat.

This mine-hunting effort will go down as one of the most professionally executed and successful operations in naval history.

PHOTO SECTION

CHANGE OF COMMAND CEREMONY FOR CRUISER-DESTROYER GROUP 1 ABOARD USS *CONSTELLATION* ON 18 JUNE 2002.

WHY WE ARE HERE

OCT 1983	MARINE BARRACKS BEIRUT, LEBANON	243
DEC 1988	PAN AM FLT 103 LOCKERBIE, SCOTLAND	244
FEB 1993	WORLD TRADE CENTER NYC, NY	6
JUN 1996	KHOBAR TOWERS DHAHRAN, SA	19
AUG 1998	US EMBASSIES KENYA/TANZANIA	224
OCT 2000	USS COLE ADEN, YEMEN	17
SEP 11 TH 2001	WORLD TRADE CENTER NYC, NY	3000 +
	PENTAGON WASHINGTON DC	
	UNITED AIRLINES FLT 93	

LIST OF PREVIOUS TERROR ATTACKS PAINTED ON THE SIDE OF USS *BONHOMME RICHARD* (LHD 6).

SHIPS OF THE *CONSTELLATION* STRIKE GROUP ON THE WAY TO THE ARABIAN GULF.

LEADERSHIP TEAM: (LEFT TO RIGHT) BACK ROW--COMMODORE BALMERT, CAPTAIN FOX, CAPTAIN FARWELL, CAPTAIN MILLER; FRONT ROW--CAPTAIN HEPFER, REAR ADMIRAL COSTELLO.

FIREFIGHTERS TAKE A WATER BREAK AFTER FIGHTING A FIRE IN 4 MAIN MACHINERY ROOM. (PHOTO BY PH2 FELIX GARZA JR.)

CHAIRMAN OF THE JOINT CHIEFS GENERAL MYERS PROVIDES COUNSEL DURING THE DECEMBER 2002 USO SPONSORED VISIT.

SAILORS AND MARINES LISTEN TO GENERAL MYERS, ROGER CLEMENS, AND
DREW CAREY.

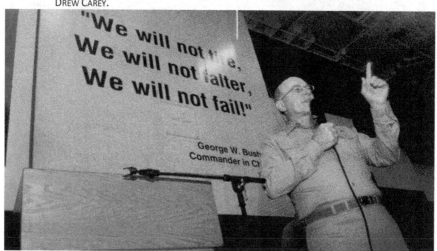

CHIEF OF NAVAL OPERATIONS ADMIRAL CLARK SPEAKS TO THE CREW DURING HIS
JANUARY 2003 VISIT.

VICE ADMIRAL KEATING MEETS WITH THE *CONSTELLATION* STRIKE GROUP LEADERSHIP TEAM IN MARCH 2003.

COALITION SAILORS ASSEMBLE IN FRONT OF RHIBS ON THE DECK OF *KANIMBLA*.

SEVERAL OF THE 147 SHIPS OPERATING IN THE 5TH FLEET AREA OF RESPONSIBILITY FOR OIF.

SUBMARINES AND HELICOPTERS PERFORMED VITAL MISSIONS IN OIF.

A TOMAHAWK MISSILE IS LAUNCHED FROM A DESTROYER.

ADDRESSING THE AIR WING PRIOR TO THE FIRST MAJOR LAUNCH INTO IRAQ.

F/A-18S LAUNCH OFF THE FORWARD CATAPULTS OF CONSTELLATION. COLORED SHIRTS REPRESENT THE VARIOUS RESPONSIBILITIES OF THE SAILORS ORCHESTRATING THIS BALLET OF OPERATIONS.

"GREEN" HANDLES THE CATAPULTS THAT THRUST THE AIRCRAFT INTO THE SKY. "YELLOW" KEEPS EVERYONE MOVING.

FLIGHT DECK CREW PREPARES WEAPONS TO BE LOADED ON THE STRIKE FIGHTERS.

"RED" LOADS THE WEAPONS.

BRIEFING THE ASSEMBLED PRESS CORPS, ENSURING STORIES OF THE HEROICS OF
BRAVE SAILORS AND MARINES ARE FULLY PUBLICIZED.

IRAQI TUG *AL JUMHURIYAH* AND BARGE ARE LOADED WITH MINES INTENDED FOR THE OPEN WATERS OF THE NORTH ARABIAN GULF.

LUGM-145 SHIP-KILLER MINES ARE DISCOVERED BENEATH DRUM SHELLS BY SAILORS INSPECTING *AL RAYIAH*.

SAILORS DISCOVER LUGM-145 MINES (CONTACT) AND IRAQI VERSIONS OF THE ITALIAN MANTA MINES (BOTTOM INFLUENCED) ON ONE OF THE PILOT BOATS FOUND ALONGSIDE THE PIER IN UMM QASR.

CAPTURED IMPROVISED IRAQI SUICIDE BOAT. CHEMICAL HORNS SHOWN WOULD INITIATE THE EXPLOSIVES IN THE BOAT UPON IMPACT (REMOVED BEFORE PHOTOGRAPHED).

COMMANDER TONY RODGERS AND HIS MINE WARFARE TEAM BRIEF CAPTAIN O'MOORE IN AN UMM QASR WAREHOUSE AS THEY PREPARE THE PORT FOR THE ARRIVAL OF RELIEF SUPPLIES.

USS CONSTELLATION PASSES BY USS MISSOURI AND THE USS ARIZONA MEMORIAL AS SHE ENTERS PEARL HARBOR, HAWAII IN MAY 2003. PROUD SAILORS MAN THE RAILS.

CONNIE, "AMERICA'S FLAGSHIP," STEAMS TO HER HOMEPORT FOR THE FINAL TIME.

To Barry Costello
With respect and appreciation,

PRESIDENT BUSH HONORS SAILORS AND MARINES IN SAN DIEGO. IN THE BACKGROUND STANDS JERRY COLEMAN WHO AS A MARINE CORPS PILOT WAS THE ONLY MAJOR LEAGUE BASEBALL PLAYER TO BE ENGAGED IN COMBAT IN BOTH WWII AND KOREA.

Vice Admiral Barry Costello and Admiral Tim Keating at the British Embassy ceremony recognizing the partnership between the U.S. Navy and the Royal Navy.

Kuwait's Major General Al-Mulla signs a Protocol dealing with the KAA waterway with his Iraqi counterpart on 11 November 2008.

CHAPTER 10 | WIND DOWN OF NAVY ENGAGEMENT

"Having successfully completed your combat service in the Central Region, please take pride in knowing that the Constellation carrier strike group delivered a firm blow for freedom across a wide operational spectrum. As you return home to families and friends, please take with you my congratulations on a job well done and best wishes for the future!"

Warm regards, General Tommy Franks

RELEASE OF CARRIERS

The naval air support from the sea was critical to the success of the ground force advance. The three carrier air wings from the Gulf and two from the Mediterranean had been flying sorties around the clock for weeks, keeping F/A-18 and F-14 fighters overhead to clear the way forward and to provide close air support when needed. Praise from the ground commanders poured in, and there was a prevailing sense of accomplishment.

It was now mid-April and time to reevaluate the role of the naval force at sea in this conflict. The number of air-launched weapons deployed in support of the ground force had been reduced to a trickle as forces moved into the Baghdad area on 5 April. Air supremacy (total control) was declared over Iraq on 6 April. The regime officially fell on 9 April. Opposition forces were now less concentrated and were moving into the shadows. Requirements for Tomahawks ceased.

The crew of *Constellation* had not had liberty since 10 February when the ship left Bahrain. Other ships had similar experiences. The air wing had not had a day off for rest since 17 March.

It had been an intense deployment. I spoke to the crew via the loudspeaker system that echoed throughout the ship. After highlighting the many accomplishments of the force, I summed up my remarks:

"The air wing crews have been superb. The flight deck team outstanding. The maintenance teams kept the wing up for 58 days at sea and 22 straight 15-hour days without a break. Combat systems teams have kept us up to speed throughout the war as well as the operations crews. The supply department has been fantastic, continuing to work hard to support the crew.

None of this would have been possible without the weaponeers and engineers. You who build the bombs have done a super job. The engineers... well, you have my deepest respect... eight boilers every day... maintaining the plant in a manner which makes "*Connie*" the most reliable ship in the Gulf!

I want to say again how proud I am of you... I could not have asked for a better team to coach. Every day you do extraordinary things and make them appear routine because of your professionalism... and that is from junior sailors to seniors. Thank you."

Vice Admiral Keating made a case for the release of the ships as the requirement for their presence had diminished. He had no desire to hold onto the ships and their support teams just for appearance's sake. It *was not* about Central Command or 5th Fleet maintaining excess capacity. It *was* about Sailors and Marines. Lieutenant General Moseley and Admiral Clark agreed with his assessment that the requirement for the power projection capability of the carriers had been reduced significantly. He then presented the drawdown proposal to General Franks who agreed that returning to a single carrier presence in the Gulf was the right thing to do. Coalition leadership followed this decision and redeployed their ships to home waters.

Vice Admiral Keating's staff planned for the gradual redeployment of the force. The submarine force was quickly redeployed. On 4 April the force reconstituted, with *Augusta*, *Providence*, and *Montpelier* transiting the Suez back to the Mediterranean; six other submarines began homeward transits to the west; four submarines began homeward transits to the east, and USS *Pasadena* and HMS *Splendid* remained on station in the Arabian Gulf. This was followed by the redeployment of the surface ships, amphibious units and carriers.

Many factors were considered in the sequencing and timing for the release of the carriers. These included: time on station, maintenance requirements, and necessity to maintain a presence in the Gulf for land component support. *Lincoln* had been in the theater for the longest by far, followed by *Constellation* and then *Kitty Hawk*.

Lincoln was released on 13 April, ultimately experiencing a ten-month deployment, having departed their homeport in Everett, Washington on 20 July 2002. Vice Admiral Keating then sent out an order for the departure of *Kitty Hawk* and *Constellation* indicating their missions were complete.

Vice Admiral Keating flew out to *Constellation* on 15 April and spoke to the crew. It had been a month since he last visited, wishing us the best of luck in the then-upcoming battle. This time he came to thank the crews for their outstanding performance during 25 days of continuous combat operations. They had met every challenge, flown every sortie tasked, including some very time-sensitive missions when no one else could get airborne due to weather. Vice Admiral Keating's enthusiasm was contagious. He exuded energy, told the *Constellation* team how proud he was of them, and walked through the hangar bay to shake as many hands as possible before departing for the last time. Later he would say:

> "We were able to keep up with the rapidly dynamic and changing war in ways that were, in my experience, unprecedented."

Kitty Hawk departed the Gulf on 15 April and left CENTCOM area of responsibility on 19 April, headed back to Japan for previously scheduled maintenance. On 16 April we turned over Task Force 55 duties to Destroyer Squadron 50 and departed the Gulf through the Strait of Hormuz for the last time in the history of *America's Flagship*.

We officially "out chopped" from 5th Fleet to 7th Fleet on 20 April 2003. *Nimitz,* having arrived on 3 April 2003, had the watch.

Here is my final message to Task Force 55:

R 151909Z APR 03
FM CTF 55
TO TF 55
BT
UNCLAS //N03000//
MSGID/GENADMIN/CCDG-1/-/APR//

SUBJ/FAREWELL//

RMKS/1. PATRIOTS IN TF 55 - YOUR COURAGE, COMPETENCE AND COMMITMENT HAS PLAYED A MAJOR ROLE IN LIBERATING THE PEOPLE OF IRAQ. ONCE IN A LIFETIME THERE IS THE OPPORTUNITY TO MAKE A DIFFERENCE OF THIS MAGNITUDE. CAREERS COME AND GO WITHOUT THE OCCASION TO FIRE A SHOT IN ANGER. YOU SEIZED THE MOMENT AND ROSE TO THE CHALLENGE. THE HARD WORK IN THE TRAINING CYCLE PAID HUGE DIVIDENDS ACROSS THE WARFARE SPECTRUM - STRIKE, MIO, MIW, IW, NGFS, SUW AND ESCORT OPERATIONS. YOU WERE SUPERB, WITH EVERY MISSION BEING EXECUTED IN A THOROUGHLY PROFESSIONAL MANNER.

2. *NEVER FORGET THAT YOU WERE A PART OF THE FINEST NAVAL FORCE THE* WORLD HAS EVER SEEN. I WILL NEVER FORGET THE HONOR OF LEADING YOU IN THIS QUEST, AND FEEL BLESSED TO HAVE SERVED IN YOUR COMPANY. YOU PROVED THAT FORTUNE DOES FAVOR BOLDNESS! RADM COSTELLO SENDS.

Following are:

- Commodore Harward's note of appreciation from Task Force 561.
- Vice Admiral Keating's farewell message.
- General Franks' "well done" note as we departed.

P 190923Z APR 03 PSN 045823T22

FM NSWTG CENT
TO RHRMAAL/CTF 561
RHRVNUL/COMCONBATGRU
INFO RHMFIUU/COMUSSOCOM MACDILL AFB FL
RUCQSOC/COMUSSOCOM MACDILL AFB FL
RHHMHAA/COMPACFLT PEARL HARBOR HI
RHRVAKS/COMUSNAVCENT

OPER/IRAQI FREEDOM//
MSGID/GENADMIN/NSWTG CENT//

SUBJ/THANK YOU TO CONSTELLATION BATTLEGROUP// POC/I

RMKS/1. RADM COSTELLO, ON BEHALF OF TASK FORCE 561, I WOULD LIKE TO THANK YOU AND THE CONSTELLATION BATTLEGROUP FOR THE SUPPORT THAT MADE OUR OPERATIONS SUCCESSFUL.

2. *DURING YOUR VIGILANT SUPPORT OF OPERATION IRAQI FREEDOM, THE* GALLANT WARRIORS OF THE CONSTELLATION BATTLEGROUP WERE DIRECTLY RESPONSIBLE FOR THE MISSION SUCCESS OF U.S. SPECIAL OPERATIONS AND COMBINED SUPPORTING FORCES. YOU WERE KEY AND ESSENTIAL PLAYERS IN EXECUTING INITIAL COMBAT OPERATIONS THAT INTERDICTED, SECURED, AND PRESERVED VITAL IRAQI OIL RESERVES. THROUGH YOUR INVALUABLE SUPPORT, OUR NAVY TEAM TOGETHER PREVENTED AN ENORMOUS ENVIRONMENTAL DISASTER AND MAINTAINED CRITICAL INFRASTRUCTURE ESSENTIAL FOR THE RAPID INTRODUCTION OF HUMANITARIAN ASSISTANCE AND ECONOMIC RECOVERY OF THE OPPRESSED PEOPLE IN THE COUNTRY OF IRAQ.
MOST NOTEWORTHY, THIS COMPLEX OPERATION WAS ACCOMPLISHED WITH NO FRIENDLY CASUALTIES WHILE ERADICATING ENEMY FORCES IN OUR TARGET AREA.

3. *YOU ENABLED OUR MISSIONS WITH YOUR ASSETS, PLANNING, AND* INTELLIGENCE SUPPORT. YOU PROTECTED OUR FORCE WITH CAS, JAMMING, AND ISR. YOU EFFECTED COMMAND AND CONTROL AND MISSION MONITORING THROUGH YOUR EXCEPTIONAL SYSTEMS, AND YOUR LEADERSHIP STYLE GAVE US THE FLEXIBILITY TO REACT ON THE BATTLEFIELD. BUT MOST OF ALL, WE REMEMBER THE PROFESSIONALISM, DEDICATION, AND FIGHTING SPIRIT OF YOUR MEN AND WOMEN. THEY TRULY CARRIED THE DAY.

4. *CONNIE BATTLEGROUP HAS BECOME PART OF OUR NAVAL SPECIAL WARFARE* HISTORY. WE ARE PROUD TO HAVE WALKED IN HARM?S WAY WITH WARRIORS SUCH AS YOU. WE WISH YOU A QUICK AND SAFE JOURNEY HOME. FAIR WINDS AND FOLLOWING SEAS!

5. *COMMODORE HARWARD SENDS.//*

P 210930Z APR 03 PSN 071195T23

FM COMUSNAVCENT
TO RHRVNUL/COMCRUDESGRU ONE
OPER/IRAQI FREEDOM//
MSGID/GENADMIN/CJFMCC CENT/-/APR//
SUBJ/BRAVO ZULU TO THE USS CONSTELLATION STRIKE GROUP//

RMKS/1. WE NOTE WITH PRIDE AND ADMIRATION THE SUPERB PERFORMANCE AND IMPRESSIVE ACHIEVEMENTS OF THE MEN AND WOMEN OF THE CONSTELLATION STRIKE GROUP DURING OPERATIONS IN THE CENTCOM AOR. YOUR SOLID DETERMINATION AND PROFESSIONALISM SERVED AS THE BACKBONE OF MULTI-NATIONAL COMBAT OPERATIONS IN SUPPORT OF OPERATION IRAQI FREEDOM.

2. *THE HISTORIC CONTRIBUTIONS OF COMCRUDESGRU ONE, CVW 2,*
COMDESRON 7, USS CONSTELLATION, USS BUNKER HILL, USS VALLEY FORGE, USS MILIUS, USS THACH, AND USS RAINIER IN OPERATION IRAQI FREEDOM ARE SINGULARLY IMPRESSIVE. SINCE ARRIVING IN THE AOR ON 14 DECEMBER 2002, THE CONSTELLATION STRIKE GROUP HAS FLOWN MORE THAN 3,700 SORTIES, ACCUMULATING OVER 12,000 FLIGHT HOURS. DURING THESE SORTIES, CVW 2 PROVIDED EXCEPTIONAL CAS AND STRIKE SUPPORT VITAL TO COMBAT TROOPS ON THE GROUND IN AFGHANISTAN AND IRAQ, AND DELIVERED NEARLY OVER 1.1 MILLION POUNDS OF ORDNANCE ON TARGET. COMBINED WITH THE 59 TOMAHAWK MISSILES FROM STRIKE GROUP UNITS, THE PINPOINT ACCURACY AND ON-CALL RESPONSIVENESS IN SUPPORT OF OPERATIONS SOUTHERN WATCH, ENDURING FREEDOM, AND IRAQI FREEDOM DELIVERED A DEVASTATING PUNCH TO OUR ADVERSARIES AND EXEMPLIFIED THE ABILITY OF NAVAL FORCES TO PROJECT POWER ASHORE.

3. *ARRIVING AT A TIME WHEN OEF AND OSW WERE IN FULL SWING AND*
QUICKLY TRANSITIONING TO COMBAT OPERATIONS IN SUPPORT OF OPERATION IRAQI FREEDOM, THE UNITS OF THE CONSTELLATION STRIKE GROUP PERFORMED MAGNIFICENTLY. YOUR PROFESSIONALISM AND SUCCESS IN COMBAT, WHILE MAINTAINING OVER 90 PERCENT OPTEMPO, HAVE INSTILLED ADMIRATION AMONG OUR ALLIES AND HAVE SHOWN THE WORLD WHAT AMERICAN NAVAL POWER CAN DO. YOU DEMONSTRATED EXCEPTIONAL DEDICATION, SUSTAINED SUPERIOR READINESS AND RELENTLESS SPIRIT. AS YOU STEAM TOWARD A WELL-DESERVED REUNION WITH FAMILY AND FRIENDS, PLEASE ACCEPT OUR BEST WISHES AND SINCERE THANKS FOR A JOB EXCEPTIONALLY WELL DONE. VADM TIM KEATING SENDS.//

P 231612Z APR 03 PSN 132904T19

FM USCENTCOM FWD
TO RHRVNUL/COMCRUDESGRU ONE

SUBJ: CONSTELLATION STRIKE GROUP BRAVO ZULU (U)//

RMKS/1. (U) BRAVO ZULU TO THE MEN AND WOMEN OF THE USS
CONSTELLATION CARRIER STRIKE GROUP FOR YOUR SUPERIOR
PERFORMANCE DURING OPERATION IRAQI FREEDOM (OIF). YOUR
OUTSTANDING DEPLOYMENT IN DIRECT SUPPORT OF OUR GLOBAL WAR ON
TERRORISM WILL BE LONG REMEMBERED BY BOTH U.S. CENTRAL
COMMAND AND THE AMERICAN PEOPLE.

2. (U) YOUR ACCELERATED DEPLOYMENT TO THE ARABIAN GULF IN SUPPORT OF
THIS OPERATION SERVED AS AN IMPORTANT DIPLOMATIC TOOL FOR OUR NATION AS
WE INCREASED PRESSURE ON THE IRAQI REGIME. READY TO EXECUTE UPON THE
FIRST DAY OF YOUR ARRIVAL IN THE ARABIAN GULF, THE COMBINED SHIP/AIR WING
TEAM OF YOUR BATTLE GROUP PROJECTED COMBAT POWER DEEP INTO THE REMOTE
REACHES OF IRAQ. YOUR SUPERB COMBAT READINESS AND WARFIGHTING SKILLS
PROVED TO BE INSTRUMENTAL TO OUR JOINT COMBAT TEAM. LIVING UP TO YOUR
MOTTO "FORTUNE FAVORS BOLDNESS," YOU FLEW MORE THAN 6500 COMBAT
SORTIES, DELIVERED MORE THAN 1,000,000 POUNDS OF ORDNANCE AND PLACED 408
TOMAHAWKS PRECISELY ON TARGET. I HAVE NO DOUBT YOUR EFFORTS DIRECTLY
HASTENED THE FALL OF SADDAM HUSSEIN'S REGIME AND THE LIBERATION OF THE
IRAQI PEOPLE.

3. (U) HAVING SUCCESSFULLY COMPLETED YOUR COMBAT SERVICE IN THE
CENTRAL REGION, PLEASE TAKE PRIDE IN KNOWING THAT THE CONSTELLATION
CARRIER STRIKE GROUP DELIVERED A FIRM BLOW FOR FREEDOM ACROSS A WIDE
OPERATIONAL SPECTRUM. AS YOU RETURN HOME TO FAMILIES AND FRIENDS,
PLEASE TAKE WITH YOU MY CONGRATULATIONS ON A JOB WELL-DONE AND BEST
WISHES FOR THE FUTURE! WARM REGARDS, GENERAL TOMMY FRANKS.//

HOMEWARD BOUND

Like Vice Admiral Keating's planning for the release of the carrier
groups from the Gulf, I was planning for our transit back through 7th
Fleet waters to Hawaii and ultimately San Diego. The team clearly
wanted to have a port visit in Australia on our return voyage. I sent a
transit plan to the appropriate staffs and followed with a message to Vice
Admiral Willard, the commander of 7th Fleet. Communications with the
upper echelon would be vital to achieving our goal of quality port visits
for our Sailors on the way home. The initial response from the 7th Fleet
chief of staff was "No Australia, don't even think of asking." The plan
was to send us directly to Hawaii with no stops in between to support a
"higher plan." 7th Fleet leadership was proceeding in the last direction
it received from higher headquarters to get the carriers back at best
speed to reset the force.

That did not sit well with me. With the dramatic naval success in the Gulf and the lack of requirement for more than one carrier to support the land forces in Iraq, I felt there would be room to *revisit* the guidance. Relationships matter. I reached out to Rear Admiral Bob Moeller, my former neighbor when we worked together in the Pentagon who was now on Admiral Doran's Pacific Fleet staff, requesting his assistance in supporting the Australia visit for the group. I was not about to let failure to communicate be the reason for a missed opportunity to get my team to a well-deserved port visit.

The next day there was an email string indicating that Admiral Doran, Pacific Fleet commander, and boss of 7th Fleet, had discussed our transit plan with Admiral Fallon, vice chief of the Navy, and they agreed that an Australian port visit would be fine! *Sometimes if you are not getting the right answer, you might not be asking the right question to the right people at the right time... or maybe we just got lucky.*

On 22 April 2003, en route to Australia, the *Constellation* Strike Group crossed the equator and conducted the traditional *Crossing the Line* ceremony. This hearkened back to days of old when Sailors who had previously crossed (and could prove it) were called *shellbacks*, and the new people were *pollywogs* who needed to be introduced to the legendary Davy Jones and other mythical figures of the deep.

That day was declared a no-fly day. As the ships had been to sea for the required number of days, a beer day was appropriate—two per Sailor/Marine... truly living the dream!

Our first stop would be Perth, Australia. We had experienced 79 continuous days at sea and looked forward to enjoying the warm hospitality of the Australian people from 29 April to 4 May. *I have never felt so welcome,* as the people expressed their appreciation to our Sailors and Marines.

It reminded me of a stop in the western Australian city of Bunbury in 1983. There, several of the older gentlemen pulled us aside, and over a cold beer asked: "Do you Yanks know why we welcome you here today?" We deferred on our answer. They said: "It is because without the U.S. Navy in 1942 supporting the fight off the northern coast in the Battle of Coral Sea, we might be speaking Japanese today." They had long memories and had not forgotten the sacrifices of the U.S. Forces.

That conversation left a lifelong impression on me. Ironically, on our way from Perth to Hawaii, we transited near the waters where the Battle of Coral Sea was fought 61 years before.

We headed northeast toward Hawaii, our next port visit. We crossed the International Date Line and entered the 3rd Fleet area of responsibility on 19 May. The following day the ship held a *CONNIE U* graduation ceremony. The U.S. Navy provided a comprehensive education program aboard the ship. The leadership team made sure personnel had the time to take classes. Many higher education degrees were awarded including a Master of Science, three Bachelor's degrees, and nearly 70 Associates degrees. This is a great indicator of a ship that valued education, and everything that this support meant for the morale of the crew.

The enlisted leadership of the strike group was superb, and I truly enjoyed working with them throughout our time together on this deployment. In the case of the air wing, Command Master Chief Peter Flores wrote me a note on the return transit. He said:

> "Sir, your leadership, guidance, and friendship during our combat cruise was an experience I will never forget. Thank you for believing in the Chiefs Mess. You placed the responsibility of Blue Jacket leadership squarely on our shoulders, exactly where it belongs. You gave us positive praise when we deserved and earned it, but also held us accountable when we may have fallen short. Sir, you were a Chief's admiral, and for that, I say thank you.
> Fair winds and following seas."

It doesn't get any better than that. Sometimes leaders never get feedback from their warriors; I was honored to receive his note.

PACIFIC COMMAND DEBRIEF

Every deploying strike group debriefs Navy leadership when they return, providing highlights and lessons learned such that training and equipping shortfalls can be addressed. Each returning group feels their uniqueness, yet the staffs of higher headquarters tend to minimize the import of these briefings as *more of the same*, feeling that they learned of events as they occurred. Four-star admirals' schedules are tight, and the staffs tend to shoehorn post-deployment briefs between other commitments and allow for a 30 to 60-minute window in an already too full day.

When we arrived in Hawaii, my team and I debriefed Admiral Doran at his Pacific Fleet headquarters and had a good exchange of ideas for over an hour. He had supported our efforts from the beginning of the deployment. I could not have asked for more.

The next day we proceeded up the hill to brief Admiral Tom Fargo, commander of *all* Pacific Forces (including Navy, Air Force, Army, and Marines). My leadership team was well prepared. We arrived at 1300 and were ushered into a conference room filled with staff officers who lined the walls, with the more senior officers taking seats. After everyone was in place, Admiral Fargo arrived and took his seat at the head of the table.

I began with an overview of our operations and then planned to hand over the briefing to each of my leaders to discuss their areas of expertise. As I hurriedly skipped over the wave tops of specific points, attempting to squeeze as much as possible into the designated time window, Admiral Fargo said, "Barry slow down—what's the rush?" As delicately as possible I informed him that the staff had allotted us 30 to 45 minutes and he had other pressing engagements on his schedule for the afternoon.

Admiral Fargo sat back in his chair, paused, and said, "I have all afternoon for this discussion. I want to hear every detail of your recent operations in the Gulf." You could hear an audible groan from his staff, as the boss had just overturned the schedule. He addressed his aide and told him to make the appropriate adjustments. Then he looked at me and said, "OK, now that we're on track, let's begin again."

At that moment, the importance of our operations became much more vivid. This was no routine deployment. Having a leader such as Admiral Fargo express that fact made the significance more profound. We spent the next several hours meticulously discussing relationships with other services and coalition partners, planning and execution challenges, and recommendations for future operations.

The admiral inquired into every facet of the events before, during, and after the opening days of OIF. Admiral Fargo fully intended to acknowledge the points made and ensure they did not end up on the trash heap of lessons learned (or identified). My leadership team was energized by this special opportunity.

RETURN TO SAN DIEGO

The strike group got underway on 26 May from Hawaii and headed east for our return to San Diego. The Navy has a wonderful program called the "Tiger Cruise," wherein families of Sailors can join them on the ship as it transits back to its homeport. It is an opportunity to showcase exactly what Sailors do in their 24-hour day. Each of the ships in our strike group hosted Tigers.

As we transited toward San Diego, it became obvious to me that among the 1000 Tigers on *Constellation* there were many Vietnam War veterans. This included two of my brothers. *Constellation* herself was a veteran of seven combat tours in the waters off Vietnam. When veterans returned home in the late 1960s and early 1970s, there were no welcomes from anyone but their families. The fact that they were fighting in an unpopular war caused very mixed emotions among the citizenry of the time. Their service was not appreciated by the American public in general.

That history caused me to awaken to an obvious opportunity. We were returning to a very appreciative hometown of San Diego. Thousands of people would be lining the channel, waving and applauding their Navy/Marine team.

We were all gathered in the hangar bay the night before we returned. San Diego Mayor Dick Murphy flew aboard in advance to give the thanks of the city to the crew. I had not intended to speak to the audience, as it was Captain Miller's show; that was until I realized the opportunity before me. As the captain turned to me to see if I wanted to say anything, I rose and spoke to the crowd of excited Sailors, Marines, and their Tigers.

First, I thanked the teams for their sterling performance over the past year. I expressed gratefulness that we returned with all our Sailors and Marines after performing incredibly dangerous missions.

Then, *I spoke directly to the many Vietnam veterans in the crowd.* I said that their lack of a return "welcome home" 30+ years before was unsatisfactory. However, tomorrow *when we entered San Diego Bay to the cheering throngs... that would also be for them, and I wanted each of them to be on the flight deck to receive a long overdue symbolic appreciative welcome home!*

Otto Kreisher of *Copley News Service* had been with us from the beginning of the embark program back in February. In a sense, he deployed with us and became an honorary crew member. He wrote his last at-sea piece on 1 June, the day before *Constellation's* final return to San Diego.

> "For an old lady out for what probably will be her last dance, the *Constellation* put on quite a show. The Navy's second oldest warship set an example for ships half its age—starting early, staying late, and meeting every commitment during the air war against Iraq. The *Constellation* and its aircraft supported the opening strikes against Baghdad on March 19.... the *Constellation* crew went on to launch more than 1,500 sorties during the conflict... The air wing's jets also spread millions of leaflets over Iraq, many of which were produced in a printing operation that was unique to the *Constellation*... Aircraft and ships from the *Constellation* Battle Group also took part in operations to capture Iraqi oil transfer platforms that could have been used to pollute the Persian Gulf, to rescue captured U.N. workers, and to stop Iraqi vessels apparently attempting to spread sea mines in the Persian Gulf... The 4,800 Sailors and Marines went more than two months without a port visit, working long hours... Morale remained high, as indicated by the reenlistment rate of 83 percent."

Mayor Murphy hosted a homecoming rally at the San Diego Broadway Pier that began at 0800 Monday 2 June for all the returning ships. Our Vietnam veterans were on the flight deck as we entered the bay, and emotions ran high as the massive crowds along the shoreline cheered. The welcomers ranged from older veterans to young children, many waving small American flags. The carrier moored at its berth on North Island at 1000. The destroyers headed to their piers at the 32nd Street Naval Station. Each group was received by crowds of delighted families and friends on that gray, foggy morning. One hundred six (106) *Constellation* Sailors and many from the other ships in the strike group met their sons and daughters for the first time.

The San *Diego Union-Tribune* quoted some of the participants the next day:

> "They're coming back to this country heroes." (San Diego Mayor Dick Murphy)

> "We are free because of the bravery and spirit and courage they have." (Gina Engels, wife of *Bunker Hill* officer)

> "This is the best time to be in the Navy." (Petty Officer First Class Scott Smart, *Constellation* crew member)

Constellation had returned home for the final time. It would be decommissioned at Naval Air Station North Island, San Diego two months later. The executive officer placed a note in the "Plan of the Day."

> "Today ends the long and legendary active service of 'America's Flagship.' Fortunately for the Navy and our country, the *"Connie Spirit"* will live on as you transfer throughout the fleet and into civilian life, just as her crews have for nearly 42 years. The heart of *Connie* always beat deep in her engineering spaces, her character was always on her flight deck, but her spirit came from her crew. It was Sailors taking care of Sailors, leading the way in education and advancement, doing things the right way and making her the operator of the fleet that defined her spirit. As you say your farewells to the best

ship, crew, and tour I have ever or will ever experience, rest assured the '*Connie Spirit*' lives on."

Captain Miller wrote a message in the last edition of the *Starscope*:

"This edition of *Starscope* marks the end of a great publishing history and the end of a grand operational career for *Constellation*. We are the keepers of a fantastic legacy and our service aboard *America's Flagship* will be a source of pride for time immemorial. I consider it a great privilege to have served during such a critical time in our nation's history, and an absolute honor to have served with the last, best group of *Starscope* readers!"

POST-DEPLOYMENT BRIEF TO CHIEF OF NAVAL OPERATIONS

On 16 June I flew with my leadership team to Washington D.C. to brief the chief of naval operations and his staff. Word of our Hawaii debriefings had reached the Pentagon, and there was a desire to hear the *Constellation* Strike Group report firsthand. We discussed a wide variety of issues, from the pre-deployment training to the operations in 5th Fleet. Included in the brief was a summary of operations in support of Operation Iraqi Freedom:

- Total sorties: strike 1082, tanking 276, other 197
- Total bombs dropped: 897
- Total deployment PDU-5 leaflet bombs dropped: 149
- Total leaflets printed/dropped: 5.1 mil/9.2 mil
- Tomahawk launched: 802
- Total ships escorted: Hormuz 324, Bab-el-Mandeb 246, Suez 203
- Warships: 147 overall in 5th Fleet
- Confirmed mines located in the water: 11 destroyed
- Mines intercepted by TF Maritime Interception Operations: 11 (in water), 140 (near piers), 86 (in tugs headed for the Northern Arabian Gulf—Total: 237

At one point, I spoke of the glowing performance of *Constellation*, from both an operational and a maintenance perspective. CNO Clark asked:

> "If I were to reconsider the decision to decommission *Constellation*, what maintenance would it require for another deployment?"

I asked Captain Miller to respond on behalf of his ship. His answer to the CNO was:

> "We would need some new boiler tubes. Other than that, the ship is ready to sail."

This was not the answer the Navy staff wanted, as the die had been cast to retain the *Kitty Hawk*, which was in same class and age; however, that ship had many significant maintenance challenges, as appropriate for its age. CNO pressed. There must be more. Captain Miller held his ground. The ship was running like clockwork after essentially a year of constant operations. It reminded me of what CNO had said when he visited back in January while the ship was at sea in the Gulf. He marveled then at the cleanliness of the ship, and its ability to meet all commitments, despite being the second oldest carrier (commissioned in 1961 along with *Kitty Hawk*) in the fleet. He said:

> "You can take a new ship, and without a good crew, make it look old in the span of a few years. Likewise, you can take an old ship, and with a great crew, make it run and look like a new ship in a matter of years. This looks like a new ship!"

CNO was also interested in the workings of multiple strike groups in the constrained waters of the Arabian Gulf. I went into the details of how the commanders worked out the division of responsibility and recommended it as a template for future JTFEX training for all strike groups.

Another area of high interest to CNO was the effort of naval air from the three carriers in support of the ground force. In Operation Desert Storm, there was a high percentage of flights allocated for the defense of the ships at sea, which caused significant blowback in post-conflict reviews. In OIF, the percentages were reversed, and 90 percent of flights from the sea were dedicated to strike and close air support missions ashore, which made a significant difference in the success of the ground force advance north.

CNO asked about the performance of the patrol craft in OIF. I told him that they performed superbly during operations in and around the KAA waterway in the Northern Arabian Gulf. *Firebolt* and *Chinook* served as motherships and command and control platforms.

This capability was critical in supporting the numerous boats that carried Sailor inspection teams across the waters to intercept fleeing dhows. The inspection teams' successes allowed combatant ships to maneuver in the shallow waters near the coast of Iraq with the confidence that the force was safe from mines. The PCs were central to the rescue of the U.N. Oil for Food representatives who were on the oil terminals at sea at the beginning of hostilities. They also provided force defense for the mine warfare ships as they proceeded up the KAA waterway in the opening days of combat operations. They provided a buffer to the north as ships and helicopters worked the waterway, ever conscious of the potential threat from enemy forces on the Al Faw Peninsula.

As I discussed the issue of operations in the shallow waters of the Arabian Gulf, the CNO posed a question. "Would you trade one Arleigh Burke destroyer for four or five of these PCs?" Without hesitation, I responded with an unqualified, "absolutely."

There was an audible groan among the staff officers present. They had recently briefed the CNO on their proposal to decommission these ships, as the ship's propulsion plant had provided challenges to the maintenance community. There was an article in the 9 June 2003 *Navy Times* that reported the Navy's plan to transfer the eight PCs to the Philippines, Columbia, and Egypt. Congress was questioning the wisdom of this move, and congressional aides were quoted as saying, "These are very young ships with a lot of life left in them."

The PCs had proven their worth when they were needed most. Admiral Clark decided to rule against his staff recommendation and invested in these PCs to remedy the maintenance issue. They continue to contribute and have supported many naval operations in the past 14 years. The Navy is now modernizing the 14 PCs with laser-guided weapons, missiles, and drones to extend their service life to 2025 and beyond.

LESSONS IDENTIFIED

We continued to feed 285 Lessons Identified to various Navy organizations over the next several months. The bulk of these lessons fell into six categories: air wing operations, Tomahawk, maritime interception operations, information warfare, intelligence, and communications. The lesson identified most was that our Sailors and Marines represented the greatest naval force the world had ever seen.

Specific requests for additional capability included: more armed helicopters, more robust RHIBs, unmanned aerial vehicles (drones) to replace capabilities being lost with the sundowning of the S-3 aircraft, and increased bandwidth for all command and control systems.

The overall assessment of the naval aviation participation from the Northern Arabian Gulf was a high-interest item. Navy flew half of the 15,000 air strike sorties through mid-April, as compared to about a quarter of these missions in the 1991 war. Captain Fox provided his perspective as he was able to reflect on his time in command of the air wing in the Gulf during OIF:

> "I think we got it right this time, both in terms of bringing flexible, credible combat power to the region and using it effectively. Some specifics include:
>
> • MUCH IMPROVED PRECISION STRIKE CAPABILITY. My baseline for comparison is Desert Storm. In Desert Storm, we had limited abilities to employ precision-guided munitions (only 14 aircraft in the air wing—A-6s—carried LGBs, and the F-14s had no air-to-ground capability whatsoever). In Iraqi Freedom, all

46 'pointy nose' aircraft (36 F/A-18s and 10 F-14Ds) could autonomously deliver LGBs, as well as carry the GPS-guided JDAM (about 75% of the ordnance dropped by Navy pilots in Iraqi Freedom were guided by lasers or GPS, compared with less than 10% in Operation Desert Storm).

- SIGNIFICANTLY IMPROVED COMMUNICATIONS AND COORDINATION. Another key to our success was the level of Navy interaction and liaison in the CAOC. Having spent well over 10 years in the AOR since Desert Fox, etc., we all understood how to operate in the region. Having both CVW-2 and 90-day Navy liaison officers in the CAOC paid big dividends. SIPRNET was essential in our ability to effectively plan and coordinate operations.

- INTANGIBLES. Hard to put into a metric, but the people in leadership positions worked extremely well together and created a synergy of getting things done despite some significant challenges. Personal friendships established well before a conflict pay great dividends when absolute trust is needed during a crisis: Captains Bill Gortney and Garry Mace in the CAOC; Captains KC Albright and Kendall Card aboard *Lincoln*; and Captain Pat Driscoll (CVW-5) aboard *Kitty Hawk*. Multiple examples—sharing congested airspace and seaspace; the 'on very short notice, can you launch your EA-6B to support the F-117 decapitation strike?'; the decision to launch the JSOW strike amid the sandstorm, etc.

- TANKER SUPPORT. In absolute terms, we had adequate strategic tanking assets available, although, at the time, it didn't feel like it. We could have generated more power projection sorties if we had had more robust tanker support. That said, I am convinced that we (USN) got our 'fair share' of the strategic tanking allocation, and ultimately had enough big wing tanking support to do the job. I would have moved the tanker tracks in country sooner than we did. We had less organic tanking capacity (S-3s only) in Iraqi Freedom than in Desert Storm (A-6s and A-7s with buddy stores). With the Super Hornet entering the fleet in significant numbers, we regain the tactical/organic tanking capability that we had 15 years ago.

- CONSTRAINTS.
  - Our ability to keep <u>real-time track of blue ground forces</u> needs to improve. We had no air-to-ground blue-on-blue, so the time and effort we devoted to Close Air Support and USMC/Army coordination obviously paid off. Using the E-2 as a coordinating facilitating agency was another means to overcome the problem.
  - <u>GPS Weapons</u>: needed 'target quality' mensurated coordinates, which are not easily generated in the Close Air Support battlefield. We need a better means to get coordinates for GPS weapons in an uncertain, fluid environment.
  - <u>Weather</u>: the sandstorm in late March was as bad an operating environment as I've ever seen in my 25-year flying career.
- AIR FORCE RELATIONSHIP. We had a strong rapport with the CAOC planners, of which many were USAF. Tactically, we worked well both in the planning process and executing the mission airborne. Having mildly complained about the number of strategic tankers available, the tanker crews did a terrific job during some incredibly difficult circumstances. I have nothing but good things to say about our brothers and sisters in AF blue."

Rear Admiral Nichols spoke of *what we validated* as opposed to *lessons learned*. In an interview at an Association of Naval Aviation symposium in Pensacola, Florida, he said:

> "The way we went out there and fought as a joint force is exactly the way we have been planning, training, and preparing to fight. The value of the EA-6B, the F/A-18, the E-2, I mean all the capability the carrier air wing brought played very well in the joint fight."

Air Force leadership convened a gathering of Operation Iraqi Freedom veterans in July 2003 to review lessons learned. Lieutenant General Moseley and his staff pointed out that the pre-war focus on southern Iraq targets in response to Iraqi firing at coalition aircraft helped to shape the coming battle. They focused on anti-aircraft artillery sites, surface-to-air missile sites, early warning radar sites, and command and control facilities. These attacks also included precision strikes on the Iraqi fiber-optic cable network, which the Iraqis used to communicate with Baghdad.

They identified two key lessons. The first was that the communications flow from the CAOC to the warfighter was not as fast and as current, as it could have been because the system could not handle all the information. The second had to do with working with ground forces on definitions of *close air support*. Seventy-eight percent of sorties flown were in direct support of Army, Marine, and special operations forces. While coordination was good, improvements were sought in certain areas.

CNO Clark remarked:

> "We invested in readiness, and that investment paid off.
> It paid off in giving the president options... I could not be
> prouder of our men and women and the way they have
> executed in the battlespace... I am convinced that this
> was not like the last war, and it won't be like the next
> one... The key for us is to create capabilities that have the

flexibility to be used with great advantage anywhere we're called to go."

He would go on to say:

"We are a Navy committed to mission accomplishment. I still vividly remember the charge to the military from the president following 9/11. His order was, 'Be ready.' For every commander and every leader in our Navy, that must remain the focus. For all the forces heading home, our mission now is to re-cock this force. I ask you to challenge every assumption; the genius of our great Sailors will assure mission accomplishment. As commanders, I'm mindful that these challenges fall on your shoulders. I make no apologies; yours is the challenge of command. We're counting on you."

RECOGNIZING A JOB WELL DONE

Each of the Navy organizations that participated in OIF recognized their Sailors via a wide variety of awards for excellence. This recognition took different forms, from Letters of Appreciation to Letters of Recognition (for specific actions), to Achievement/Commendation/Meritorious Service medals. Also, there were some recognized by Air medals. These awards would be signed by commanding officers or forwarded to 5th Fleet for signature by Vice Admiral Keating.

The goal was to recognize the superb work of the Sailors in a timely way, with award ceremonies conducted in front of their shipmates. Done correctly, this is a huge boost to morale. The military does not have the authority to award extra pay or bonuses for jobs that exceed goals unlike counterparts in private industry. These Sailors worked 24-hours-a-day in stifling hot weather, deployed for 7+ months, and flawlessly executed the president's direction. They do not work for additional pay. They work for the love of country. The recognition in front of their peers, who fully understand their achievement, is satisfying enough.

These ceremonies, many before we departed the Gulf, caused the Sailors to swell with pride, and gave their leadership a chance to demonstrate that achievement matters. In every ceremony in which I was privileged to participate, I came away inspired by the greatness of this American youth.

Having taken care of our Sailors first, I turned my attention to leadership recognition. This was a "Band of Brothers," and I intended to recognize them equally with a ceremony in the Pentagon. The Bronze Star Medal is awarded to a member of the U.S. military for heroic or meritorious achievement or service. Each of these commanding officers rose to the level of accomplishment to warrant that recognition. We were honored with the Bronze Star, and more importantly, peer approval, the true coin of the realm for excellence. Thus, on 17 December 2003, we gathered in a Pentagon conference room. Admiral Mullen presided over the ceremony. There were nine of us there for the reunion, and the sense of camaraderie prevailed. It was a moment in time of which I was most proud and honored to be among these leaders. These officers represented all that is good, and their professionalism ensured that we accomplished the mission and returned home safely with all hands.

CDR ANDREW WHITSON, CDR DAVID DOBER, CDR KEVIN ANDERSEN, LTCOL GARY THOMAS, RADM BARRY COSTELLO, CAPT MARK FOX, CAPT JOHN MILLER, CDR JEFFREY HARLEY, AND CDR MICHAEL GILDAY

BRITISH EMPIRE RECOGNITION

Rear Admiral Snelson rotated back to the U.K. but did not forget those who assisted him in ensuring success for the U.K. forces, both their ships at sea and the Royal Marines as they stormed the Al Faw Peninsula. He nominated Vice Admiral Keating and me for special recognition by Queen Elizabeth II.

Admiral Clark was informed by the U.K. via official correspondence dated 30 August 2004 from Rear Admiral Dymock, Defense Attaché, British Embassy, that Vice Admiral Keating and I had been endorsed and approved in principle for Honorary Orders of Knighthood. The U.S. Navy leadership would have to concur in the granting of the award. Vice Admiral Tom Church, chief of the Navy staff, made sure that the concurrence was forwarded expeditiously. On 25 January 2005, the British Foreign Office sent a note to Sir David Manning, the British ambassador to the United States, indicating that Queen Elizabeth II had formally approved the recommendation, and we could be officially informed.

Vice Admiral Keating and I were presented with options to receive the awards in Washington D.C. or London. Admiral Keating was in command of Northern Command in Colorado Springs, and I had taken command at 3rd Fleet in San Diego. The urgency of our new duties guided our judgment on selecting the British Embassy in Washington, D.C. as the investiture site.

Ambassador Manning hosted the ceremony at his residence on 28 July 2005. The British Embassy team performed superbly. As always, our friends from across the pond put on a first-class ceremony. The military staff was dressed in their formal uniforms. The setting was elegant. The reading of the citations proceeded first with the award of the "Companion of the Most Honourable Order of the Bath" to Admiral Keating. The ambassador read the citation, and then made the presentation of the medal, a cross with "For God and the Empire" inscribed. Then I was summoned forward for the presentation of the "Commander of the Most Excellent Order of the British Empire."

Vice Admiral Keating and I noted that we were there only as representatives of the Sailors who performed magnificently in 2003 to ensure success from the sea.

PRESENTATION OF INSIGNIA

of honours bestowed by

HER MAJESTY THE QUEEN

♦♦♦♦♦♦

BRITISH EMBASSY, WASHINGTON

Thursday, 28th July, 2005

♦♦♦♦♦♦

COMPANION OF THE MOST HONOURABLE ORDER OF THE BATH

Admiral Timothy Keating

COMMANDER OF THE MOST EXCELLENT ORDER OF THE BRITISH EMPIRE

Vice Admiral Barry Michael Costello

CHAPTER 11 | THE WAY FORWARD

LEADERSHIP ASSIGNMENTS AFTER OPERATION IRAQI FREEDOM

Our military success resulted from excellence and dedication of junior personnel from all services. Their success was ensured by a team of outstanding leaders directing the action in OIF. Evidence of this truth is found by following the careers of some of these leaders after the war. I have listed these individuals with their ranks during OIF and then indicated their later promotions to higher ranks and responsibilities.

U.S. ARMY

LTG JOHN ABIZAID—Commanded CENTCOM (four-star general). He led efforts through the next several turbulent years to get other government departments to play a role in the reconstruction of Iraq.

LTG DAVID MCKIERNAN—Commanded all forces in Afghanistan (four-star general).

U.S AIR FORCE

LT GEN MICHAEL MOSELEY—Served as the chief of staff for the U.S. Air Force (four-star general).

U.S MARINE CORPS

LTGEN JAMES CONWAY—Served as commandant of the Marine Corps (four-star general).

MAJGEN JAMES MATTIS—Relieved LtGen Sattler as commander I Marine Expeditionary Force, commanded Joint Forces Command and Central Command (four-star general). He currently serves as secretary of defense.

MAJGEN JAMES AMOS—Followed General Conway as commandant of the Marine Corps, a first for a Marine with an aviation designator (four-star general).

MAJGEN JOHN SATTLER—Commanded I Marine Expeditionary Force and became Director of the Strategic Plans and Policy Directorate (J5) on the Joint Staff in the Pentagon (three-star general).

MAJGEN TERRY ROBLING—Commanded 3rd Marine Aircraft Wing, 3rd Marine Expeditionary Force and Marine Corps Forces Pacific (three-star general).

MAJGEN KEITH STALDER—Commanded II Marine Expeditionary Force and Marine Corps Forces Pacific (three-star general).

COL JOSEPH DUNFORD—Served as commandant of the Marine Corps, and currently serves as Chairman of the Joint Chiefs of Staff (four-star general).

COL JOHN KELLY—Commanded Southern Command (four-star general). He currently serves as the White House chief of staff.

LTCOL GARY THOMAS—Currently serves as assistant commandant of the Marine Corps (four-star general).

U.S. NAVY

VADM TIMOTHY KEATING—Commanded Northern Command and Pacific Command (four-star admiral).

RADM SAMUEL LOCKLEAR—Commanded 6th Fleet and Pacific Command (four-star admiral).

RADM JOHN HARVEY—Commanded U.S. Fleet Forces Command (four-star admiral).

CAPT HARRY HARRIS—Commanded Pacific Fleet and Pacific Command (four-star admiral). He currently serves as U.S. ambassador to South Korea.

CAPT WILLIAM GORTNEY—Commanded 5th Fleet, Fleet Forces Command, and Northern Command (four-star admiral).

RADM BARRY COSTELLO—Chief of Legislative Affairs, and commander 3rd Fleet (three-star vice admiral).

RADM DAVID NICHOLS—Commanded 5th Fleet and was the deputy commander Central Command (three-star vice admiral).

CAPT MARK FOX—Commanded 5th Fleet and was the deputy commander Central Command (three-star vice admiral).

CAPT JOHN MILLER—Commanded 5th Fleet (three-star vice admiral).

CDRE ROBERT HARWARD—Deputy commander, Joint Forces Command and deputy commander Central Command (three-star vice admiral).

CDR MICHAEL GILDAY—Commanded 10th Fleet and currently serves as the Director for Operations, J3, Joint Staff (three-star vice admiral).

CDR JAMES LOEBLEIN—Currently leads the Navy Legislative Affairs office (two-star rear admiral).

CDR JEFFREY HARLEY—Currently serves as president of the Naval War College (two-star rear admiral).

CAPT RUSSELL PENNIMAN—Served as deputy commander Pacific Fleet (two-star rear admiral).

CDRE MARK BALMERT—Commanded an expeditionary strike group (one-star rear admiral).

This is but a sampling of the varsity team that led from the front in OIF. Several of them will continue to advance in rank and responsibility. Each of them would attest to the honor of leading "America's treasure" in conflict.

3RD FLEET INITIATIVES

My next assignment after commanding Cruiser-Destroyer Group 1 was as the Navy Chief of Legislative Affairs in the Pentagon. This was a two-year tour (2003–2005) where I supported the Secretary of the Navy and Chief of Naval Operations in their interaction with the Congress. I had previously served as the Navy liaison to the Senate (1998–2000), so it was a natural progression as I knew the procedures and personalities on one side of the Hill. This was another assignment where *relationships matter*.

Early in 2005, Admiral Clark called me into his office and told me I would be the next commander of 3rd Fleet, responsible for naval operations from the west coast to the International Dateline. I was honored to head to San Diego to lead this team.

MULTI-STRIKE GROUP TRAINING

The experiences in combat in 2003 provided the basis for many initiatives I would champion when I took command of 3rd Fleet. A large element of the responsibility of this fleet was to prepare deploying strike groups for missions they would execute in forward operating areas.

One area I focused on was ensuring that each departing group had the training to contend with the challenges associated with operating with multiple strike groups in proximity. This was training *Constellation* Strike Group lacked when it headed west in 2002. The following questions would need to be addressed:

- How is the waterspace managed (where will ships be stationed)?
- How is the airspace managed (there will be three carrier air wings flying, nearly 216 aircraft)?
- How do the warfare commanders divide up the ships and aircraft for the support of air, surface, subsurface defensive, and offense operations?
- How does the leadership determine command relationships within the three groups (which admiral has the lead for air, surface, and subsurface operations)?
- Who is the senior officer to coordinate with higher authority? With other components? With coalition forces?

Strike group training would include operating with two other groups. This would be achieved by coordinating the schedules of returning deployed groups with those in training for deployment. Additionally, one of the group *staffs* in homeport would be tasked to interact with the training, playing the role of a third strike group via synthetic input to the radar systems. This group and their *synthetic* ships and aircraft would show up in training as clear as the *real* assets.

This provided the elements necessary for training in the most robust environment that the group would face in a combat situation. Additionally, we injected requirements for interaction with coalition forces and other U.S. military components (Army, Air Force, Marine Corps, and Coast Guard). Each of these opportunities provided the staffs a challenging environment where they would need to create the necessary harmony for success.

WEST COAST TEAMMATES

The strength of the force in Operation Iraqi Freedom was significantly enhanced by our coalition partners. Their capabilities meshed with the U.S. warfighting expertise and, in several instances such as mine warfare, their skills and equipment were cutting edge. We learned from each other. With that experience in mind, I redoubled the efforts of 3rd Fleet to reach out to our partners along the Pacific Rim.

The *U.S. Coast Guard* was an important partner, and we initiated regular warfighter talks to ensure alignment. I traveled with my 3rd Fleet staff leadership team to Alameda, California to get a better understanding of their command center operations. Vice Admirals Harvey Johnson and Charlie Wurster were outstanding teammates. We met to deal with the very real terrorist threat to our west coast ports. Additionally, the success of counter-drug operations in the eastern Pacific was attributed to this professional partnership.

Our *Canadian* teammates possessed great skill in anti-submarine warfare. We partnered with them in defense of the approaches to the Strait of Juan de Fuca, a boundary between our countries. There were occasions where U.S. Navy ships and aircraft teamed with U.S. Coast Guard and Canadian navy assets to deal with smuggling occurring in the strait. Additionally, a Canadian ship would regularly exercise with U.S.

Navy strike groups and sometimes deploy as a part of the team. Commodore Roger Girouard was my partner in Esquimalt, Canada and we communicated regularly.

The *Mexican* navy patrolled the waters to our south. I traveled to Manzanillo, Mexico to meet with Rear Admiral Sainez to discuss combined operations with his ships. He was very interested in pursuing initiatives that would prevent seams along our shared ocean border. The next day I headed to Mexico City to get the approval for these operations from Mexico's chief of the navy and the secretary of the navy. As in the Manzanillo talks, there was great enthusiasm to move on this initiative. Once again, face-to-face meetings were key to this success.

The *Chilean* navy is a very professional organization. I took my staff on a road trip to Valparaiso, Chile to meet with its leadership. Their navy has deep roots in the independence of their country. Heroes like Prat, Cochrane, O'Brien, and O'Higgins were responsible for the birth of their navy and laid the foundation for excellence. My counterpart was Vice Admiral Gerardo Covacevich, and we established a solid relationship, resulting in mutually beneficial training opportunities. The Chilean navy provided a diesel submarine for training 3rd Fleet ships off San Diego. The U.S. Navy sent ships and aircraft to Chile to work with their navy in an exercise termed Teamwork South. Additionally, the Chilean navy leadership took on increased responsibilities in the Rim of the Pacific exercise, held every two years in the Hawaiian operating areas.

I did not visit Peru but utilized the talents of the *Peruvian* navy liaison officer in my headquarters to ensure that our navies worked together in the eastern Pacific.

I mentioned the role of liaison officers earlier in the book, and the value they bring. At 3rd Fleet, we utilized liaison officers from Australia, Canada, Chile, Japan, Mexico, Peru, and the United Kingdom. They were future leaders of their navies, and their presence in the headquarters was a win-win situation. They gained experience that would be very valuable as they progressed in rank and responsibility, and I gained insight as to the thinking of their leadership as well as the capabilities of their navies.

Relationships matter. These outreach activities helped to build a coalition of navies from the southern tip of South America to the northern waters of Canada.

WARFARE COMMANDERS CONFERENCE

After being in command of 3rd Fleet for a few months, I came to appreciate that there was no venue established for the three and four-star Navy leaders to discuss *warfighting* issues. This surprised me, as I had always thought that such a gathering must exist, but it was above my paygrade. I felt it was imperative that *fleet commanders* gather on a regular basis to share views. There was an immense amount of experience and talent that was not being tapped.

I pursued this line of thinking with Admiral Nathman at Fleet Forces Command in Norfolk, Virginia. Once I made a case for this gathering, he tasked me to be the host and set up the attendees and the agenda. I crafted it as a *warfighter* conference to discuss warfighting issues (versus maintenance, personnel, or other prominent issues relevant to another forum).

Fleet commanders came from Norfolk (2nd), San Diego (3rd), Bahrain (5th), Italy (6th), and Japan (7th). Additionally, the four-star commanders from Hawaii (Pacific Fleet), Norfolk (Fleet Forces Command), and Naples (Naval Forces Europe) came to San Diego to support this initiative.

It was an insightful professional gathering that was unprecedented in the scope of attendees and agenda. We discussed: ballistic missile defense, anti-submarine warfare developments, surface warfare issues, and the oncoming cyber warfare threat. This brain trust really dug into the details of each issue and created a roadmap for future initiatives in each of the areas covered by the agenda. It was a tremendous success by any measure.

I tell incoming fleet commanders about this forum and encourage them to carry the mantle forward and continue warfighting talks at the highest level. Our Navy is more than putting ships to sea, as Admiral Arleigh Burke so eloquently said regarding the new class of destroyers named after him:

"This ship is built to fight. You had better know how."

U.S. NAVY AND U.S. MARINE CORPS RELATIONSHIPS

BGEN JOE MEDINA/BGEN CARL JENSEN CHANGE OF COMMAND REMARKS

As 3rd Fleet commander, I had the privilege of presiding over a U.S. Marine Corps Change of Command event. This was my responsibility because the Navy and Marine Corps had agreed to an experiment where a Marine general would command the ships of an Expeditionary Strike Group. This group consisted of amphibious ships with embarked Marines, supported by a cruiser, destroyer and a submarine. This was an experiment that lasted only a few years due to several good reasons.

The Change of Command event occurred in 2005 in San Diego at the 32nd Street Naval Base Pier 7 aboard USS *Belleau Wood* (LHA-3). My public affairs staff prepared a lengthy speech as a draft for my consideration. I knew my appearance at this primarily Marine Corps audience would be a dismal failure if I read this tome to them. Hence, I was still considering what to say up to the morning of the event. At first light, my vision cleared, and my role crystalized in my mind.

Marines are superb public speakers. They speak from the heart, with no notes. They practice their remarks such that they can walk and talk, as opposed to being anchored to a podium while they read their speeches. It is very professional, and frankly, I admire their approach.

With this in mind, I headed to the event, confident in my direction. After Brigadier General Joe Medina welcomed the guests, and Brigadier General Carl Jensen kicked off the ceremony by introducing me, I headed to the podium. No speech—no notes. I simply looked out at the audience and began without the usual introductory salutations. I told them honestly that a few hours ago I had no idea what I would say that morning. But a call to my brother Tom, a Marine, provided focus. I asked for Tom's advice, and he quickly responded that he had two suggestions. I eagerly awaited his counsel. He said, first... the Marines did not want to hear from a "squid," so I should just decline the invitation! Secondly, if I must proceed, keep it short to lessen the pain for the audience. With that levity as a start, I launched into a simple and heartfelt discussion of the state of Marine-Navy relationships.

I remarked about how impressive it was at that time to have General Peter Pace as the first Marine Chairman of the Joint Chiefs, and how the European Command was led by General Jim Jones—another first. These Marine officers were chosen for a reason, they were *best qualified* for the positions of responsibility. They were typical of the high caliber of Marine Corps leadership.

The Marine generals in the front row—Sattler, Paxton, and Natonski—were all my friends. The Navy-Marine team was much closer than in the past when I was growing up in the service. My generation appreciated the importance of this relationship; it needed care and feeding every day.

The Navy-Marine leadership team worked hard to ensure the flow of communication was a part of the *daily* routine and conducted regularly scheduled *warfighter talks* to tackle the tough issues. It was not perfect, but the country has been much better served as a result.

U.S. Navy/Marine Corps Warfighter Conference held in 2005. Front row: (left to right) ADM Roughead, ADM Mullen, GEN Hagee, and ADM Nathman

LtGen John Sattler and LtGen Jim Mattis Teammates

An example of this connective tissue between the Navy and Marine teams came during the first week of my command of 3rd Fleet in May 2005. I asked my staff if my Marine counterpart at I MEF in Camp Pendleton (just north of San Diego) was in his office that day. They asked if I wanted to make an appointment to see Lieutenant General John Sattler. I replied in the negative, just let me know if he is at his office. Once the answer returned in the affirmative, I jumped in a car and headed north for the 45-minute drive. When I entered the outer office, the young Marines' expressions were priceless. I could see the wheels turning, "What the heck was this Navy vice admiral doing here? Did they miss something in the schedule?" I smiled, inquired as to the whereabouts of their boss, and walked into his office. John looked up, surprised but pleased (I think!). I told him that I was his Navy teammate in San Diego and came north to tell him directly that I was intent on working closely together and supporting him in any way possible. Together we would work to eliminate seams created by our well-intentioned staffs.

Several months later, Lieutenant General Sattler headed south for a reciprocal visit. On his way, I called him and asked him to come to my residence in Coronado, rather than visit the headquarters at Point Loma. I told him that some people wanted to see him. He agreed, not knowing what was to follow. We periodically hosted wounded Marines and Sailors who were receiving treatment at Balboa Hospital. This would typically be an all afternoon respite from the wards to our backyard for a cookout with their families. When Lieutenant General Sattler arrived, I took him into the backyard. The young Marines were agog, as Lieutenant General Sattler was a demigod to them, leading from the front in numerous battles. He was and continues to be an inspiring leader. As excited as the young Marines were, I sensed that he was equally as excited to be among his heroes.

Eighteen months later, my staff announced that I had an unscheduled visitor at the 3rd Fleet headquarters. There in the front office stood Lieutenant General Jim Mattis, who had relieved Lieutenant General Sattler as commander I MEF. He simply said, "I heard what you did two years ago, and I am here to continue the tradition." As good as it gets.

FLEET HEADQUARTERS AS MARITIME OPERATIONS CENTERS

Each service is a learning organization. Leaders appreciate that to fight yesterday's war is to invite failure. Ongoing modifications to command and control systems are important to keep the sword sharp.

The planning depth of Navy was lacking. Navy had been content to execute plans constructed by others up to this point. There was simply no emphasis on this skillset. If we needed planners—look to the Marines or Army officers—they lived and breathed the planning process. It was past time to be able to *plan at the operational level*. This was imperative to ensure maritime capabilities were fully integrated into the overall theater plan.

Additionally, Admiral Gary Roughead and other leaders recognized the challenge of strike groups operating under 3rd Fleet guidance in the eastern Pacific, modifying to fit into the 7th Fleet rules as they transited to the western Pacific, and finally accommodating 5th Fleet procedures as they approached the Arabian Gulf. These differences had crept into the system over decades of fleets choosing to do their own thing procedurally.

Navy leadership in 2005 took on the challenge of evolving the existing fleet headquarters into Maritime Operations Centers (MOCs).

There was an appreciation of the need to more effectively *command* Joint Forces at the fleet headquarter level and to establish systems commonality. The model they employed was the system of Air Operations Centers (AOC) established by the U.S. Air Force across the world. These AOCs operated on common systems and common doctrine—such that their people could transfer easily between commands.

The Navy needed to take on the positives of the AOC example. The Naval War College stood up an organization under the College of Strategy and Leadership. Led by Professor Richard Findlay (retired USMC colonel), a team was formed to craft a vision of the *Maritime Operations Center*. They then went forth to each of the fleets to collect *best practices* and infused the document with fleet input.

The Naval War College training and assist teams have been deployed for over a decade, working closely with teams from U.S. Fleet Forces Command. Because of their work, the fleets are much more capable of planning and executing operations in a joint environment. This was tangibly demonstrated when one of the forward fleets was recently assigned the responsibility for planning theater operations by a combatant commander. Additionally, with procedures aligned, deploying strike groups transitioned seamlessly among fleets.

The Navy has moved well along the track to becoming a full partner in the planning and execution of Joint Operations.

COMBINED FORCE MARITIME COMPONENT COMMANDER COURSE

As officers advance in rank and responsibility, there is a need to "up their game" as far as thinking at the next level. On the day that officers get selected to rear admiral or brigadier general, they are *not* miraculously struck by a miter to receive higher levels of intelligence, vision, and judgment. The thought process was that you were selected because you did well as a tactician and showed the potential for higher responsibility and authority. Good enough. Grow into the job and figure out the rest. Often that was enough, as officers learned on the job, and hopefully had mentors that assisted them in making the transition. But couldn't the services do better to prepare our leaders as they entered a new phase of their careers? There was a clear need to pass along the *lessons learned* in wartime to the leaders of the future Navy, so we learn from both our successes and failures.

In 2004, the Naval War College took on the responsibility to lead a greater focus on the operational level of war. Initially, the college developed a *U.S. only* Joint Force Maritime Component Commander (JFMCC) course that included students from all services.

This was soon followed by recognition of the need for a *Combined Force Maritime Component Commander* (CFMCC) course where students from regional navies join a cadre of U.S. officers. This initiative was viewed as an opportunity to develop a network of leaders, increase regional trust and confidence, and address barriers to coalition command and control. The first course was held in 2006. Nearly a thousand senior leaders from the U.S. and partner navies around the world have attended these courses, which are conducted in Hawaii at the Pacific Fleet headquarters, in Bahrain at the 5th Fleet headquarters, in Naples at the 6th Fleet headquarters, and in Miami at the Southern Command headquarters on behalf of the 4th Fleet. Each participating officer is hand selected and has the potential to lead their respective country's navy.

I am convinced, after facilitating these classes for a decade, that *there is no other gathering in the world as rich in talent or as far-reaching in effect as these CFMCC courses. Hearing the perspectives of other country and other service leaders is priceless.*

In addition to operational planning, other tenets that senior facilitators stress throughout the week-long course include the role of the commander to:

- Anticipate—what is beyond the next move.
- *Feed the beast* proactively—provide information to higher headquarters.
- Consider what is happening one and two levels above, and one level below.
- Assess risk, and *take* well-thought-out risk.

It is heartening to get feedback from students several years after they participate in the course. In 2017, I was at a security conference in Panama, and several former students were participating in the event. I was looking forward to seeing them, and hearing of their successes. One of the CFMCC students in 2013 was Rear Admiral Felix Alburquerque Compres, now a vice admiral, deputy minister for Naval and Coastal Affairs of the Dominican Republic. He gave me a hug, and said, "I did not forget the priorities! I followed them and have enjoyed great success ever since." He had experienced the same awakening that I had back in 1990 when I first heard the guidance of self, family, and job from Lieutenant General Armstrong on the Joint Staff. General Armstrong' legacy lives on, one service member at a time.

Another wonderful reality was seeing the Iraqi student in the 2017 CFMCC course in Bahrain in discussion with Major General Al-Mulla from Kuwait. The Iraqi student was a young lieutenant in command of a LCAC vehicle in the Port of Az Zubayr in 2003. He was relating how his life had changed for the better in the past 14 years. He had attended the Naval War College in Newport, Rhode Island and was now a captain in charge of the Iraqi ships based in Umm Qasr. The ability to foster that conversation is a greatness of the CFMCC course <u>and</u> the fruit of the OIF coalition navy success in 2003.

EPILOGUE

There you have it. I hope you have enjoyed reading this story as much as I have enjoyed living and writing about it. My request now is that you take a few minutes to read the story of my upbringing in "Blessed" in Appendix A, "Mentors and Early Lessons Learned" in Appendix B, Letters from Commanders in Appendix C, and Daily Press Briefings in Appendix D. I promise you they will be well worth the read. They provide an essential context for the entire book and my thinking as I approached the challenge of writing about our national heroes.

In this book, I wanted to fill in some of the blanks of naval activities in 2002–2003 leading up to and through the opening days of Operation Iraqi Freedom. I wanted to respond to Lieutenant Commander Nelson's prod in his *Proceedings* article, referred to earlier in this book, to write about these operations so that future generations could benefit.

It has been said that the U.S. intelligence apparatus bats 100% when predicting the future... that is... 100% *incorrect*. Despite our best efforts, we cannot foresee the intentions of leaders around the world. It is now 15 years after OIF, and Iraq continues to struggle. There were many missteps in the wake of the initial coalition military success. Iraq is complex, with many factions, and its future remains uncertain.

That said, because of the efforts of the coalition naval forces in 2003, the navies of Kuwait and Iraq now conduct exercises *together* as they patrol the waters of the Khor Abd Allah waterway and the Northern Arabian Gulf. They have signed a bilateral security cooperation initiative based on international law and have developed protocols for operations at sea. This is a major step forward for peace in the region.

FORTUNE FAVORS BOLDNESS documents the incredible professionalism of our Sailors, Marines, and Coastguardsmen who operated successfully in the dangerous waters of the Northern Arabian Gulf, on the ground in Iraq and in the air over the country in 2003. The American people should be rightly proud of them. I know I am.

Thanks for reading.

Appendix A | Blessed

I am a native of Rutland, Vermont... and proud of it. It is a wonderful place to raise a family as it provides the opportunity to learn basic tenets that form the foundation for the rest of your life. My family refers to it as "Camelot." It is an idyllic spot. The four seasons are very distinct. Summer is a beautiful time to enjoy the Green Mountains. Lakes abound, and camps teem with youngsters learning the basics of water sports, archery, and crafts. Music flows from the bandstand in the center of Main Street Park. Golfers enjoy good lies (on the course and after the round) and true greens (unlike the stories). They have a choice of Rutland Country Club or Proctor-Pittsford, both challenging tracks. The usual suspects can be found at each clubhouse, enjoying one of the many fine cold New England beers.

As the long summer days wane and Labor Day approaches, it is time to return to school. The air gets crisper... the days shorter. The leaves begin their annual ritual of taking on the colors of the rainbow. Tourists flock to Vermont to view this bonanza, hoping they have chosen a peak viewing weekend.

The leaves fall and are raked up as winter approaches. Storm doors and windows are affixed. Furnaces are checked to ensure their reliability for the cold months ahead. Final rounds are played on the links.

Then it arrives... the first snow. The winter comes in as the days grow shorter... much shorter. Hopefully, the snow is bountiful because the ski industry is an economic engine for the area hotels, restaurants, and merchants. Okemo, Pico, Killington, and others are packed with "flatlanders" (those from Southern New England, New York, and New Jersey).

Finally, spring arrives. The sun begins to melt the snow. The maple sap runs. Spring skiing is wonderful. The crocuses and daffodils begin to peek out of the snow, and planning begins for summer adventures.

Rutland is a city that has a comfortable feel. It has a constancy that is refreshing in a world full of change. Father Mayo had been in charge at Christ the King Church, as Monsignor Kennedy was for decades before him. The market remains a meeting place. The downtown sculpture of a dog on leash memorializes my Uncle Dick walking his terrier "Butsy" all over the city. The local donut shops provide the best home cooked delicacies. If you are from Rutland and meet another native anywhere in the world—a quick comparison of family names and street addresses form a common bond. And, as in the TV show "Cheers," when you return—everybody knows your name. My brothers contend that there are more *characters* in and from Rutland than anywhere else in the world... *not* per capita, but total.

My mother and father came from humble means, growing up during the Depression. Nothing came easily, but anything was possible... anything. They worked hard to provide their four sons the opportunity to succeed in life. "Aim for the stars" was my mother's charge. She believed that an idle mind was the devil's workshop and had many chores to keep us busy... we were *never* idle.

My father worked hard as a lawyer to provide for our family. He came from a family of nine and lost his father to pneumonia in 1928 (my dad was 14), with my grandmother pregnant with twins. To say that that family faced daunting challenges would be a gross understatement. But they faced them together. There was suggestion by others that the children be split up to be raised by families with more means and a father figure. How could a mother raise nine children during the Great Depression and beyond? She did, and every member of this brood had a success story of their own. This was "family" at its best.

My father showed us the way by his integrity. I recall listening to a local lawyer one day as he mused that my father was the most honest person he had ever known. At my father's wake, the line of those who had come to pay their respects extended out to the street. I met people whom I had never known, each with a story I had never heard, of how my father had helped them—quietly without fanfare. As is often the case with that wonderful generation, I got to know him better in death than in life.

My parents were a constant. They were always there for us and enjoyed living vicariously through our exploits. They would express their dissent for some of our ideas; however, once it was clear that the decision was made—that dissent disappeared, and full support took its place. And despite disappointments—I certainly provided my share—they were eternally loyal, for which I am eternally grateful.

The 1960s were tumultuous years for our country. Vietnam, hippies, and the clash of cultures dominated the media. My brothers BJ (Navy) and Tom (Marines) went off to fight in Vietnam for a cause they believed was just. My parents had funded three college educations, and two years of prep school for me. Thus, I should not have been surprised when my brother Tom "suggested" that I take the Navy ROTC test to try to get a scholarship. I was offered a scholarship by the College of the Holy Cross and began an odyssey that continues today.

My success from those early tentative steps is wholly attributed to my mentors along the way, who provided me constant examples of how to do it right. In Appendix B, I expand on their role in my professional development. They are the leaders I wanted to emulate. They provided me with the lessons learned that I want to pass along to the next generation.

APPENDIX B | MENTORS AND EARLY LEADERSHIP LESSONS

To a certain extent, we are products of our culture. I had great mentors and experiences, both of which helped me when I took command of Cruiser-Destroyer Group 1, *Constellation* Strike Group. People tend to emulate the qualities they admire in their mentors, or they note traits and tell themselves—do not ever be like that. From each of my mentors, I took a page and made it my own.

My early mentors were my three older brothers. Being the "Rookie" or "Little Beaver" of this foursome was wonderful and instructive. Each of my brothers took on the traits of our parents.

BJ exemplified my mother's mantra that *"To those whom much is given, much will be required."* He has dedicated his life to serving the less fortunate in a wide variety of causes, from founding a home for women suffering from addiction, to serving on the board of The LaSalle School in Albany, New York (residential treatment center for at-risk boys), to spearheading the effort to keep the doors of Mount Saint Joseph Academy open in Rutland, Vermont, despite their significant financial challenges. It was the Sisters of Saint Joseph who assisted our grandmother in keeping her family together. BJ remains intent on carrying forward that tradition of service, as taught to us by our father, so that other young people can experience a Catholic education and all the values that come with it. *He leads by example every day!*

He is also the chairman of the board for the USS *Slater* (DE 766), the last of the 563 World War II destroyer escorts, berthed in Albany. It is a living museum that has been restored by the hands of destroyer Sailors who served during and since World War II. It is a labor of love that serves as a schoolhouse for young and old alike and preserves the stories of the gallant Sailors of that era.

One of my favorite BJ stories began when he was doing his usual New York State Capitol walk (he advocates for several worthy causes). One of the senators saw him and inquired as to his less than normal cheery disposition. BJ related a difficult challenge he was presented with that day in support of a high school principal. Without hesitation, the Senator said, in his thick Italian accent, "BJ, if there were no dragons, there would never have been a Saint George." With that he headed out on his mission, not realizing how much of a foreshadowing the counsel would be. As he ventured out to central New York State on his mission, he stopped to ask for directions as he approached the high school where the hearing was to occur. The passerby told him to go up to the corner where he would find *Saint George's Church* and take a right. Clearly, there was Divine intervention working. He went forth with renewed confidence that he could accomplish what was earlier believed to be impossible and slew his dragon.

Tom took me under his wing at an early age, and I have been there ever since. He is a decorated Marine (Bronze Star and Purple Heart from Vietnam). He exemplifies the phrase often used by General Jim Mattis that Marines can be defined as *"no better friend, no worse enemy."* He defines the word "passion." He is *relentless in pursuit of his goal of improving the lives of others,* crafting legislation while serving several tours in the Vermont House of Representatives. He has worked to support the underprivileged his entire life in the courtrooms of Vermont, creating new law by his persuasive arguments.

Brother Brian followed my father's early career choice, teaching. While my dad taught in a one-room schoolhouse for grades one through eight, Brian spent his career laboring in the fertile minds of the high school students in Rutland. *His ability to inspire his students might have been the template for Robin Williams in the movie "Dead Poet's Society."* Walking with him around Rutland today is entertaining, as young adult after young adult come up and say "Mr. Cos, remember me" and tell stories of how Brian turned their lives around and was responsible for their current success.

I consider my cousin Tim Collins, my fourth brother. In addition to managing a successful career, he dedicated his life to raising three wonderful children, and the results of that effort along with his wife Sandy are a testament to his leadership. He inspires me to be a better father every day.

In each of my assignments from early command of a destroyer to admiral, I actively sought out officers who had been in the job. "What were the issues that dominated your tour? What worked for you? What did *not* work?" It is helpful to have a historical perspective on any assignment and to understand how things got to be the way they are before you go about instituting change.

To the point about historical perspective, I had an interaction with **Admiral Richard Mies,** then commander of Strategic Command in Omaha in 2002. As I was preparing to go into the "tank" (a special conference room in the Pentagon) to brief the Joint Chiefs of Staff, he asked me, "What did you find when you went back in the Joint Staff history on this issue... how did they handle it five to 10 years ago?" He indicated that *we tend to revisit issues over time, and how our predecessors handled them should be instructive.* He was right.

Therefore, here is a snapshot of many who have contributed to my leadership style. They get a large amount of credit for any success I experienced, and for the *positive attitude and the can-do spirit that permeated the Constellation Strike Group.*

———

My first assignment after commissioning in 1973 was to the USS *Brownson* (DD 868). It was a WWII vintage destroyer and the perfect place for Ensign Costello to learn the surface warfare trade. Our commanding officer was **Commander Charlie Alves**, nicknamed the *Silver Fox* for his shock of gray hair. He was on a mission to turn *Brownson* from the non-deploying test ship with a poor reputation into the best ship in the new squadron—and he succeeded. We won the Battle E award for operational excellence (best ship in the destroyer squadron of seven ships, all newer than *Brownson*, sometimes by decades). He had to face significant personnel challenges head-on; many of the crew he inherited had alcohol abuse issues. His leadership was a fitting example for me when I later commanded USS *Elliot* (DD 967). *Sometimes, despite everyone's best efforts to address issues, it is best to remove people to get the right team in place.* It is much better to operate with an undermanned situation than to be fully manned, with an element of malcontents.

He was a good evaluator of talent and *empowered junior officers and chiefs to take ownership of ship events, creating a pride that became emblematic of Brownson Sailors. We were winners... make it happen.* We were fortunate to have several high draft choices in the Wardroom and Chiefs Mess, people who led by example.

He was relieved by **Commander Jack Roundtree** who was also a keen evaluator of talent. I recall a situation where I was the officer of the deck on the bridge late at night. I called him in his cabin to address a particularly close quarters situation with another ship. He listened to my recommendation and said to proceed. In the past, the commanding officer would usually come to the bridge, would affirm the recommendation, and let you off the responsibility hook—because he was there. Commander Roundtree did *not* come to the bridge... what the heck, he was leaving it up to a lieutenant junior grade?! The answer was a qualified "yes." I later learned that he was evaluating his officers of the deck by walking unobserved on the torpedo deck below the bridge and watching the situation develop. If handled professionally, you would not see the commanding officer on the bridge. If he felt uneasy, that officer of the deck would get a few visits on the bridge during maneuvering events. *He was an early advocate of trust but verify.*

After a five-year adventure in the Navy, I left to attend Albany Law School. Law school was a fantastic experience; job opportunities awaited. However, after two years it was clear that the gravitational force of Navy life was pulling me back. I missed the camaraderie of the Wardroom and the challenge of leading young Sailors. I consulted with my mother regarding this dilemma. As usual, her counsel was spot on. She said that my desire to return to shipboard life was "interesting," but I would first complete law school, take (and pass) the New York State Bar Exam, and *then* return to the Navy. *Finish what you start before embarking on the next adventure.* And that is the course I followed. I took and passed the bar exam on a Wednesday and Thursday, and on Monday I was in Newport in Surface Warfare Department Head School. I owe a detailer for his flexibility in making this happen. During the next

26 years, I drove ships while at sea, but my law school training came in handy every day in identifying issues and crafting solutions.

My first ship after Department Head School was USS *Whipple* (FF 1062), commanded by **Captain George Miller**. He was an incredibly intelligent nuclear-trained officer who was equally patient. He had to be, as we had an "interesting" Wardroom and a ship that had little to no redundancy. *He taught me the value of recognizing that the first report was usually only partially correct (at best), and the prudent leader waited for the follow-up information to arrive before making dramatic adjustments.* Additionally, he accepted that his leadership team was a work in progress and understood mistakes would be made. The only question was, were the mistakes due to a lack of preparation or simply unfortunate confluence of circumstances? If it were the latter, he would provide the appropriate counsel and training. I received a lot of mentorship under his wing, and only through his patience was I able to continue my career. He later went on to command the nuclear-powered cruiser USS *Texas* (CGN 39).

Commodore Hal Sexton was my next boss—*the* Navy expert on anti-submarine warfare. I served as his operations officer. He gave me a great deal of leeway in managing operations of Destroyer Squadron 5, always backing me up when there were tough decisions to be made. *I have a vivid memory of him going to bat for his commanding officers.* In 1985, USS *Marvin Shields* (FF 1066) was on the point in the North Arabian Sea as the eyes of the USS *Ranger* (CV 61) Carrier Strike Group operating to the south. An Iranian P-3 Orion surveillance aircraft approached *Marvin Shields*. The crew went through the designated pre-planned responses, going down a checklist of asking for identification, delivering warnings, going to general quarters, and manning their sole gun mount. The ship appropriately reported each of these steps to the staffs on the *Ranger*. The P-3 continued its course directly overhead the ship. The initial reaction (without all the facts) by the admiral in charge and his staff was to send a message to the captain of *Marvin Shields*, blasting him for his failure in dealing with the situation by allowing the P-3 to overfly his ship. The admiral's staff tasked Commodore Sexton to draft the "blast" message to the ship. Commodore Sexton contemplated the situation, gathered the facts, and returned with a message to the admiral's staff for his release. But it was not what they expected. It was a message for the admiral to send to the commander of the 7th Fleet asking for clearer guidance for ships dealing with these types of situations. *He took a misguided negative and turned it into a positive, resulting in additional clarification of Commander's Intent by the fleet commander.* He also sent a "well-done" to the *Marvin Shields*.

Commodore Malvin Bruce followed as commander of Destroyer Squadron 5. *He took care of his people.* When I was working my next set of orders and was having a "failure to communicate" with my detailer, he did not hesitate to get involved to ensure his people received what they deserved—nothing more or nothing less. *This loyalty up and down the chain of command was something I embraced, and I tried to perpetuate the concept in every subsequent command.* He worked hard and played hard (a racquetball titan), and the members of the staff loved being on his team.

As executive officer (XO) of USS *Harry W. Hill* (DD 986), I learned from two dynamic leaders with very different styles. **Captain Dan Salinas** *taught me to be myself—no matter what the job* (XO was traditionally the "bad cop," while the captain (CO) took the "good cop" role). Faking a personality to fit a job did not work. I appreciated this, as I espoused a positive leadership style. He allowed me to run the business of the ship. It was exhilarating to work under his hands-off approach, knowing he was always there to assist as required. At sea, he would step in to run the anti-submarine warfare prosecution of Russian submarines, and he was a master. He studied hard, and his work paid off by the ship achieving frequent contact on the target in the middle of the Pacific Ocean, well in advance of other ships in the squadron. He later went on to become commanding officer of the cruiser USS *William H. Stanley* (CG 32) and commander of Destroyer Squadron 13. Dan was also the best blackjack player I have ever known; he taught me how to not lose my shirt at the tables!

Dan was followed by Commander **Cutler Dawson**. The change in style was immediate and dramatic. Cutler had a more hands-on approach. Like the other mentors I have described, he had a passion for winning, but even more so. He was a superb athlete—captain of the Naval Academy tennis team, and a versatile basketball player (a killer on the inside). This attitude carried over from the courts to every facet of shipboard operations. *Being second was never an option.* The ship excelled under his leadership. He later commanded the USS *Princeton* (CG 59), became the chief of legislative affairs for the Navy, and was promoted to the rank of vice admiral when he commanded the 2nd Fleet out of Norfolk, Virginia.

While I was in command of USS *Elliot*, the ship was attached to Cruiser-Destroyer Group 5/USS *Kitty Hawk* Battle Group commanded by **Rear Admiral Phil Coady**. Our interactions were not frequent, but each encounter left an indelible impression. He spoke in measured tones, with each word having significance. I listened intently as he provided his thoughts on command. I felt privileged to be in the presence of a master. He was proud of his Navy and put every ounce of effort into making it better. I would want to go to war with this man in the lead. When he retired in 1995, his ceremony was aboard the USS *Barry* (DD 933) at the Washington Navy Yard. In his final remarks on active duty, he reminded all present what true service was all about. He talked of his early years in the Navy:

> "I found my initial inspiration in the enlisted men who manned the engineering departments of those ships who served in hellishly hot and hazardous places well out of view from the bridge. Their willingness to serve in conditions that were unimaginable in a bank in Boston* and were invisible from any seat in the Pentagon, calibrated me to a wholly new concept of service. Their unselfish dedication was framed in the belief that they were doing a job tougher than any other afloat and they wore their rating patches as proudly as any French Foreign Legionnaire wore his kepi. *Where do we get such men? Once I bonded with them, as MPA (Main Propulsion Assistant), DCA (Damage Control Assistant) and Chief Engineer, I could not imagine leaving the Navy until I met their measure of sacrifice and service.*"

*Phil's father was a Boston banker.

Rear Admiral Joe Prueher chose *Elliot* as his flagship for the annual Portland Rose Festival. Upon learning of this designation, I wrote him a note indicating that we were honored to be selected to host him and his staff, knowing this would potentially be a very intrusive event for the ship. I visited the admiral in his office to get firsthand guidance on his priorities. Admiral Prueher came directly to the point, indicating that his needs would be minimal. He was confident the ship would excel, and we should expect to enjoy the event. His chief of staff was in the meeting, and looked at me and said, "He is serious, do an excellent job, but don't sweat the small stuff." I left thinking this was a good gesture, but reality would be quite different. I was wrong, and he held to his word... *a true professional who prided himself in being "low maintenance" for the crew.* This was another in the long line of lessons I took aboard and tried to make my own. Rear Admiral Prueher was later promoted to admiral, led Pacific Command, and was ambassador to China.

Vice Admiral Jerry Unruh commanded 3rd Fleet when I reported onboard to join the Operations and Plans department. *He taught me many lessons in dealing with subordinates who had disagreements.* During one exercise two admirals were having a squabble. Admiral Unruh heard each of their versions of the facts separately—once. From then on, he refused to meet with them unless they came together. The problems ceased. Admiral Unruh frocked me to the rank of captain one evening at sea on the deck of the USS *Coronado* (AGF 11). It came to his attention that I had been selected by the promotion board; and that my promotion had been approved by the Secretaries of the Navy and Defense and forwarded to the U.S. Senate for confirmation. In a very simple and memorable ceremony, we stepped out on a forward deck after dinner, and he pinned on my eagles. It was fantastic! It did not cost the government a penny (the associated pay raise would occur a year later when my number came up), but it was truly priceless to me.

Vice Admiral Connie Lautenbacher relieved as commander 3rd Fleet, and I became his operations officer. He was a Rhodes Scholar, brilliant in every respect. His demeanor was always calm and attentive.

You knew he was listening, and you had better be prepared for a series of very logical questions. *He recognized that a large part of his job was to train his officers for greater responsibility.* Sessions with him were not "stump the dummy," but rather times when he could provide his perspective from years of experience that we lacked. Rather than simply providing the answer, he would often ask "Have you considered...?" This was his way to cause us to think at the next level, the operational level vice the tactical level where we were all so comfortable. I recalled these sessions as I advanced in rank and responsibility and thank Vice Admiral Lautenbacher for his example.

Rear Admiral Lyle Bien was my battle group commander when I took command of Destroyer Squadron 23. *He allowed each of his commanders to do their job, with very little meddling. He was involved—but appreciated the reality that he had a varsity team.* It included five captains who would go on to become admirals:

- Gary Roughead: captain of USS *Port Royal* (CG 73), our Aegis cruiser.
- Al Harms: captain of the USS *Nimitz* (CVN 68), the carrier.
- Barry Costello: commodore, Destroyer Squadron 23 (note: Kevin Green, whom I relieved, was also promoted to admiral).
- Joe Enright: chief of staff for Rear Admiral Bien (a submariner by training).
- J.J. Quinn: executive officer of USS *Nimitz*.

Rear Admiral Bien spoke with quiet confidence. We had a memorable meeting of the minds once in Bahrain at 5th Fleet headquarters. There was a disagreement regarding command and control of the naval forces deployed in the Arabian Gulf. The commander of the amphibious force (a captain) felt he should always remain independent, reporting directly to the 5th Fleet commander (a vice admiral). Rear Admiral Bien's team felt that if the two forces (amphibious ready group and carrier strike group) were in proximity, there should be one reporting chain to the 5th Fleet commander, the amphibious force folded under the strike group. An admiral flew in from San Diego to support the amphibious point of view. The 5th Fleet commander, Vice Admiral Scott Redd, drew various command and control diagrams on a chalkboard. Rear Admiral Bien sat in silence throughout a prolonged debate. Finally, Vice Admiral Redd asked for his views on the matter. The room became quiet. Rear Admiral Bien paused. Then he said, in a straightforward way, that when he was coming up in the Navy, the highest-ranking man at sea was in charge. That simple. End of discussion. End of issue. End of meeting. *Boil a complex problem down to its essence—what is the real issue, and the rest will fall into place. Find simplicity on the far side of a complex problem.*

I had wonderful tutelage from **Rear Admiral Norb Ryan** at Navy Legislative Affairs. He was the chief, and I was his deputy for Senate Affairs. Norb was another true competitor. He possessed grace, poise, and disarming ease that partially disguised his intensity and killer instinct, on the basketball or tennis court, or as he worked the Navy legislative agenda in the halls of Congress. *He had great tenacity, a trait I tried to emulate. Issues were worked out successfully with the Congress solely due to his professional efforts.* Rear Admiral Ryan went on to earn a third star as vice admiral when he was confirmed as the chief of naval personnel.

I worked for **Lieutenant General John Abizaid** in my first assignment as an admiral, as deputy director for Strategy and Policy in the J-5 organization on the Joint Staff in the Pentagon. He was an incredibly gifted officer who had an uncanny ability to get to the central issue quickly. His arrival as the J-5 gave the entire organization a huge boost in morale. He moved issues forward for decision to the Director of the Joint Staff and on to the Chairman of the Joint Chiefs. *He recognized that the 90% solution was good enough and moving forward was more important than drilling another three to six months to achieve the "perfect" product, which might not survive the first engagement with the director or chairman. He was never happy with the status quo, and continually asked: "Why not?"* He engaged the "nuclear mafia" and the Office of the Secretary of Defense (OSD) staff with revolutionary approaches to nuclear weapons and relations with the Russians. *He had a wonderful balance.* He came in early but was on the way out of the office before 1900—complete with Red Sox cap and gym bag. He earned our trust and respect, and we worked very hard to not let him down.

I have discussed the leadership qualities of **Vice Admiral Tim Keating** throughout the book. This list of influential leaders would be incomplete without mentioning him here. *He provided us the tools and environment to succeed, allowed us to operate, and provided top-cover with senior leaders when required—the epitome of great leadership.*

I relieved **Rear Admiral Gary Roughead** as Chief of Legislative Affairs. He lived a tenet that I tried to emulate: *a firm commitment to setting up his successors for excellence.* There was no desire for self-aggrandizement, but rather a professional goal for the mission to continue regardless of leadership change. He included me on all correspondence from Legislative Affairs months in advance (well before I arrived) such that I could appreciate the issues. It made for a smooth turnover process (only a few days), which provided the staff continuity of operations versus any disruption to educate the new commander. The professional rapport continued when I later worked for Admiral Roughead when he was the Pacific Fleet commander, and I commanded 3rd Fleet.

Admiral Vern Clark was the chief of naval operations leading the Navy with Gordon England. *He brought his business acumen to the Navy*, and the rise in readiness under his tenure reflected efficiencies he was able to achieve. Our success in the opening days of Operation Iraqi Freedom can be partly attributed to this focus on ensuring ships had parts, fuel, and ammunition.

Gordon England was the secretary of the Navy while I was the chief of Legislative Affairs. *"Forthright, direct, and honest,"* were his guiding principles. I had served with or observed several secretaries of the Navy, but none approached Secretary England's ability to earn the respect of the Congress and Department of Defense. He was comfortable walking the halls of the Senate and House office buildings, and his approach was very disarming to several potentially explosive interactions with senators and congressmen. They knew he would give them a straight answer and knew that he would quickly and effectively address their concerns. He had a self-effacing style that covered an intense desire to do the right thing for Sailors and Marines—his primary concern—above all others. He earned respect, and people gravitated toward him as a result.

These leaders provided me with many examples to emulate. They represent the highest caliber of talent in our country, and I was most fortunate to work under their tutelage. The American people need to know how fortunate they are to have people of such integrity, courage, and wisdom leading their sons and daughters, brothers and sisters, and fathers and mothers in peace and during war.

APPENDIX C | LETTERS

Canadian Task Group 307.1/
Task Force 151

15 April 2003

RAdm Costello
CTF 55
Aboard USS CONSTELLATION

Admiral,

It is with the greatest of appreciation and admiration that I offer you, your staff and the team of the CONSTELLATION Battle Group best wishes and a fond farewell. AS CTG 307.1 and CTF 151, I have enjoyed a most positive and professional relationship with the OEF team, and I sincerely appreciate your own leadership, guidance and collegiality. These have been challenging times for all, and my insights only offer a glimpse of the courageous efforts undertaken by your OIF team, but from my perspective in the margins of this troubled region you have a great deal to be proud of.

Last night the boarding team in IROQUOIS visited the TARGET 1, a small tanker with a checkered past once involved in the last decade's oil smuggling enterprise out of the KAA. ...   When our Boarding Officer queried the master as to where he was from, he responded "from the FREE country of Iraq!" He went on to introduce his crew of nine as being all from 'free' Iraq, and then described to the boarding party, through our linguist, stories of life under the regime and how each had lost family members to its horrors. ... The tales and mood of the crew offer the strongest measure of success that I can imagine for your efforts in the NAG.

Sir, your support and forbearance through this deployment have been tremendous. I have always felt comfortable with the access I have had to you, and with the candid and professional nature of our discussions. ...

Let me close by wishing you a safe and swift journey home to family and friends, and a well-deserved respite from the pace of the Gulf. The legend of the CONSTELLATION will be all the richer for what she has accomplished under your guidance in these, the twilight months of her service life. I offer you and your team the respect and admiration of just one more simple sailor.

Yours Age,

Roger Girouard
Commodore
Commander

P 210056Z MAY 03 ZYB PSN 146080H19

FM COMPACFLT PEARL HARBOR HI
TO RHOVNUL/COMCRUDESGRU ONE

SUBJ/BRAVO ZULU TO CONSTELLATION STRIKE GROUP//

RMKS/1. WELL DONE TO THE MEN AND WOMEN OF CONSTELLATION STRIKE GROUP
FOR YOUR OUTSTANDING PERFORMANCE DURING DEPLOYMENT. FROM EXERCISING
WITH THE REPUBLIC OF SINGAPORE TO COMBAT OPERATIONS AGAINST IRAQ, YOU
EXCELLED IN ALL MISSION AREAS.

2. *YOUR LIST OF ACCOMPLISHMENTS IN OPERATION IRAQI FREEDOM IS*
IMPRESSIVE: CONDUCTING AIRSTRIKES DEEP INTO IRAQ; LAUNCHING 107 SURFACE
AND 19 SUBSURFACE TLAMS; DESTROYING IRAQI NAVAL VESSELS;

SEIZING THE MABOT AND KAAOT OIL TERMINALS; AND CLEARING KHOR ABD AL TO
ENABLE ACCESS TO UMM QASR. AT EVERY CALL, YOU DEMONSTRATED
CONSUMMATE SKILL AND TENACITY IN EXECUTING YOUR MISSIONS.

3. *FOR USS CONSTELLATION: THANK YOU FOR YOUR SUSTAINED EXCEPTIONAL*
PERFORMANCE THROUGHOUT 21 DEPLOYMENTS AND 42 YEARS OF SERVICE TO OUR
COUNTRY. THE LEGACY YOU LEAVE BEHIND WILL NOT BE SOON FORGOTTEN.

LOOKING FORWARD TO VISITING PRIOR TO YOUR ARRIVAL IN PEARL HARBOR.

4. *TO ALL, I SALUTE YOUR DEDICATION TO DUTY AND PROFESSIONALISM AS*
WARRIORS. AS YOU PROCEED TOWARD A WELL DESERVED RETURN HOME AND
REUNION WITH LOVED ONES PLEASE PASS TO THE MEN AND WOMEN OF YOUR STRIKE
GROUP MY VERY BEST WISHES AND SINCERE THANKS FOR A JOB EXCEPTIONALLY
WELL DONE.

5. *ADM DORAN SENDS.//*

P 191453Z MAY 03 PSN 104031H09

FM COMTHIRDFLT
TO RHOVNUL/COMCRUDESGRU ONE

SUBJ/WELCOME BACK TO COMTHIRDFLT (U)//

RMKS/1. (U) WELCOME HOME WARFIGHTERS.

2. *BRAVO ZULU ON A JOB WELL DONE AT THE TIP OF THE SPEAR IN*
SUPPORT OF OPERATION IRAQI FREEDOM AND THE GLOBAL WAR ON TERRORISM.
THE CONSTELLATION STRIKE GROUP HAS PERFORMED SUPERBLY IN ALL WARFARE
AREAS, FROM LAUNCHING 408 TOMAHAWKS AT ENEMY TARGETS, EXECUTING OVER
6500 COMBAT SORTIES, PLACING OVER 500 TONS OF ORDNANCE ON TARGET ISO
GROUND FORCES IN AFGHANISTAN AND IRAQ TO MAINTAINING THE EVER IMPORTANT
MARITIME SUPERIORITY. YOU HAVE RE-EMPHASIZED THE NAVY'S SEA BASE ROLE AND
THE EFFECTS WE CAN PROVIDE FROM SEA. THE CONSTELLATION STRIKE GROUP HAS
BEEN PART OF AN HISTORIC COALITION FORCE THAT LIBERATED A COUNTRY AND
BROUGHT FREEDOM TO ITS PEOPLE. YOU SHOULD BE VERY PROUD OF YOUR
ACCOMPLISHMENTS.

3. *AS YOU RETURN HOME TO ENJOY YOUR WELL-DESERVED LIBERTY AND*
RETURN TO YOUR FAMILIES. KNOW THAT YOUR COUNTRY APPRECIATES YOUR
TREMENDOUS EFFORTS. MY PERSONAL THANKS FOR YOUR PROFESSIONALISM AND
HARD WORK, VADM MIKE BUCCHI SENDS.//

P 011800Z JUN 03 ZYB PSN 381951H27

FM COMNAVAIRPAC SAN DIEGO CA//N00//
TO RHOVNUL/USS CONSTELLATION
RHOVNUL/COMCARAIRWING TWO

SUBJ/WELCOME HOME USS CONSTELLATION AND CARRIER AIR WING 2 TEAM//

RMKS/1. CONGRATULATIONS TO AMERICA'S FLAGSHIP ON AN EXCEPTIONALLY SUCCESSFUL SEVEN MONTH DEPLOYMENT, YOUR LAST IN OVER 41 YEARS OF DISTINGUISHED SERVICE. YOUR EFFORTS IN DIRECT SUPPORT OF THE GLOBAL WAR ON TERRORISM HAVE BEEN MOST IMPRESSIVE. YOU HAVE EARNED THE RESPECT AND ADMIRATION OF THE ENTIRE NATION.

2. *SINCE YOU LEFT IN NOVEMBER, YOU HAVE SUPPORTED THREE MAJOR*
OPERATIONS - SOUTHERN WATCH, ENDURING FREEDOM, AND IRAQI FREEDOM. IN DOING SO, YOU COMPILED AN IMPRESSIVE LIST OF ACCOMPLISHMENTS: OVER 20,000 FLIGHT HOURS, MORE THAN 10,000 SORTIES FLOWN, AND MORE THAN A MILLION POUNDS OF ORDNANCE DROPPED ON TARGET. YOU HAVE PROVED THE INHERENT STRENGTH AND FLEXIBILITY THAT IS FOUND ONLY WITH THE CARRIER STRIKE GROUP - A TESTIMONY TO NAVAL AVIATION'S SUPERB COMBAT READINESS AND STRIKING CAPABILITY.

3. *AS YOU COMPLETE YOUR JOURNEY HOME, LET US ALL REMEMBER THAT*
THERE IS STILL WORK TO BE DONE IN REBUILDING THE COUNTRY OF IRAQ, BUT YOUR EFFORTS WERE ESSENTIAL IN SETTING THE RIGHT COURSE FOR FREEDOM AND DEMOCRACY.

4. *YOU EPITOMIZE NAVAL AVIATION'S VISION OF "FLY, FIGHT, LEAD."*
YOU HAVE EARNED THE RESPECT OF THE ENTIRE NAVAL AVIATION COMMUNITY. ENJOY YOUR WELL-DESERVED HERO'S WELCOME HOME!

5. *VADM MIKE MALONE SENDS.//*

APPENDIX D | DAILY PRESS BRIEFINGS

The daily morning press briefings covered a broad range of topics, usually from activities of the *prior* day. For brevity, I only note a few of the unique events. I captured them here as a group to give a sense of the flow of the information to both the press and the American people, my target audience.

13 March:
- Sandstorms—divert seven aircraft to Bahrain.
- Ballistic Missile Defense and Tomahawk exercises.
- Board suspect Iraqi vessels *Zenaida* and *Al Assad*.

14 March:
- Boarding of suspect dhows by HMAS *Darwin*.
- 20 dhows attempt to break out of the KAA waterway.
- USS *Gary* rescues eight Iranian nationals at sea.

15 March:
- Vessels escorted through the Strait of Hormuz and the Bab-el-Mandeb Strait.
- Mine warfare vessels conducting exercises in preparation for operations.
- Search-and-Rescue program started with *Kitty Hawk*.

Indicative that shipboard life goes on as all these activities occurred, I spoke to the press that day of:

- Sailors taking advancement examinations.
- Reenlistments of Sailors.
- *Constellation* would be alongside *Rainier* to take on fuel/supplies/weapons.

- I would fly to HMS *Ark Royal* to meet with Commodore Jamie Miller and Brigadier General Jim Dutton of the Royal Marines.
- Showing teamwork in action—a Sailor suffered head trauma on USS *Toledo* (submarine) in the Red Sea, was treated by medical personnel from USS *Arleigh Burke* (destroyer), and then flown to Cairo Al Maadi Military Hospital via helicopter from USS *Deyo* (destroyer)—coordination at its best.

16 March:
- No-fly day for the air wing.
- 30 dhows attempted to breakout from the KAA waterway.
- Leaflets were dropped in Iraq yesterday.
- Media transferred to USS *Bunker Hill*.

17 March:
- Safety stand-down.
- Locating beacon for "Hefe," a dolphin who had gone on unauthorized absence to take a swim in the Arabian Gulf, was picked up.
- Ships transited the Suez Canal from the Mediterranean Sea to the Red Sea because of Turkey's refusal of Tomahawk overflight rights.

18 March:
- Resume flying tonight.
- Authorized 58 dhows to exit the KAA waterway, transiting south; 14 boarding teams inspected these vessels for illegal contraband or mines—dhows followed the route established by coalition surface forces.
- Air wing trained on Rules of Engagement, deconfliction procedures, and communications.

Other topics to address:

- Crew had heard President Bush's 17 March address to the nation—Saddam Hussein had 48 hours to leave Iraq.
- Prime Minister Blair went to the House of Commons for a debate on action against Iraq; vote was passed to support.
- Iraqi MiG pilot defected to Italy, providing important intelligence to coalition forces.

19 March:
- Aircraft attacks against Iraqi radar sites.
- F/A-18 leaflet drops Basra/An Nasarhya — 108,600 pounds worth — "Surrender to coalition forces."
- 250 dhows outbound Arabian Gulf.
- 47 steel hulls exit KAA waterway.
- U.N. inspectors rescued from Iraqi vessel.
- Naval Gunfire Fire Support ships in position.
- Preemptive Tomahawk missiles fired from ships/subs in both Red Sea and Arabian Gulf.
- Oil platforms isolated.

Other topics to address:
- VADM Keating came out to *Constellation* and addressed the Sailors and Marines.
- Execute order given for Plan 1003V—Operation Iraqi Freedom.
- Operation Telic (U.K. war plan) and Operation Falconer (Australia war plan) were formally executed.

20 March—Operation Iraqi Freedom Begins:
- TF 561 Special Forces seize oil platforms and pumping station.
- USAF AC-130 aircraft sinks Iraqi missile patrol boat PB-90 in KAA waterway.
- 13 coalition mine warfare vessels are underway (U.S./U.K./Australia).

Other topics to address:
- President addressed the nation—indicating that the coalition of 35 countries has begun striking selected targets of military importance. (It was 19 March in Washington, D.C., but 20 March in the Arabian Gulf due to the eight-hour time difference.)

21 March—G-Day and A-Day:
- 105 combat sorties launched from *Constellation* air wing (CVW-2); Tomahawk strikes continue.
- U.K. force lands on Al Faw Peninsula and U.S. Marines move north.
- Preparing to commence mine clearance operations in KAA waterway.
- Intercept tugs/barge carrying 86 mines (evening of 20 March).
- Two Sea King helicopters from HMS *Ark Royal* collided.

Other topics to address:
- Four Iraqi suicide speedboats exit Shatt Al-Arab waterway. Chased by Iranian Revolutionary Guard vessels until grounded ashore.

22 March:
- Tomahawk missile strikes continue.
- U.S. Marines discover sea mines staged ashore in Umm Qasr.
- Combat air strikes: close air support to ground forces; destruction of Iraqi surface-to-air missiles.

23 March:
- Combat strikes continue against Iraqi Special Republican Guards.
- U.K. Tornado fighter downed—Search-and-Rescue ongoing.

- 12 mines on two dhows destroyed in KAA; discovered six pilot boats in Umm Qasr modified to deliver mines; captured mine warehouse in Umm Qasr.

24 March:
- 65 sorties/72 precision weapons versus:
  o Surface-to-air missile support facilities
  o Artillery positions (south of Baghdad)
  o Field ammunition storage areas
  o Surface-to-air missile system (Karbala)
- Missile patrol boat and training ship destroyed (Basra).
- TF 561 work in vicinity of KAA.

25 March:
- Iraqi OSA patrol boat and presidential yacht attacked.
- Coalition aircraft attack targets in vicinity of Baghdad and Al Kut.
- Sandstorms and 80 MPH winds cause several aircraft diverts to land bases; hail damage to two aircraft.
- Escort U.S. Army IV Corps through Suez Canal (moving around the Arabian Peninsula due to Turkey's refusal for access rights).

26 March:
- Marine mammals (dolphins/sea lions) transported to Umm Qasr (on 25 March).
- 56 aircraft attack command and control nodes/field artillery.
- Final prep of KAA for transit of humanitarian assistance.

27 March:
- Air wing attacks in Baghdad, Al Amarah, An Najaf, and Al Kut.
- Tomahawk strikes continue (+700 to-date).
- Army IV Corps advances to Bab-el-Mandeb Strait.

28 March:

- Five mines found/exploded in northern KAA; underwater vehicles/marine mammals clear water area at Port of Umm Qasr.
- *Sir Galahad* docks in Umm Qasr with 300 tons of aid.
- Coalition forces, U.N., State Department, Red Cross working together.
- Air wing engaged across Iraq; first EA-6B High-Speed Anti-Radiation Missile (HARM) launched.

29 March–1 April:

- Continued close air support to ground force.
- Tomahawk strikes continue.
- Meet with MG Al-Mulla, chief of Kuwaiti navy.
- MANTA mines found on shore.

2 April:

- Close air support and strikes continue against pre-determined targets.
- EA-6B supported a B-2 bomber and F-117 on a mission over Baghdad.
- Iraqi suicide RHIB and arms cache found by *Dextrous* and *Chinook*.

3–8 April:

- Entire air wing engaged in support of ground forces.
- F-14s strafe targets in support of ground advance.
- *Sir Galahad* and *Sir Percival* continue to deliver relief supplies.

9 April:

- EOD destroys Iraqi weapons cache.
- SPS (Spanish) *Galicia* transits to Umm Qasr.

10 April:

- Low-level flight over Al Najaf to disperse riot.
- UAE ferry Manar transits to Umm Qasr.

Acknowledgments

I want to first thank my family, particularly my sons, Aidan and Brendan, for understanding that my many deployments away from home were part of a career dedicated to the defense of our country. It is very challenging to grow up in a military family where deployments for extended periods are required. I continue to be proud of their accomplishments today as they cut their own path in life.

This project has been a wonderful odyssey, reconnecting me with those who were teammates in 2003 during Operation Iraqi Freedom, from the CCDG-1 staff to the *Constellation* leadership to the air wing commanders and to the operators on the point. It has been an honor and joy to engage with them to fill in details that ensured the richness of *Fortune Favors Boldness*.

There have been innumerable rewrites of the manuscript. My brothers were very helpful in providing suggestions. The editing process is laborious, but Sharon made it a fun exercise with her wit, style, and constant encouragement. Each time through we would find areas for improvement. We could continue that exercise forever but finally agreed to put pens down and launch the story. The document is so much better because of her eye for detail and passion for excellence.

Dennis Lowery of Adducent has been the ultimate professional teammate. His "can do" attitude from day one was refreshing, and he worked with us to successfully resolve every issue.

Thanks to everyone for your support!

GLOSSARY

Brig Gen (USAF)/BG (USA)/BGen (USMC)
Brigadier General (one-star)

Maj Gen (USAF)/MG (USA)MajGen (USMC)
Major General (two-stars)

Lt Gen (USAF)/LTG (USA)/LtGen (USMC)
Lieutenant General (3-stars)

Gen   General (4-stars)

RDML   Rear Admiral Lower Half (1-star)
RADM   Rear Admiral (2-stars)
VADM   Vice Admiral (3-stars)
ADM   Admiral (4-stars)
FADM   Fleet Admiral (5-stars—from WWII)

1MC   One Microphone System (loudspeaker)
1003V   Operation Iraqi Freedom War Plan
A-Day   Commencement of Air Operations
AAA   Anti-Aircraft Artillery
AAW   Anti-Air Warfare
ACE   Air Combat Element
ADC   Air Defense Commander
AEW   Airborne Early Warning
AMCM   Air Mine Countermeasures
AOC   Air Operations Center
AOR   Area of Responsibility
ASOC   Air Support Operations Center
ASUW   Anti-Surface Warfare
ASW   Anti-Submarine Warfare
ATACMS   Army Tactical Missile System
ATO   Air Tasking Order

AVIP	Anthrax Vaccine Immunization Program
AWACS	Airborne Warning and Control System
AWOL	Absent Without Leave
BDA	Battle Damage Assessment
Blue-on-Blue	Attack where forces are injured by their own force
CAG	Central Arabian Gulf; also, Commander Air Group
CAOC	Coalition Air Operations Center
CAS	Close Air Support
CATCC	Carrier Air Tactical Command Center
CBR	Chemical, Biological, and Radiological
CCDG-1	Commander Cruiser-Destroyer Group 1
CENTCOM	Central Command (Responsible for U.S. Operations in the Middle East)
CENTRIX	Combined Enterprise Regional Information Exchange
CFACC	Combined Force Air Component Commander
CFLCC	Combined Force Land Force Component Commander
CFMCC	Combined Force Maritime Component Commander
CINC	Commander in Chief
CJCS	Chairman of the Joint Chiefs of Staff
CNO	Chief of Naval Operations
CO	Commanding Officer
COMPTUEX	Composite Training Exercise
CONOPs	Concept of Operations
COPE	Challenge/Opportunity/Professional/Education
CSAR	Combat Search-And-Rescue
CSSC-3	Coastal Defense Seersucker Cruise Missile
CSSE	Combat Service Support Element
CVW-2	Carrier Air Wing 2
CWO	Chief Warrant Officer
D-Day	Day for Launching an Operation
DCA	Damage Control Assistant
DCFACC	Deputy Combined Force Air Component Commander
DDG	Guided Missile Destroyer
DLQs	Deck Landing Qualifications (helicopter landings on combatants)
DoD	Department of Defense

DSMAC	Digital Scene-Matching Area Correlator
EOD	Explosive Ordnance Disposal
ESG	Expeditionary Strike Group
EW	Electronic Warfare
FAC	Forward Air Controller
FACDAR	Forward Area Combined Degaussing and Acoustic Range
FAST	Fleet Anti-Terrorism Security Team
FDNY	Fire Department of New York
FS	French Ship
G-Day	Commencement of Ground Operations
GCC	Gulf Cooperative Council
GCE	Ground Combat Element
GOA	Gulf of Aden
GOO	Gulf of Oman
GPS	Global Positioning System
HARM	High-Speed Anti-Radiation Missile
HE	High Explosive
HMAS	Her Majesty's Australian Ship
HMS	Her Majesty's Ship
HOA	Horn of Africa
HS	Helicopter Support
HSV	High-Speed Vessel
INS	Inertial Navigation System
IO	Information Operations
ISIC	Immediate Superior in Command
ISR	Intelligence, Surveillance, Reconnaissance
ITS	Italian Ship
IW	Information Warfare
IWC	Information Warfare Commander
JAG	Judge Advocate General (lawyer)
JASK	Iranian Naval Port
JCS	Joint Chiefs of Staff
JDAM	Joint Direct Attack Munition
JFACC	Joint Forces Air Component Commander
JFLCC	Joint Forces Land Component Commander

JFMCC	Joint Forces Maritime Component Commander
JFSOCC	Joint Force Special Operations Component Commander
JSOW	Joint Standoff Weapon
JTFEX	Joint Task Force Exercise
KAA	Khor Abd Allah Waterway
KAAOT	Khor al Amaya Oil Terminal
KAS	Khawr As Subiyah Waterway
KAZ	Khor Al-Zubair Waterway
KNB	Kuwait Naval Base
LAC	Launch Area Coordinator
LGTR	Laser-Guided Training Round
Link-11	A secure digital link that exchanges airborne, land-based, and shipboard tactical data
LUGM	Iraqi Produced Naval Moored Contact Mine
MABOT	Mina al Bakr Oil Terminal
MAGTF	Marine Air-Ground Task Force
MANPAD	Man-Portable Air-Defense System
MANTA	Multi-Influence Shallow Water Sea Mine
MCM	Mine Countermeasures
MEF	Marine Expeditionary Force
MEFC	Marine Expeditionary Force Commander
MEU	Marine Expeditionary Unit
MEZ	Missile Engagement Zone
MIF	Maritime Interception Force
MIG	Soviet-Made Fighter Aircraft
MILDEC	Military Deception
MIO	Maritime Interception Operations
MOBI	Man Overboard Indicator
MOC	Maritime Operations Center
MPA	Maritime Patrol Aircraft
MSF	Main Space Fire
NAG	Northern Arabian Gulf
NALE	Naval Amphibious Liaison Element
NCW	Naval Coastal Warfare
NECC	Naval Expeditionary Combat Command
NGFS	Naval Gun Fire Support

NSA	National Security Administration
NSW	Naval Special Warfare
OEF	Operation Enduring Freedom
OIF	Operation Iraqi Freedom
OPCON	Operational Control
OPSEC	Operational Security
ORM	Operational Risk Management
ORP	Polish Ship
OSD	Office of the Secretary of Defense
OSMDS	One-Shot Mine Disposal System
OSW	Operation Southern Watch
PAO	Public Affairs Officer
PC	Patrol Craft
PIM	Position of Intended Movement
PRC	People's Republic of China
PSAB	Prince Sultan Air Base
PSYOP	Psychological Operations
RAN	Royal Australian Navy
REMUS	Remote Environmental Measuring Unit System
RFA	Royal Fleet Auxiliary
RHIB	Rigid-Hulled Inflatable Boat
RIO	Radar Intercept Officer
RN	Royal Navy (United Kingdom)
RO	Response Option
ROE	Rules of Engagement
RS	Red Sea
SAA	Shatt al-Arab Waterway
SAG	Southern Arabian Gulf; also, Surface Action Group
SAM	Surface-to-Air Missile
SAR	Search-And-Rescue
SCC	Sea Combat Commander
SEAD	Suppression of enemy air defenses by nonlethal jamming or lethal missiles
SEAL	Sea Air Land–Navy Special Forces
SHAPE	Supreme Headquarters Allied Powers Europe
SIPRNET	Secret Internet Protocol Router Network

SLAM-ER	Standoff Land Attack Missile—Expanded Response
SOCAL	Southern California
SOC-R	Special Operations Craft—Riverine
SOF	Special Operations Forces
SOH	Strait of Hormuz
SRA	Ship's Restricted Availability
SRBM	Short-Range Ballistic Missile
SWIMS	Shallow Water Influence Minesweeping System
SUBPAC	Commander Submarine Force Pacific
TAOC	Tactical Air Operations Center
TBM	Tactical Ballistic Missile
TBMDC	Theater Ballistic Missile Defense Commander
T-EFP	Expeditionary Fast Transport Vessel
TERCOM	Terrain Contour Matching
TF	Task Force
TFCC	Tactical Force Command Center
TIBS	Tactical Internet Broadband System
TLAM	Tomahawk Land Attack Missile
TST	Time-Sensitive Target
TTGP	Tactical Training Group Pacific
UAE	United Arab Emirates
UMCM	Underwater Mine Countermeasures System
UNSCR	United Nations Security Council Resolution
USA	United States Army
USAF	United States Air Force
USAID	United States Agency for International Development
USCG	United States Coast Guard
USCGC	United States Coast Guard Cutter
USMC	United States Marine Corps
USN	United States Navy
USO	United Service Organizations
USWEX	Undersea Warfare Exercise
VFA	Strike Fighter Squadron
VMFA	Marine Fighter Aircraft Squadron
VTC	Video Teleconference
WPB	United States Coast Guard Patrol Boat

XO   Executive Officer
3rd Fleet   Responsible for Naval Operations in the Eastern Pacific
4th Fleet   Responsible for Naval Operations in the Latin America
               Area
5th Fleet   Responsible for Naval Operations from the Arabian Gulf
               to the Red Sea
6th Fleet   Responsible for Naval Operations from the
               Mediterranean Sea to Northern Europe
7th Fleet   Responsible for Naval Operations in the Western Pacific
               to India
10th Fleet   Responsible for Cyber Operations
COMPACFLT Commander Pacific Fleet—3rd and 7th Fleet report to
               this Command
PACOM   Commander of all U.S. Forces in the Pacific (all
               Services)

Ship Types:

AGS: survey
AO/AOE/AOR/AOT: oiler/replenishment
ARL: repair
ARS: rescue and salvage
ASP: tanker
ATS: salvage and rescue
CG: cruiser
CV/CVN/CVS: aircraft carrier
DD/DDG: destroyer
FFG/FFH: frigate
LCC: command and control
LHA/LHD/LSD/LSL: amphibious
MCM/MHC: mine warfare
OPV: offshore patrol vessel
PC: patrol craft
SSN/SSK: submarine
T-AE: ammunition
T-AFS: combat stores

T-AGM: missile range instrumentation
T-AOT: military prepositioning tanker
T-ATF: fleet ocean tug
T-AVB: aviation logistics support container
TAH: hospital
WLB: buoy tender
WPB: Coast Guard patrol boat

BIBLIOGRAPHY

- Donald, Kirkland H. Rear Admiral. "Commander's War Diary"—Operation Iraqi Freedom Submarine Force Perspective. 2003.
- Fox, Mark I Captain. "Air Wing of Destiny." *Foundation*, Naval Aviation Museum, Fall 2004, Volume 25 Number 2: 70—83.
- Grant, Rebecca. *Battle-Tested, Carrier Aviation in Afghanistan and Iraq.* IRIS Press, 2005.
- Holmes, Tony. *U.S. Navy F-14 Tomcat Units of Operation Iraqi Freedom.* Osprey Publishing, 2005.
- Jones, P.D. Commodore. "Maritime Interception Operations Screen Commander in the Gulf."
- Morgan, Edmund. *American Heroes, Profiles of Men and Women Who Shaped Early America.* Norton, 2009.
- Nelson, Christopher Lieutenant Commander. "Where Have All the Naval Memoirs Gone." *Proceedings, U.S. Naval Institute*, May 2014; 18.
- Patch, John Commander. "Taking Out Saddam's Floating Pleasure Palace—Smart move or mindless destruction." *Proceedings, U.S. Naval Institute*, September 2008.
- Thiesen, William H. "Tip of the Spear": Combat Operations of Adak and the WPBs in Operation Iraqi Freedom (Atlantic Area Historian, United States Coast Guard).
- Stout, Jay A. *Hammer from Above.* Presidio Press, 2005.

CPSIA information can be obtained
at www.ICGtesting.com
Printed in the USA
LVHW060813280219
609026LV00004B/48/P